THE SORROWS OF MEXICO

*An Indictment of Their Country's Failings
by Seven Exceptional Writers*

LYDIA CACHO
ANABEL HERNÁNDEZ
SERGIO GONZÁLEZ RODRÍGUEZ
DIEGO ENRIQUE OSORNO
EMILIANO RUIZ PARRA
MARCELA TURATI
JUAN VILLORO

*Preface by Elena Poniatowska
Introduction by Felipe Restrepo Pombo*

MACLEHOSE PRESS
QUERCUS · LONDON

First published in Great Britain by MacLehose Press
An imprint of Quercus Publishing Ltd
Carmelite House, 50 Victoria Embankment, London EC4Y 0DZ

An Hachette UK company

This book has been selected to receive financial assistance from English PEN's Writers in Translation programme supported by Bloomberg. English PEN exists to promote literature and its understanding, uphold writers' freedoms around the world, campaign against the persecution and imprisonment of writers for stating their views, and promote the friendly co-operation of writers and free exchange of ideas.

A CIP catalogue record for this book is available from the British Library

ISBN (TPB) 978 0 85705 620 7
ISBN (Ebook) 978 0 85705 621 4

10 9 8 7 6 5 4 3 2 1

Designed and typeset in Sabon by Libanus Press Marlborough
Printed and bound in Great Britain by Clays Ltd, St Ives plc

This book is dedicated to the murdered journalists
and photojournalists of Mexico

E.P., F.R.P., D.E.O., J.V., E.R.P.,
A.H., S.G.R., M.T., L.C.

Everyone has the right to freedom of opinion and expression; this right includes freedom to hold opinions without interference and to seek, receive, and impart information and ideas through any media and regardless of frontiers.

Article 19 of the Universal Declaration of Human Rights

CONTENTS

ACKNOWLEDGEMENTS

The publishers gratefully acknowledge the editors of the publications in which some of the pieces in this book first appeared:

Anabel Hernández, "The Hours of Extermination" in *Nacional*, 19 September 2015

Diego Enrique Osorno, "I'm the Guilty One" in *Gatopardo*, June 2010

Sergio González Rodríguez, "Anamorphosis of a Victim" in his book *Campo de Guerra* (Barcelona: Anagrama, 2014)

Emiliano Ruiz Parra, "The Wreck of the Tangerines" was originally published in *Reforma* in 2010, in *País de muertos* (Mexico: Debate, 2010) and later included in a revised version in his book *Los hijos de la ira* (Mexico: Océano, 2015)

Marcela Turati, "War Made Me a Feminist" in February 2006 in *Altaïr* (www.altairmagazine.com) in a special issue called "A bordo del género"

Juan Villoro, "Collateral Damage – Living in Mexico" was originally published in *El País* in 2010

Articulo 19, "About Article 19 (Mexico and Central America)" and "Register of Murdered Journalists" are published on the Article 19 (Mexico and Central America) website <www.articulo19.org>

The publishers gratefully acknowledge the advice of the consulting editors Michael Schmidt and Bill Swainson, of Felipe Restrepo Pombo, editor of *Gatopardo*, and of Gala Sicart Olavide.

Grateful acknowledgement is made to New Directions (in the U.S.A. and Canada) and Carcanet Press (in the U.K. and Commonwealth) for the right to reproduce "Interruptions from the West (3) (Mexico City: The 1968 Olympiad)" and lines from "Sunstone" from Octavio Paz: *Collected Poems 1957–1987*. Copyright © 2012 by Marie José Paz, heir of Octavio Paz; Translation Copyright © 2012 by Eliot Weinberger; reprinted by permission of New Directions Publishing Corporation and of Carcanet Press

Finally, the publishers would like to thank the fifteen translators of the essays and other material in this book for their enthusiastic commitment to this project.

UNITED STATES

Rio Grande

HUILA

Nueva
Laredo

GULF OF MEXICO

Reynosa

Torreón
Lerdo

ECAS

NUEVO
LEÓN

SAN
LUIS
POTOSÍ

TAMAULIPAS

Monterrey

San Luis Potosí
Bledos
Villa de Reyes

Ecatepec
Mexico City
Cuernavaca

Huimanguillo

YUCATAN

CAMPECHE

QUINTANA
ROO

Morelia

ÓACÁN

VERACRUZ

TABASCO

BELIZE

GUERRERO

OAXACA

CHIAPAS

GUATEMALA

HON.

Iguala
Ixtla
Chilpancingo
Acapulco

Ayotzinapa
Huitzuco

EL S.

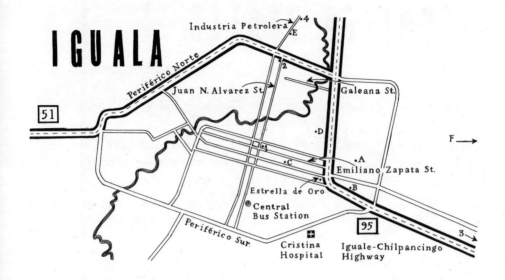

A 27th and 41st Infantry Battalion (Military Zone)
B Federal Police base
C Strategic Operations Centre of the Attorney General's office (P.G.R.)
D Municipal Police base
E C4, Iguala
F State Police base in the Regional Police Training Centre (C.R.A.P.O.L.)

1 First attack at the corner of Juan N. Alvarez and Emiliano Zapata
2 Second and fifth attack at the corner of Juan N. Alvarez and Periférico
3 Third attack in front of the Palace of Justice
4 Discovery of the flayed body of Julio Cesar Madragón

GLOSSARY

C4   Centre for Control, Command, Communications
                    and Computing. There are C4 surveillance centres in
                    all the major cities of Mexico

C.C.A.   Cuerpo Consultivo Agrario – Agrarian Advisory
                    Board

C.E.F.E.R.E.S.O.   Centro Federal de Readaptación Social – Federal
                    Social Readaptation Centre

C.I.M.A.   Centro Internacional de Medicina – Centre of
                    International Medicine, one of a number of private
                    hospitals in Mexico and Latin America

C.I.D.H.   Comisión Interamericana de los Derechos Humanos
                    – Inter-American Commission on Human Rights
                    (I.A.C.H.R.)

C.N.D.H.   Comisión Nacional de los Derechos Humanos –
                    National Commission for Human Rights

C.I.A.   Agencia de Investigación Criminal – Criminal
                    Investigation Agency

C.I.S.E.N.   Centro de Investigación y Seguridad Nacional
                    – Centre for Intelligence and National Security

C.O.N.A.L.E.P.   Colegio Nacional de Educación Profesional
                    Técnica – National College of Professional Technical
                    Education

D.E.A   Drugs Enforcement Administration

D.I.F.   Desarrollo Integral de la Familia – Integral Family
                    Development Clinic

E.M.A.F.   Equipo Mexicano de Antropología Forense –
                    Mexican Forensic Anthropology Team

F.E.A.D.L.E.   La Fiscalia para la Atención de Delitos cometidos
                    contra la Libertad de Expresión – The Special
                    Prosecutor for Crimes against Freedom of
                    Expression

F.E.M.O.S.P.P.   Fiscalía Especial para Movimientos Sociales y
                    Políticos del Pasado – Special Prosecutor's Office for
                    Social and Political Movements of the Past

G.I.E.I.	Interdisciplinary Group of Independent Experts
I.A.C.H.R.	Inter-American Commission on Human Rights
I.M.S.S.	Instituto Mexicano de Seguridad Social – Mexican Social Security Institute
INSYDE	Instituto para la Seguridad y la Democracia – Institute for Security and Democracy
I.S.S.S.T.E.	Instituto de Seguridad y Servicios Sociales de los Trabajadores del Estado – Institute for Security and Social Services for Public Sector Workers
O.A.S.	Organisation of American States
O.B.I.	Órgano de Búsqueda de Información – Intelligence Gathering Authority
O.E.C.D.	Organisation for Economic Co-operation and Development
P.A.N.	Partido Acción Nacional – National Action Party
P.G.R.	Procurador del Gobierno de la República – Attorney General of the Republic
P.G.J.G.	Procuraduría General de Justicia del Estado de Guerrero – Guerero Attorney General
P.I.P.S.A.	Productora e Importadora de Papel S.A. – Production and Importation of Paper S.A.
P.V.E.M.	Partido Verde Ecologista de México – Green Ecologist Party of Mexico
P.R.I.	Partido Revolucionario Institucional – Institutional Revolutionary Party
S.E.I.D.O.	Subprocuraduría Especializada en Investigación de Delincuencia Organizada – Assistant Attorney General's Office for Special Investigations on Organised Crime
S.P.P.	Security and Prosperity Partnership of North America
S.S.P.	Secretaría de Seguridad Pública – Ministry for Public Safety
U.P.O.E.G.	Unión de Pueblos y Organizaciones del Estado de Guerrero – Union of Towns and Organisations of the State of Guerrero

PREFACE

Elena Poniatowska

ONCE UPON A TIME drivers on their way to Acapulco would stop off at Chilpancingo in order to refuel or fix a puncture. Today Chilpancingo is a key city in the denunciation of governmental abuse, thanks to the authoritative voice of a 98-year-old social campaigner, a former GP, Doctor Pablo Sandoval Cruz. A few kilometres off the Autopista del Sol you can find the Ayotzinapa Rural Teacher Training College, where forty-three students on their way to becoming school teachers were abducted and disappeared.[1]

Ever since September 26, 2014, their parents have been on the road in the United States and Europe, to denounce this crime against humanity. Many years ago, a teacher by the name of Lucio Cabañas, observing that the authorities never once addressed themselves to the desperate poverty of his students, took to the sierra with a band of local peasants from the State of Guerrero, committed to putting their lives on the line. The same path was taken by Genaro Vázquez Rojas, a teacher at the same college, named after Raúl Isidro Burgos who was murdered on February 2, 1972.

The teacher training college was deemed a nest of guerrillas and has been continually demonised by the government of Guerrero, a state known for its violence and narco-trafficking. Corrupt state governors – from Caballero Aburto to Ángel

Aguirre – made the region a byword for catastrophe. Due to corrupt government, the state has become notorious for dishonest politicians and an army repeatedly accused of collusion in narco-trafficking.

Juan Villoro knows better than anyone else how just how much the people of Guerrero live on a knife edge, most of all those who are vital in the support of their mothers, and younger brothers and sisters. Getting involved in narco-trafficking brings far better returns than dedicating one's life to subsistence farming. Becoming a teacher is – against all the odds – one rare area of choice for young peasant boys. "I want to be a teacher, I could become a bilingual school teacher." In Guerrero, some twenty indigenous languages coexist – among which the most common are Nuhuatl, Amuszo, Tlapanec and Mixtec – and only 30 per cent of native speakers are also fluent in Spanish.

Ayotzinapa Teacher Training College accepts these young hopefuls, although it has little to offer them than a daily bowl of beans. As Juan Villoro has said elsewhere: "Guerrero has long been a land of shame and disgrace, but also one of resistance."

Villoro knows all about children's living conditions in Mexico City because he, too, once decided to lose himself on the streets. A writer of Villoro's stature, a member of the National College and honoured with Spain's Herralde Prize for his novel *El testigo* (The Witness), stands out among the contributors to *The Sorrows of Mexico* thanks to the particular slant of his writing and his opinion pieces in the daily newspaper *Reforma*. His attitude to life is equally striking, as is his trenchant skill in criticising the present government. As far as he is concerned, in Mexico carnival co-exists with the apocalypse. Street children in Mexico City survive without fathers or mothers, without even a dog to bark for them. They can only share the extreme poverty of their comrades on the street, and marijuana and cocaine as their fate. To have a mate is to be able to rely on someone, whether or not they happen to rape you or – worse – abandon you.

Let me illustrate Juan Villoro's words with a personal anecdote about Guerrero, one of the most corrupt regions in Mexico. In 1943, my mother, Paula Amor de Poniatowski, took my sister and I in her car to Acapulco. In other words, she drove her Chrysler from Mexico City to the coastal port, unafraid of taking the sharpest hairpin bends along the Cañón del Zopilote (Vultures' Canyon) on her own. We arrived safe and sound at the one hotel which used to exist there. It overlooked the beach and was called *El Papagayo* (The Parrot). In those days the only people living in Acapulco were peasants, fishermen and B. Traven, author of *Rebellion of the Hanged* and *The Treasure of the Sierra Madre,* who hid his identity behind Mexican palm fronds.

Later on the King of Acapulco, otherwise known as Teddy Stauffer, founded the Tequila-a-Gogo Cabaret, and played host to Rita Hayworth, Orson Welles, Diego Rivera, Lola Olmedo and the rest of the stars who came over from Hollywood. In the blink of an eye, Acapulco became a magnet for international tourism and Miguel Alemán, then President of Mexico, either built or permitted to be built skyscrapers just like those in Miami. He presented his lover, Leonora Amar, with a fully equipped beach and round-the-clock police protection. Other members of his Cabinet selected the best spots on the bay for themselves, and the rightful owners of Acapulco – the fishermen and peasants – either sold up their properties for no more than a few cents, or simply lost them outright. They were left with no alternative but to go back to the mountains where they were obliged to live without electric light or drinking water, without anything to show for their sacrifice. Their sole chance of work, if they did not return to the mountains again, was to work out their days washing dishes or cleaning rooms in the new luxury hotels. From that time onwards, Guerrero witnessed the start of a grotesque inequality, one which fed one successive guerrilla movement after another.

Guerrero may be among the most poverty-stricken regions of Mexico, but it bears Acapulco stuck like a gold medal on its chest. The influx of tourism and the boom in night-clubs, discotheques and prostitutes underwrite its prosperity. Johnny Weissmuller, the US film industry's Tarzan, died (without Chita) in Acapulco; Henry Kissinger, Secretary of State to President Richard Nixon, enjoyed special access to the Yacht Club in the same way, as did Elvis Presley, Carlos Santana, Ringo Starr, Sofia Loren, Dolores del Río, María Félix and Alain Delon. A Film Festival in the Fort at San Diego crowned Acapulco's cosmopolitanism for "having become internationalised ever since the opium trade was able to compete on a par with Afghanistan".

Due to political corruption in recent years, many Mexicans have reached the conclusion that a drugs overlord could prove the most likely benefactor. In Mexico City, "benefactors" have come to mean the pimps and rapists who have been so extensively documented by the journalist, Lydia Cacho.

Diego Enrique Osorno is, by any standards, one of the most respected of all our combative reporters. With extraordinary courage, which he has proved time and again, he exposes himself to arguably more dangers than anyone else. Carlos Slim (the richest man in Mexico who appears on the Forbes List just below Bill Gates) agreed to give him an interview, and Osorno turned their discussion into a book, *Slim*. Osorno is an expert in drugs journalism, winning international awards which place him at the forefront of non-fiction writing, while inside Latin America he causes a similar sensation to that of Federico Mastrogiovanni in Italy, whose catch phrase is "violence as a new form of government". Diego Enrique Osorno risks his life by denouncing the Zetas, the Sinaloa cartel, the meddling of the United States in our country and in making documentary films such as *El poder de la silla* (The Power of the Throne) produced by Andrés Clariond Rangel, which focused on four Mexican State governors.

In "I'm the Guilty One", and in parallel with the way in which Villoro has documented narco-trafficking and street children, Osorno tackles the fire at the A.B.C. Children's Nursery in Sonora, one of the major catastrophes in our country's recent history. On June 5, 2009, forty-nine infants died due to the negligence and corruption within our institutional authorities. Since these child deaths were threatening to occlude the election of Sonora's next governor, the issue was played down: there was a cover-up. Osorno gives an agonising description of the rage of Roberto Zavala Trujillo, who ran to search for his baby son Santiago, following the plumes of smoke rising from the nursery and clearly visible from kilometres away at Hermosillo. He failed to find him in every hospital he visited, each time coming up against further human stupidity: "The receptionist still had not realised that a tragedy was unfolding in the city, and reacted in the off-hand manner typical of overworked hospital staff. 'Hey, say something! I'm looking for a boy, Santiago de Jesús Zavala, from the A.B.C. nursery,' Roberto shouted.' 'Ah, yes: carry on down that way.'"

In only one hospital did the nurses hang up the children's clothing to help with their identification. Roberto Zavala Trujillo's search ended in the institute of the forensic medical services. It was there they handed over to him his dead son.

At a demonstration of nearly 10,000 people, Roberto Zavala Trujillo declared himself guilty of the death of his son: "Because I am an honest person who has a job, who has to fulfil his working hours, who pays into Social Security for giving me the chance to send my boy to that nursery, where I was told they had adopted all the proper safety measures. I am guilty for trusting them . . . I am guilty for the death of my son."

In just the same way, his article "Lily Sings Like a Little Bird", is a song to the child-woman whose voice can no longer sing as she becomes a sex slave, dishonoured in the hotel beds where she has to earn at least three or four thousand pesos a day. Not that the dealers or pimps do much better out of the arrangement, since the poor women who migrate from Central America cannot succeed in improving their lot from low to better paid. They come and go along the streets around the La Merced market, where women are treated no better than an onion or a carrot. They spend all day standing on the streets waiting for a client, only to have to hand over what they earn to their pimps, who once declared their love and promised the stars in the heavens to them.

I had never before read such a harrowing account as that given by the writer Emiliano Ruiz Parra in "The Wreck of the Tangerines". It is impossible not to be moved by a text such as his. *Moby Dick* has nothing on him and Herman Melville fell short when set beside this living horror! The shipwreck of the workers on the Usumacinta Pemex oil rig in the Campeche Sound will remain in our minds forever, thanks to the extraordinary account from an exceptional documentarist. Emiliano Ruiz Parra was a journalist on the daily newspaper *Reforma*, and published his remarkable "The Wreck of the Tangerines" there. Any reader, however indifferent, will feel in their guts the full force of eight-metre high waves threatening to crash down upon the platform anchored in the waters of the Gulf of Mexico, where a small oil rig is little better than a floating islet, struggling not to topple over with everything and everyone upon it and all its crude oil into the depths of the ocean.

Before I'd read Ruiz Parra, I had no idea of the destruction that could be caused by a "cold front", nor did I know that the front could transform itself into a hurricane. The head of maintenance ordered everyone to remain at their work stations but Pensamiento (Thinker), a nickname given to him by his friends and fellow workers, "worried that hydrogen sulphide, a gas heavier than air, might concentrate below the platform, where a single spark could blow it to pieces. He also knew that even the briefest exposure to hydrogen sulphide could be lethal." Alfredo de la Cruz, a.k.a. Pensamiento, was one of the Pemex employees working shifts of twelve hours a day on the rig in fourteen-day stretches before being allowed off, to take fourteen days' leave on dry land.

In "The Dream of Jesús Fragoso", Ruiz Parra relates how Don Jesús Fragoso Aceves – known, to all as El Chango (Country Boy) – "dressed like a peasant, in cowboy hat, homespun trousers, and sandals, a rough bag slung over his shoulder . . . like a poor Indian" dared to set foot in the Supreme Courts of Justice of the Nation to defend his community's right to his land and was murdered in cold blood.

Mexico appears to be scarred by tragedies which exclusively impact upon the marginalised, those whom socioeconomic studies tend to label "vulnerable groups".

Lydia Cacho, Anabel Hernández and Marcela Turati; Juan Villoro, Diego Enrique Osorno, Emiliano Ruiz Parra and Sergio González Rodríguez are outraged by Ayotzinapa and what can be considered "one of the worst tragedies in the recent history of Mexico". How many more "worst tragedies" still await us? How many more are to be added to the victims already buried all across the nation, their bodies still waiting to be disinterred? How many more mass graves remain for us still to uncover? From Mexican soil and its skeletons buried deep within spring pain and rage. We shall no doubt never learn how many forced abductions there have been, and how many dead remain to be counted, ever since President Felipe Calderón's government began his vain and absurd war on narco-trafficking. Nor shall we ever learn how many women and men lost their identities by becoming just one more corpse among so many others, buried in one of yet another clandestine grave, and as Sergio González Rodríguez reminds us: "A body is a person", not a lost identity.

I have been impressed by the fact that my friend, the literary critic Sergio González Rodríguez has recourse to *anamorphosis*, a way of seeing that derives from the Renaissance and is linked to the development of optics as a scientific discipline. It was the Italians who first began to polish mirrors, and they eventually succeeded in making telescopic lenses, along the lines of the Newtonian telescope. Caravaggio used them to experiment with light in his paintings as Canaletto would do later. They both used the *camera obscura*: a mirror on which it was possible to paint a reflection of the artist's features, as they look both normally and also when distorted. González Rodríguez – perhaps the most attacked and persecuted of all the contributors to this book (his injuries having incapacitated him for long periods of time) arguably used the process of *anamorphosis* to overcome the suffering to which he was exposed in the years a denunciation of femicide in Mexico City, so giving us the impression that he is on the point of either leaving (or returning) like Holbein's "The Ambassadors", who appear to be emerging from the picture frame. González Rodríguez succeeded in emerging from the horror he lived through via his writing and his focus on art.

Information is power, and those exalted by public office turn it to their advantage. To the Mexican government, an individual who thinks is more dangerous that one who carries a gun. From this derives the disaster that passes for education in our country, and the scorn we express for culture, along with a mistrust and contempt for intellectuals and the well-founded criticism expressed by the Inter-American Commission on Human Rights (C.I.D.H.), which quite clearly – and justly – considers Mexico to be a country that is both dysfunctional and a disgrace.

On March 2, 2016, following a visit to our country from September 28 to October 2 of the previous year, the C.I.D.H. detailed how in Mexico forced abductions are more than a common occurrence, they are a regular one, to which the state's response is wholly inadequate. "According to the National Register of Data on Persons Missing or Disappeared, those persons 'not located' on September 30, 2015, amount to 26,798." Yet another statistic attaching to Peña Nieto's six-year presidency are the 94,000 victims of murder.

The 200 pages of the report summarise the violence which overwhelms our country. In addition to our failed human rights record it "analyses the situation regarding murder, violence and threats made against journalists, which together render Mexico one of the most dangerous countries in the world in which to exercise their profession".

Few workers here have the privilege of being able to count on the protection of the law, or even believe that their basic rights would be respected if they did. The tragedy of the oil rig in the Campeche Sound where twenty-two oil workers died, along with two crew members of the boat attempting a mid-ocean rescue, exemplifies the state of abandonment in which the vast majority of Mexicans live.

Their only option was to take to lifeboats, known as "tangerines" because of their bright orange colour, and abandon the rig. Emiliano Ruiz Parra explains to us here that while the workers "were experts in welding, operating cranes and engines, drilling, preparing concrete and feeding a legion of workers . . . Some could not swim".

Twenty-two of their number who should not have died there did so.

The National Commission on Human Rights (C.N.D.H.) concluded: "We observed that the human rights of the 23 individuals who lost their lives on 23rd October 2007 were grossly violated in the Campeche Sound, as were those of the further 68 persons wounded." Not a single state official was either sacked or sanctioned.

These "worst tragedies", at Ayotzinapa, of the A.B.C. Children's Nursery, or in the Campeche Sound are the consequence of poor government; and those who die through violence, are qualified as collateral damage by former president, Felipe Calderón. His idiotic war on drugs trafficking left thousands more dead in its wake.

Sergio González Rodríguez's essay is indispensible because it shows the pain of a victim who not only needs to struggle with criminal atrocities but who confronts the infinity of locked doors inside the "Mexican justice" system. "Given that their access to justice is blocked, victims can only be certain of one thing: that they hover on the periphery of the law. They can never be sure they will receive a hearing and their very identity as individuals connects them to a pattern linking them to people who share the same predicament. The conforming and conformity of victims makes it probable that they will end up as mere statistics alongside others in some official compilation."

González Rodríguez recounts the case of the model and events organiser Adriana Ruiz from Tijuana who was abducted, tortured, decapitated and flung onto a rubbish tip. "A victim's murder is a repeated occurrence: first in reality and later, as sensationalist news items powered by what can be reproduced from images taken by the criminals."

According to González Rodríguez, to be honest in Mexico is to put your life at risk. So it occurred in the case of Daniel Arriaga, who uncovered examples of government corruption and negligence which he denounced in a letter to Felipe Calderón, the former president of Mexico. He did not receive a reply, but some time later he found a suitcase full of money on his doorstep. "He took it to the office of the individual he suspected had sent it: someone higher in the chain of command . . . who threatened him with two options: either he should accept the money or resign and keep quiet, otherwise he and his family would be killed."

In Mexico, power renders ill those who exercise it. The best analysts of our country have observed that it is impossible to tell criminals and politicians apart.

Lydia Cacho, a leader writer and a heroine of our times, has lived in her own flesh the risks that single her out among all the social campaigners and defenders of children. Her two books *Los demonios del Edén* (The Demons of Eden) and *Memorias de una infamia* (Memories of an Outrage) had a major impact on Mexican society.

Lydia Cacho Ribeiro, tall and slender, with a mass of dark hair, became famous as a result of being denounced by the wealthy entrepreneur Kamel Nacif, who used his influence with the former governor of Puebla, Mario Marín, to have her stripped of her freedom and subjected to a legal process in the course of which the only winner could be Marín's friend Kamel Nacif. Brave,

honourable Lydia, knew that her life was at risk while she was
suffering such persecution. She was imprisoned, following which
daily harassment forced her to live abroad, rather than continue
to live avoiding threats and relentless pursuit between Puebla,
Mexico City or in Cancún. She denounced child pornography,
judicial corruption and the zero interest the authorities had in
granting her any degree of protection. On the contrary, the
government just as much as organised crime were on the point
of doing away with her. Might they just possibly be one and the
same? She was afraid she would become the next journalist to be
assassinated in Mexico.

To tell the truth is to run a massive risk. Anabel Hernández, a
contributor to the daily newspaper *Proceso*, knows as much from
her own experience, through having her home broken into, and
through her own persecution. With her cropped hair and round
face, she looked almost like a young girl when I first saw her during
a television interview, together with Virgilio Caballero. I admired
her self-possession and her cool head. She reveals that there are
numerous scapegoats among those assumed to be responsible for
government massacres and names names; in some cases they are
labourers like Patricio Reyes Landa. One by one, she documents
the stories which were smuggled between prison bars, leading later
to denunciations by wives and relatives. If those assumed guilty
were victims of rape, asphyxiation, beatings, electrocution and
other forms of torture, it becomes too easy to ask oneself: what on
earth have they done to the students, the rebels, the poor, or the
forty-three Ayotzinapa College trainee teachers?

Anabel's investigative journalism caught in the crossfire of
bullets flying from both police and army guns, between life and
death, puts her own life in danger. Curiously, she employs the same

language as her aggressors and her writing harnesses police terminology. Her book *La Familia Presidencial* (The President's Family), about the personal enrichment of former President Vicente Fox Quesada created a sensation: in 2010, she published *Los señores del narco* (*Narcoland: The Mexican Drug Lords and their Godfathers*) and soon learnt of a plan to murder her "so it would all look like an accident". That was the reason why the National Commission on Human Rights provided her with two bodyguards. "The fact that a journalist has to go about accompanied by armed guards is a disgrace to any nation. I am in constant fear for my own and my family's physical safety, but fear only drives me onwards, and convinces me I'm on the right track."

How can it be possible that Marcela Turati, Lydia Cacho and Anabel Hernández are obliged to live in such danger in their own country? On November 21, 2015, Anabel published a letter of denunciation in *Proceso*, when four men raided her home, as a result of the publication of her report on the forty-three disappeared Ayotzinapa college students.

Such a degree of aggression has become normal: "On December 21, 2013, a group of at least eleven armed men, who claimed to come from the Federal Police and the Zetas drugs gang, seized control of the street where I live, in a suburb of the Federal District of Mexico City. They broke into my housing complex, pointing guns at my neighbours and demanding to know where I live, before violently breaking into my home". Rubén Espinosa, the photojournalist murdered on July 31, 2015, was not so lucky.

Marcela Turati, Lydia Cacho and Anabel Hernández live under conditions of "exceptional risk", in the words of the "Mechanism for the Protection of the Defenders of Human Rights and Journalism", produced by the Ministry of the Interior. Ricardo Nájera, Head of the Special Prosecutor for Crimes against Freedom of

Expression (F.E.A.D.L.E.), has promised to give them the "historic truth" about the attacks made on them. No doubt this is the same historic truth intended to close "the Iguala case", one that Anabel calls into question in her article. On November 21, 2015, Hernández declared: "I've struggled for a long time not to become another name on the long list of murdered journalists. The types of aggression I have suffered over the past five years have completely overturned my life and that of my family."

James Cavallaro, President of the C.I.D.H., was firm: "The challenge to the Mexican state is to close the persistent breach between its official norms and the daily reality experienced by the greater part of the population, when they come in search of swift and effective justice."

The federal government could not let such "an affront" go. Also, on March 2, it declared itself amazed that the report from the C.I.D.H. "does not reflect the general situation in the country", now that the state insists it has made advances on human rights not taken into account by the Inter-American Commission on Human Rights. The communiqué concludes categorically: "Our country is not living through a crisis in the field of human rights . . ."

Naturally enough, what government functionary, sitting in his luxurious office, is going to know anything about the harm done to our indigenous people, to migrants and women, or about the inhumane days our street children have to endure, washing car windscreens on the streets of Mexico City? Who or what is more to blame: the corrupt bureaucrat behind his desk or the report produced by the Inter-American Commission on Human Rights?

The Ministries of State for the Interior, External Relations and the General Office of the Republic protested: "The methods employed by the C.I.D.H. in order to assemble their report had but one particular slant. Instead of producing an assessment of the state of compliance in the state's obligations, it focused on seeking out and dwelling on specific violations, taking into account the six federal states, in order to reach their baseless conclusions."

If the C.I.D.H. were to expand its investigation to all the thirty-two federal states, debts would rise, and the Government of the Republic would need to do something more than express irritation. We everyday Mexicans, and we the outraged, are more numerous than the government. We cannot overlook, still less forget the atrocities taking place in Tlatlaya, Apatzingán, Tanhuato and Ayotzinapa between 2014 to 2015.

"Violence changed my sense of identity," says Marcela Turati, a journalist on *Proceso* and the most tender and responsible person one could possibly know. "My training taught me non-intervention, how not to get myself involved, stay always neutral, not become the protagonist of any cause. Only now have present circumstances obliged *Periodistas de a Pie* (Grassroots Journalists) to request help from international human rights organisations, provide them with necessary information, tell them what is going on in Mexico, so now I have become a different person".[2]

In Washington Marcela Turati received the Washington Office on Latin America (W.O.L.A.) Prize in 2013, alongside Senator Tom Harkin – who has struggled for human rights for more than forty years – and Ambassador Milton Romani Gerner from Uruguay, who combats drugs trafficking.

An independent journalist, who graduated from the Iberoamericana University, Marcela never imagined that reporting on poverty would lead her to the subject of the victims of narco-trafficking. In 2006, she co-founded the organisation *Periodistas de a Pie* to assist journalists investigating the subject of poverty. "Violence came looking for journalists without warning". Marcela had been forced to change the focus of her career drastically; and she came to prepare her comrades not to die. She brought them psychological and legal support, even founding a shelter for persecuted journalists. She also provided advice to child survivors of a massacre, providing additional information on how not to run unnecessary risks inside conflict zones. In consequence of the war on drugs, the role of a reporter was transformed into an act of resistance.

By 2010, the border city of Ciudad Juárez "had already turned into a national scrapyard of the dead, and newspapers published the scores for murders on a daily basis. Known as the 'execution-ometer'." Marcela met with groups of mothers, daughters, and wives in the most violent neighbourhoods, to share the enveloping horror, and to help them have the courage to come through.

All the women had been through the hardest experience of their lives: the disappearance and murder of a child. Marcela listened to the question of an old woman brought before a judge: "If they give me a bag of bones and tell me it's my son, how do I know it's him?"

Nowadays it is easy to see these women on every demonstration outside government offices waiting to see a bureaucrat who may well not even look at them. It is also easy to encounter them in civic organisations. They swell the lines of demonstrators, holding up photographs of their missing loved ones.

Official indifference obliges the women to undertake their own searches, sometimes alone, sometimes under the wing of a fellow civic organisation.

Marcela Turati's text conveys their role in the struggle: "It is they who travel the length and breadth of the country . . . to uncover the whereabouts of the husband, son or brother, any or all of them disappeared . . . It is they who remain on the home front – at homes now without a man, but with an abundance of children to feed."

Ciudad Juárez was the first city to epitomise violence against women. The cries and the abuse they suffer are endorsed by a *macho* society, even including assassination. The word "femicide" has joined the lexicon to describe the daily atrocities taking place in our country.

What is life composed of? What composes the weave of the infinite fabric of our unfolding destiny? In Mexico, there are thousands of women who have no other project that matters in their lives beyond their children. These three women journalists – Lydia Cacho, Marcela Turati and Anabel Hernández and the great Carmen Aristegui[3] (sacked from her programmes on state media) – reverse their fate and, without realising it, they become Marxists, Indianists, heroines and Antigones. By saving their children from oblivion they save their country.

All those who have joined in creating *The Sorrows of Mexico* are well-known writers and journalists. Villoro is just barely sixty years old; Osorno began writing in *Milenio*; Turati and Hernández in *Proceso*. Their articles are a reference point in Mexican litera-ture and current affairs columns. Not only have they published best-selling books but they take the side of what is in effect a suppurating wound, in other words they support Ayotzinapa, and make their denunciations at the risk of their own lives in a real but shadowy Mexico. These authors are a window opening onto a cleansing process, or, perhaps to put it better, a process of clarifica-tion and lucidity, as Octavio Paz calls it in his poem sent back from India where he was the Mexican ambassador following the massacre of probably hundreds of students in Mexico City on October 2, 1968.

Interruptions from the West (3)[4]

(Mexico City: The 1968 Olympiad)
for Dore and Adja Yunkers

Limpidity
              (perhaps it's worth
writing across the purity
of this page)
                     is not lucid:
it is fury
         (yellow and black
mass of bile in Spanish)
spreading over the page.
Why?
    Shame is anger
turned against oneself:
                              if
an entire nation is ashamed
it is a lion poised
to leap.
              (The municipal
employees wash the blood
from the Plaza of the Sacrificed.)
Look now
              stained
before anything worth it
was said:
              lucidity.

The feminist Marcela Turati is the most pained of all, for she
experiences at first hand the search followed by the opening up

of mass graves. Devastated, she is the person who has had most contact with mothers and fathers who she has witnessed "scratching at the earth with open hearts, with their own bare hands". To her, forced abductions and murders "encapsulate what this country has become". Many of these mothers turn to Marcela, knowing that from her they will receive the care and compassion our government is incapable of giving them. In many cases, the journalists have functioned as a bulwark against iniquity. Their articles were not enough, so today they walk hand in hand with the victims.

Translated by Amanda Hopkinson

INTRODUCTION
NARRATING THE DOWNFALL

Felipe Restrepo Pombo

MEXICO IS A VAST TERRITORY, almost a continent, with a diverse and sometimes impenetrable terrain. It is a difficult place for anyone to travel around, and especially for a foreigner. Above all, it is a complicated country. The Colombian writer Santiago Gamboa, who lived in India, used to say: "In the first month I thought I knew everything about India. When I had been there for many years, I realised I had understood nothing." The same could be said about Mexico, a country described by Juan Villoro – cited by Elena Poniatowska who contributed the preface to this book – as a place where "carnival lives alongside apocalypse".

I moved to Mexico in the summer of 2006, and found myself in the middle of a severe political crisis. At that time a bitter election campaign was being fought between Felipe Calderón, the National Action Party (P.A.N.) candidate, and Andrés Manuel López Obrador, the candidate for the Party of the Democratic Revolution (P.R.D.). After a violent confrontation that culminated in public protests – and profound social division – Calderón was declared the winner.

In those first years, I explored this new arena like an unsuspecting witness right at the heart of the fire. I thought then – and still do today – that Mexico was one of the most fascinating countries on the planet. I am not going to start listing all of its qualities here, but I will say that I immediately felt at home.

Yet even as I enjoyed the carnival, I began to detect signs of the apocalypse. One of the first I remember – which I described at the time in a story for the Colombian newspaper *El Espectador* – took place on September 15, 2008, the eve of Mexico's Independence Day. A group of masked men threw two grenades into the crowd celebrating in the town square in Morelia, the capital of Michoacán state. This was the first attack carried out by narco-traffickers against civilians in the country's history, and it was no coincidence that it took place in Calderón's hometown. It was an act of retaliation against his policy of waging war on organised crime.

Later, in mid 2009, I remember the arrest of Arnoldo Rueda Medina – nicknamed La Minsa – an important member of the criminal organisation known as La Familia. Rueda Medina was arrested during a shootout in the neighbourhood of Chapultepec Sur, also in Morelia. Just a few hours after his arrest, the powerful cartel he belonged to set out on a macabre act of revenge. They started by attacking a police station, shooting at it from armoured trucks and throwing grenades. This was followed by several random attacks. The Monday after the arrest, twelve bodies were found on a motorway: their hands were tied behind their backs and they showed signs of having been tortured. They were all police officers. Next to their corpses was a hand-written message on a white cardboard sign saying: "Come for another one, we're waiting for you."

In March 2010 I had the chance to watch a strange video that had arrived at the editorial department of one of the country's most popular TV news programmes. The footage, sent in by an anonymous contributor, chronicled the events that took place in the early hours of March 15 of that year in Creel, a town in Chihuahua state. The images showed a group of heavily armed men taking control of the town's main streets. Rather more than twenty hitmen took up position outside a wealthy-looking house, before going in and murdering nine people. They then burst into other homes in the neighbourhood and kidnapped some young women who they forced into their trucks. Next, without a care in the world, they began stopping the cars driving through the streets and beating up their drivers. Finally, they celebrated by sharing out a whole bag of cocaine between them. This all took over an hour, during which time no authorities appeared at any moment. After the video was broadcasted, the office of the Attorney General of Chihuahua announced that they had identified the criminals. Soon after that, the state's Assistant Attorney General, Sandra Ivonne Salas García, was murdered.

Scenes like these began invading Mexico's body politic like tumours. In Tamaulipas, one of the most violent zones, some Al-Jazeera reporters said they had never been anywhere so danger-ous or precarious. In Nuevo León, the authorities started handing out leaflets advising citizens on what to do if they happened to find themselves caught up in a gunfight. In Chihuahua, people stopped going to the local bars, preferring to cross the border into the United States for a night out.

For a long time the violence was seen as a marginal phenome-non, but eventually the outbreak spread to the big cities. The rise of organised crime began to be felt in Monterrey and Guadalajara. Even Mexico City, which had been considered an oasis, was no longer safe: not even la Condesa, one of the capital's most touristy, cosmopolitan areas, could escape the gunfights and murders. "People are beginning to see violence as something normal. There is no large-scale censorship of crime," said Ernesto López Portillo,

Director of the Institute for Security and Democracy, when I asked him about this issue a while ago.

"Organised crime has been gaining ground little by little. Its strikes are getting more and more spectacular, demonstrating how powerful it has become," explained Alberto Islas, director of Risk Evaluation, a consultancy firm that advises various governments on matters of security. An atmosphere of uncertainty and impunity began to grip the country: each day crimes took place that people no longer spoke about and which were never even investigated by the authorities. The level of impunity is thought to be at 90 per cent, and that is only for the crimes that are reported. "It's like a Swiss cheese: there are some parts where the holes are deeper. In some of these regions the State no longer has any control," Islas told me.

Finally, one of the most decisive events in recent decades took place in September 2014: the disappearance of 43 students from the Raúl Isidro Burgos Rural Teachers College in Iguala, Guerrero State.

The case provoked all kinds of reactions. However, for me the words of the courageous Elena Poniatowska stand out once more as a particularly emotional memory. At the awards ceremony for the National Journalism Prize, where she won the lifetime achievement award, she made a statement about the forty-three students. She went up on stage, turned to face the audience – which included various government officials – and said firmly: "Receiving this prize forty-one days after the disappearance of the forty-three teaching students from Ayotzinapa is a blow to the heart. Who gave them a prize? What did Mexico give them? Awards are never bestowed on the people who most deserve them: to the poor, to those who live each day as a thankless task for which the only reward is sleep. Guillermo Haro once gave a lift to a rural worker on the road between Puebla and Mexico City. To break the silence he asked him: 'What do you dream about?' The man replied, 'We can't afford to dream.'"

The disappearance of the students, which is still unresolved, confirmed that in some states crime has not only infiltrated the authorities: it is now crime itself that rules. And Guerrero, like so many other states, is trapped between desolation and brutality: an abandoned place, given over to violence and the cruel power of drug trafficking. And this all happens under the indifferent gaze of a political class that never fails to surprise us with its cynicism and corruption. This is Mexico's downfall.

* * *

Mexican journalists have suffered first-hand from the rise of violence and impunity. According to data published by Article 19 (Mexico and Central America), an independent organisation promoting freedom of expression and defending the free practice of journalism, a journalist was attacked every 48 hours during president Calderón's six-year term. This figure has increased dramatically in the three years since Enrique Peña Nieto has been president: a journalist is now attacked every 26.7 hours. Most disturbingly, around half of these assaults are carried out by people working for the State.

The National Human Rights Commission (C.N.D.H.) has 433 open cases on file regarding assaults on media outlets or journalists since 2010. The situation is particularly serious in Veracruz, Michoacán and Tamaulipas, the states with the highest number of reported attacks, murders, disappearances and instances of torture. In 96 per cent of cases, the affected journalists were covering stories relating to insecurity and corruption involving civil servants or organised crime.

Between December 2010 and February 2016 alone, nineteen journalists from Veracruz were murdered without the cases being resolved. Names like Regina Martínez, Gregorio "Goyo" Jiménez and Anabel Flores Salazar have become tragic symbols of the attacks against freedom of expression that have taken place during Javier Duarte's reign as governor of Veracruz.

Speaking in early 2016, the former director of Artículo 19 Darío Ramírez described Mexico as "the country with the highest number of missing journalists in the world". The organisation reported the forced disappearance of twenty-three journalists between January 2003 and January 2016. In other words, on average two journalists go missing every year.

Meanwhile, the online news site Animal Político has reported that 219 journalists requested State protection between November 2012 and May 2016 after becoming victims of attacks or threats. According to data from the Interior Ministry given to the Washington Office for Latin American affairs in May 2016, half of these attacks took place in the states of Veracruz, Guerrero, Oaxaca and Chiapas.

Some powerful voices are emerging from this suffocating atmosphere. In my role as editor of Gatopardo magazine I have had the opportunity to meet, read and edit the work of dozens of reporters who seek to portray the injustices being experienced in their country. Among them are Juan Villoro, Lydia Cacho, Marcela Turati, Emiliano Ruiz Parra, Diego Enrique Osorno, Sergio González Rodríguez and Anabel Hernández: seven extraordinary writers who have, through narration, risen up against the silence.

Despite coming from different generations and backgrounds, all of them have struggled with the difficulties of producing narrative, independent journalism. They have faced the dangers of reporting from inhospitable locations with no protection. They have battled with censorship – both the official kind and that of the various powers trying to silence them. And they have found that traditional media outlets either refuse to publish their work or pay only pittances. I should point out here that this is not only a Mexican problem: all Latin American journalists suffer to some degree from the same injustice. And I like to think of *Gatopardo* as a valuable space, offering an exceptionally committed platform that contributes to the production of quality journalism from across the region.

The texts that appear in this book do not just offer explanations. They are living portraits, powerful descriptions, precise dramatisations of fundamental moments in Mexico's recent history. They are hair-raising stories that also carry the weight of great responsibility. As Diego Enrique Osorno says in his "New Manifesto of Infrarrealist Journalism" (also published in this volume):

> The blank page of a reporter
> must be a weapon
> not a rag to soak up tears
> Journalistic *crónica* is subversive
> And subversive has nothing to do with nice[1]

The work of the journalists who appear in this anthology – as well as all those who do not – is hardly gratifying. It involves taking risks, both physically and as a writer, and facing up to a world of uncertainty. I hope that this book makes their work better known. And that it raises awareness of – and helps to end – all the sorrows of Mexico.

It is necessary to say that the writers whose work is in this book do not live and work in an environment where they can expect public servants to be accountable, or that information provided by the organs of state will be reliable. They live and work in an environment where they have come to expect that anything proffered as an official version of the truth must be viewed with natural scepticism. They have witnessed, at first hand, some of the events that they describe – indeed, some have been victims of those events themselves. They have interviewed people directly involved in the events. They live and work amongst these outrages and, through what they have written here, provide to the outside world the best available accounts of the current events as they see them, of incidents that might without their courage have no impact on the wider world.

Research assistant: Marcela Vargas
Translated by Catherine Mansfield

NEW MANIFESTO OF INFRAREALIST JOURNALISM

Diego Enrique Osorno

A migrant
a ghost
a battered woman
are riding right now along
the curve of death

Left far behind are the hills of a Mixteca song
or the underground tunnels of Mitla
the labyrinth of Yagul rising in Valles

Before the cries of this Mexican pain
the murmur of a common potoo
breaks a hidden cavern
among mountains filled with cacti and hunger

* * *

To write about this
at the hotel in a village of murderers
To write there
about a village of victims
Writing against the politically correct
the politically corrupt
Writing ceaselessly and more than ever
because infrarealist journalism

is wounded
distorted
confronted
but still standing
a
n
d
b
e
l
o
w

* * *

Francisco Goldman and Father Solalinde
walk around Oaxaca
they speak of the truth
they expand our consciousness
guide infrarealist journalism

John Gibler is a sensitive Mexican
whose name rhymes with Guerrero
We see him board a bus
destined for Ayotzinapa
But on the way
the bus and John
Disappear

Carlos Montemayor has died
And also some of the 54 million
Mexican poor
have had more children

The son of a policeman from Coahuila
In pain

tweets – to emptiness –
denouncing his extreme solitude

A photojournalist stays at home petrified
and doesn't attend the funeral of his assassinated colleague
Another photojournalist leaves his camera on the floor
during the press conference
where an official spokesperson
– even though he was a journalist in his past life –
is a voice from the afterlife
narrating the historical truth

A tortured man from Oaxaca
does not know what to do at the Guelaguetza
he just watches the afternoon from the Cerro del Fortín

The anarchist from Mexico City
who sets the door of the National Palace on fire
knows he is not telegenic
and that he is right

A young girl from Tenancingo
writes a poem
which, though clichéd,
no-one will decipher

* * *

More than 100,000 Mexicans have been executed in this
    first quarter of a century
We already hold them up in our memory and indignation
And who and what kind of Mexicans are the other 100,000
who were executed,
dumped in a lorry,
cooked in acid,
hanged from a bridge?

On the answer to that question
hangs the secret of governing
It's not that there is barbarity in our democracy:
Barbarity is our democracy

* * *

To write is an attack against the self
or it is not writing

Truth must be told to power
we must look it in the eye
strip it of something
Without mercy

The blank page of a reporter
must be a weapon
not a rag to soak up tears
Crónica is subversive
And subversive has nothing to do with nice
just as class struggle has nothing to do
with Mexican *lucha libre*
Although it's true that *crónica* has become fashionable
And at times it's as high and mighty
as the Cirque du Soleil
On the plus side *crónica* will outlive
journalists
crónica detractors
and *crónica* writing workshops

Narrative journalism
Is not infrarealist journalism
Narrative journalism
Is the dangerous curve
On which this manifesto began
It is also a misunderstanding

A slap in the face
A dirtied river in Veracruz

* * *

Infrarealist journalists
fall silent when they enter Mitla
In that silence there is a very scant
bit of
Transparency

They know that the strong Mexican state
is a brilliant myth
Spanning a few political columns
and three or four news shows on radio and television

Infrarealist journalists are autonomous
They do not play
the electoral game
Political parties are schools of deceit
and elections are a distraction
if what is really wanted
is to change something

We are not arithmetic
We are alive
And we want to die in peace
Aflame

Infrarealist journalists
are street dogs
Who traverse Masaryk
They are sad paths
Or Trotskyists who have never read Trotsky
although they know the proletariat
was decapitated by some Zetas and marines

Infrarrealist journalists
are backhoe excavators
of governmental shit

Infrarrealist journalism
is an insect, phosphorescent against the holocaust
A song by Arturo Meza in Acteal
A successful liver transplant
A weimarainer peering out the window
A shrimp that survives a Guinness cocktail
A dream Alberto Pathistán dreamt in prison

* * *

The rebel *campesino* is executed extrajudicially
At a roundabout of lilies
Before midnight
And the peoples are massacred on the equinox
When their spring water sprouts up
And gas explorers have arrived
All this remains unremembered
Unremembering: the real enemy
of infrarrealist journalism
of any authentic journalist

It's not enough to light a candle for peace

Artefact designed in 2015 during research, workshops and funerals held in areas of Oaxaca such as Mitla, Huajuapan, San Antonino Castillo Velasco, Putla de Guerrero and Santa Catarina Lachatao.

Translated by Jennifer Adcock

I

OUTRAGE

COLLATERAL DAMAGE – LIVING IN MEXICO

Juan Villoro

Capitalism without copyright

In 2010, I was invited on a tour of the recently renovated Red Cross Hospital in Mexico City with its president, Daniel Goñi Díaz. Justifiably proud, Goñi Díaz showed me the technology in the spotless operating theatres and wards. All of a sudden, we arrived at an entire corridor where there were only four single rooms. A special luxury?

The president of the Red Cross is a notary public. Up to this moment, he had been speaking in the tone of someone pronouncing statements with which one can only agree. In a grave voice, he added: "These rooms allow for greater vigilance." He was not referring to medical attention, but to police custody: "This is where we attend to criminals; our obligation is to give assistance to everyone."

I asked him what had been the biggest challenge to the Red Cross. The swine flu epidemic? "That was a false alarm. From the beginning we knew it was exaggerated. My son is a competitive swimmer and he had a race in Veracruz, near the first outbreak. I told him to go. Our greatest challenge is something else: keeping the wounded *inside* the ambulances. Many of them have connections to organised crime. Our ambulances get stopped and people are finished off right there." Once in hospital, they have to be kept under guard.

As chance would have it the Red Cross is located on avenida Ejército Nacional (National Army Avenue). Every day more war wounded arrive at this emergency room.

Far away to the north, in the municipality of Villa de Reyes, San Luis Potosí, is an extensive desert where coyotes are now as scarce as people. Hunting and emigration to the United States have emptied the territory. Clusters of houses are scattered here and there. I spent the 2010 Easter Holidays in Bledos, one of these towns that seem on the brink of disappearing under a cloud of dust. There, a cousin of mine struggles to preserve the ruins of a hacienda that produced mescal before the 1910 Revolution.

At night, the town is shrouded in a silence only occasionally broken by the howling of a dog. The aim of the journey was to show my daughter, who was ten years old back then, the place where her paternal great-grandmother had lived and where many of her relatives spent their holidays. We found a wasteland where the main distractions had to do with legends: ghost stories and tales of an era, even more implausible, when the region was inhabited. In such circumstances, we were enthusiastic over the arrival of a travelling circus. An old patched-up tent was erected with fantastic screeches and creaking. The ring was a circle of dust where scorpions nested. The main attractions were not the bold trapeze artists, but the clowns, who concentrated on squashing scorpions with their supersized shoes.

We thought that would be the decisive thrill of our Easter holiday, but when we returned to the hacienda my cousin told us that the drug cartels were on holiday too and a gang of Zetas had arrived in Bledos looking for some fun. Three black vans, full of hired killers, were driving around town.

We locked the gate with a medieval bolt while they spread terror. They kidnapped a teenage girl, beat up a farm worker and robbed a gas station. Around five in the morning, seizing on a quiet moment of respite, we escaped to Mexico City. I had wanted my ten-year-old daughter to travel back into her past; dreadfully, we confronted her present.

The Mexican desert has shifting masters. "The hills are my house, my family, my protection, my land," said the drug trafficker Ismael (El Mayo) Zambada in an interview he gave to Julio Scherer García, the only relevant encounter between a *capo* and a leading journalist. Four times the army had been close to capturing him, but he managed to escape: "I fled to the hills, which I know completely, every branch, every creek, every stone. They'll nab me if I sit still or get careless." That fugitive said more than he appeared to. His ability to escape is less significant than the fact that he has an enormous territory available. The abandoned Mexican countryside offers refuge, landing strips and hiding places for drug trafficking.

A hundred years ago Pancho Villa rode across a nation where 80 per cent of the population lived in the country. That proportion has reversed. Except in the fertile zones, the countryside is a desolate place where almost nothing is produced. Collective ownership of the land prevents private investment. The expropriation and reallocation of agrarian lands following the Mexican Revolution was to a large extent a demagogical operation that wiped out formerly productive units. From a statistical point of view, justice was done, but people received useless lands. A short story by Juan Rulfo, "They Have Given Us the Land", records the tragedy of those who became proprietors of dust.

After receiving useless properties, the *campesinos* went from being subjugated peons to defenceless proprietors. Their only way

out was to emigrate to the United States. This allowed drug trafficking to avail itself of an *empty country*. The countryside is its
no man's land, its hinterland, its rear-guard. There is no lack of
Mexicans in the world, but there is in rural Mexico.

In the desert everything happens as an exception. Daniel Sada's
novels demonstrate that any event there is decisive. In times of
technology and poverty, lands with nobody on them offer local
shelter to globalised illegality planned on computers.

Cinema, music, literature and painting were all obsessively
concerned with this territory until the 1950s. Then, the countryside
dropped out of our imaginations. The *campesinos* moved to the
cities or the United States. Few perceived, as Sada did in his novel
Porque parece mentira, la verdad nuca se sabe (Because It Seems to
Be a Lie, the Truth Is Never Known), that something was changing
in the largest hiding place in the Americas.

According to Leonardo Valdés, who in 2010 acted as chairman
of the Federal Electoral Institute, the absence of security conditions
hinders the installation of polling stations in at least 15 per cent of
the national territory. A strip on the margins of sovereignty.

In 2006 President Felipe Calderón launched the war against
drug trafficking. The problem, of course, had been around for a
long time. But the strategy failed. We were sitting on dynamite
and Calderón lit a match to prove it. "The only thing a war on
drugs does is raise the price without significantly reducing the
demand," explains Marcelo Bergman, who holds a doctorate in
the sociology of law from the University of California. After more
than a hundred thousand violent deaths and thirty thousand forced
disappearances it is clear that any one of us could become "collateral damage" in a war we did not ask for.

Economist David Konzevik has a gift for understanding markets
and a superior gift for explaining them: "Mexico's main economic

problem is employment. The worst thing is not that formal occupations are disappearing, but that unemployed people have other options. And they're all illegal." The arms trade, the drugs trade, human trafficking, a trade in which women are classed as products, are the options Konzevik is talking about. In this capitalism without copyright, piracy coexists with tax-avoiding monopolies. Piracy, human trafficking and drug dealing account for more than 10 per cent of the money in circulation. Another similar amount comes from the remittances migrant workers send back home, which are not accountable. But even the formal economy avoids legality; large consortiums evade taxes by way of careful fiscal engineering and favours they receive from the government. The "Panama Papers" revealed that Juan Armando Hinojosa, to cite just one example, had a hundred million dollars in offshore accounts. Hinojosa is the boss of the Higa group and has wholeheartedly supported president Enrique Peña Nieto. The secret accounts in Panama come from profits his construction company made when Peña was governor of the State of México and from the tenders it continues to obtain with the backing of the presidency. In exchange, Higa supported Peña Nieto's presidential campaign and gave the first lady, Angélica Rivera, a plot of land on which to build a mansion. This network reveals influence-trafficking and a lack of fiscal transparency. Drug traffickers as well as many big businessmen participate in an economy that avoids accountability, a capitalism without responsibilities. Foucault pointed out that books began to be signed, not so much to recognize authorship, but rather to know where to assign blame. Copyright protects, but also holds an author responsible. In a country where 120 journalists have been murdered in the last twenty-five years for writing what they think, those who do business in the shadows are faceless.

Mexico is an especially young country, where seven and a half million kids can be described as *ninis*, people who neither study nor work (*ni estudia ni trabaja*). What can be on the horizon for these young people without alternatives? There are no choices they could make to do with work, education, religion or sports that might bring them as strong a sense of belonging as organised crime. The sociologist Rossana Reguillo has done brilliant studies of this cultural variable of the subject. Unable to include the young, the state tends to criminalise them in advance as "juvenile delinquents". This works as a self-fulfilling prophecy: the cartels offer identity and shared codes.

The strangest toll of the battle against drug trafficking is that we do not know some of the decisive protagonists. We know little about the army and the various perspectives within it. But most of all, we know nothing about the United States. The D.E.A. has made Mexican *capos* into celebrities. This exterior policy has no internal correlation. The main consumer of drugs and guns operates in the shadows. Mexico contributes the dead, that is, the stories. Where is the other part of the narrative?

Culture can help the social fabric to recover. In Medellín and Bogotá two mathematicians who became mayors, Fajardo and Mockus, understood that libraries combat violence. Including young people in society is a more expensive and slower task than buying weapons, but also more worthwhile. Mexico will not be saved by bullets, but by its people.

"Do you know who contributes most to Red Cross coffers?" Daniel Goñi Díaz asked me at the end of my visit. "The poor."

The forgotten do not forget their country.

The ecology of fear

The Autopista del Sol, which leads to Acapulco, serves as therapy to the drivers of Mexico City and is as expensive as psychoanalysis. On 18 July 2015 I recovered the sensation of freedom that clear roads provide and discovered that it has its price.

After passing Cuernavaca, I left behind the Fonda Cuatro Vientos (the Four Winds Truck Stop), celebrated bastion of *cecina* (a thinly sliced, cured meat), confident we would find another place to have breakfast.

Our destination was Ayotzinapa. Along with eleven other writers and artists, I was going to be a godfather at the graduation party for the class of 2011–15, at the Raúl Isidro Burgos Teacher Training College.

Studying to become a teacher has turned into one of the most difficult ambitions to achieve in Mexico. An unwritten law closes down rural schools if there are no applicants for two years. The government has not dared to cancel this kind of education, but has done everything possible to make it unfeasible. Learning to read and write has become a threat.

To be able to enrol at the Normal School, the future students organise protests and continue to struggle for the entire academic year. If not, they lack support. The generation that I was going to sponsor began their course in tragic conditions. So poor and desperate were they that in 2011 they set up a roadblock on the Autopista del Sol to collect funds for their studies and the federal police murdered two of them. In 2014, forty-three members of the class disappeared.

The four-hour drive was an immersion in the mistrust that rules our lives in Mexico.

Past Cuernavaca, just over 70 kilometres from Mexico City, we still had several tollbooths ahead of us. We had not had a bite to eat since dawn and were still hoping to find a place to have breakfast. However, unlike other roads, where taco stands are more frequent than petrol stations, the first restaurant we found was near Ixtla, not far from Ayotzinapa.

We walked into a place with colourful wooden furniture and *piñatas* hanging from the ceiling. The toilets were clean and in good working order, there was a well-stocked bar and the menu offered enough casseroles and stews to make up for the austerity of the *cecina*.

A tall, swarthy man with a thick moustache that accentuated his smile served us. He brought some complimentary tortilla crisps and told us to look over the menu at our leisure.

I went to wash my hands. When I came back to the table, my companion said: "They asked where we were headed and I didn't know what to say."

Was it safe to tell people we were on our way to Ayotzinapa? Paranoia has many ways to reach the Mexican mind. Going to the place where the forty-three disappeared student teachers had studied opened uncertain possibilities.

The manager came back to take our order. Then he went out to the road. He saw my car, took out a mobile phone and made a call. Why did he not speak inside the restaurant? Maybe the signal was better outside, or maybe he did not want us listening in.

He came back in and handed us a copy of the newspaper *Sur*: "To keep you entertained while you wait."

Were we going to have such a long wait? A plot began to compose itself in my mind: the man had asked where we were going (although he did not receive an answer, our destination seemed obvious, since there was a celebration at the Isidro Burgos Normal School). He also checked out my car. Who had he called? Did he lend us a newspaper to justify the delay of our breakfast? In that interval someone could come and get us. I saw the place had two doors; I put the car keys on the table to give to my companion and said to escape through the other door if anyone suspicious arrived.

A pick-up truck parked beside the restaurant. I stood up to look out the window. The recent arrivals did not look like narcos or cops, more like office workers. When I got back to the table, the *chilaquiles* were waiting for me.

We ate breakfast in peace and I regretted being so paranoid. Fear ruined my trip more than the tollbooths.

We went to the Ayotzinapa students' graduation, which I was sponsoring. After a moving ceremony, where indignation gave way to hopefulness, we spent time with the students and the legion of activists who turn up in the most unexpected corners of the country to campaign for a whole range of causes.

At four in the afternoon we verified that strong emotions can be just as draining as too much sunshine. Exhausted, we began the return journey.

We decided to eat in the same place where we had breakfast. There were not too many choices before reaching Mexico City. Besides, I like to think I have rituals and that in repeating an action I am confirming some sort of belief.

The manager greeted us with even more warmth. After the day in Ayotzinapa, and now without the slightest fear that something might happen to us there, we enjoyed the food, seasoned with the our host's conversation. He told us that he had worked behind a grill in Mexico City for fifteen years, but the tensions of the capital made him ill. He was admitted to hospital in Chilpancingo; later, life in the provinces worked miracles in his body. The restaurant belonged to him and his brothers.

When we said goodbye he gave us some sweets and we promised to return.

"Well, let's hope you'll find me here," he said enigmatically.

We asked him what he meant. He told us that the drug traffickers were the real rulers of the region and they exerted rights over the ground. He had calculated the amount that would sink him and his brothers: "If they ask for ten thousand pesos a month, we'll close."

Up till now they had not touched him, but he feared the arrival of the fatal emissary.

Before we got back in the car, we looked at the landscape of green hills. It was raining softly and the breeze carried the scent of herbs. The place was idyllic, but it was in Mexico. In the morning we had been afraid of something happening to us there. At dusk, the manager told us of his fear, as if we had transferred ours to him. Dread was the ecosystem that united us.

We had mistrusted someone who mistrusted others, someone who deserved the best luck in a country where there is not much luck left.

We are all extras

Our life goes on between frights, fiestas and ceremonies. Fear can assault you on a deserted highway, whether or not it represents a real danger, and later you might attend a mise en scène that might entail greater risks. If the world of facts is defined by bullets, that of politics is defined by histrionics.

On March 26, 2015, six months after the disappearance of forty-three students from Ayotzinapa, a march took over the streets of Mexico City. Simultaneously, the Zócalo filled with handcrafted skeletons, skulls and sharp-looking scythes. A helicopter was filming this festival of the dead. Curiously, the funereal disguises were not part of the protest demonstration, but of the filming of "Spectre", the new James Bond movie. Even so, it was a political gesture: there is no way to see a skull in Mexico and not think of the disappeared.

In this most recent super-production, 007 drinks martinis while seducing irrefutably gorgeous girls of questionable conduct. One scene has him getting his hair ruffled in Mexico City. What role did the local population play there? The same one as in the political arena: they were extras.

A climate of false participation determines our democracy. Maybe because we take unpunctuality to epic proportions, it took us seventy-one years to free ourselves from one-party rule. During most of the twentieth century, our politics were like a hippodrome where the same horse wins every race. Based on a careful strategy of pacts with various social sectors and the elimination of dissent, the Institutional Revolution Party (P.R.I.) was able to govern, representing ideologies that changed according to the needs of the times. In a strict sense, more than a political party the P.R.I. has been an immense labour exchange, which allowed business to be conducted with the support of power.

In the year 2000 we finally discovered the idea of *la alternancia* or the transfer of power. What has happened since then? Scandals have spattered the entire political class, the parties' slogans are interchangeable and no candidate seems capable of fulfilling them.

Without any regulation other than their own, the parties discovered the industry of conflict, where it is most profitable not to resolve problems but to preserve them. This allows negotiations to proceed on which they obtain dividends (on the condition that the solution is postponed and future negotiations planned).

The Green Ecologist Party of Mexico (Partido Verde Ecologista de México, P.V.E.M.) has been fined more than forty million dollars for violating the advertising law. However, they pay the fines with the kind of optimism that approves of the death penalty.

The punishment affects few because lies are spread, and its alliance with the P.R.I. guarantees them 7 per cent of the votes, which means securing perks in excess of the fines, which are actually an investment in the future. The P.V.E.M. is not an anomaly in our political system; it is simply the group that best takes advantage of the way it works.

With Olympic disdain, Borges referred to democracy as "that curious abuse of statistics". In Mexico, the phrase acquires a disturbing radicalism. Votes do not oblige anyone to act in a certain way; they serve as a pretext or, in the best of cases, as a poll to justify the business of the parties. In this atmosphere of a charity bazaar, it is not surprising that Morena, the left-wing group, should select its plurinominal candidates by raffle.

On Sunday, June 7, 2015, we Mexicans abused statistics in mid-term elections. Voting is preferable to not voting because abstention favours the most powerful party (in this case, the P.R.I.); nevertheless, we were facing the most soulless election since 1976, when there was only one candidate for the presidency – José López Portillo of the P.R.I. Fed up with the electoral farce, the opposition parties refused to put forward any candidates. The novelist Jorge Ibargüengoitia wrote an article about this contest without adversaries that began: "The election is this Sunday. How exciting! Who will win?"

Nowadays, "alternatives" abound, but all the parties distance themselves from the citizens and the government opts for isolation, protecting themselves from criticism. Pressures against journalists intensify; Article 19 has identified more than three hundred incidents of aggression in the past year. Not long ago, Virgilio Andrade was named Secretary of Public Administration; however, this "anti-corruption prosecutor" lacks autonomy because he is accountable to the president. Heinrich von Kleist renewed German comedy with "The Broken Jug", in which a judge investigates a crime he committed himself. In Mexico, this has another name: "legality".

More than a year after the Ayotzinapa disappearances there is no reliable version of what happened. In an attempt to change the uses of language, the Attorney General in charge of the investigation called a hypothesis a "historical truth": the students were handed over by the police to drug gangs who murdered and incinerated them. However, to reduce bodies to ashes in the open air would have required a quantity of firewood or rubber tyres of which there are no traces. I spoke with Berta Nava, mother of one of the disappeared boys. After visiting the alleged site, she said with eloquent simplicity: "All around the edge, it was green." There were no signs of a huge pyre. For its part, the international forensic team charged with reviewing the remains have complained about interference and the manipulation of data.

The government condoned the "historical truth" to prevent the investigation of the army, which does have crematoriums at its disposal, and used them against the civilian population in the "dirty war" of the 1970s.

No-one seems to be responsible for the incident. On May 11, 2015, the Interdisciplinary Group of Independent Experts, named by the Inter-American Commission on Human Rights, criticised the "fragmentation of the investigation". "More than thirteen cases filed in six different courts in various cities around the country" make it difficult to have a complete overview of the events.

That summer I travelled with my family to Nayarit on Mexico's Pacific coast. The only airline that flies there is Aeromar, which operates small propeller planes. Half of the passengers were hand-cuffed prisoners on their way to one of the largest penitentiaries in the country. None of them had committed crimes in the region and their accomplices had been sent to other prisons. An example of

the kind of dispersion that turns justice into an impassable labyrinth. Since it can no longer sanction, the judicial system prefers to
confuse in order to hide its incompetence.

"Dead bodies: places please!"

In *La guerre des images* (*The Image War*), Serge Gruzinski describes
the population of Mexico City as a "chaos of doubles". We might
say that this is the current function of the citizenry (given the violence, we could specify that we are talking about "stunt doubles",
like those who take Daniel Craig's place in the dangerous scenes
in "Spectre").

Super-productions offer involuntary metaphors of Mexico. In
1997, three years after the signing of N.A.F.T.A. with the United
States and Canada, the movie "Titanic" was filmed on the beaches
of Baja California. The blocks of "ice" in the water were pieces of
polyurethane, and the "drowned" were Mexican extras. This
symbol of the unequal exchange between north and south, to which
Mexico contributes floating corpses, has also been made flesh in
science fiction. In "Total Recall" (1990) and "Elysium" (2013),
Mexico City was used as a *natural* setting of devastation and its
inhabitants participated as a needy horde, beggars of a future age.

But it was a stateless writer who best understood the meaning
of the Mexican people in international super-productions. Born in
Romania, Gregor von Rezzori wrote in German, lived in France
and spent his final years in Italy. In 1965 he spent five months
in Mexico participating in the shooting of the film "Viva María!"
directed by Louis Malle and starring Jeanne Moreau and Brigitte
Bardot. The novelist had a modest role. Like Malcolm Lowry or
D. H. Lawrence, Rezzori was fascinated and horrified by Mexico
in equal measure. The literary result of his stay was *Die Toten
auf ihre Plätze. Tagebuch des Films Viva Maria* (The Dead in their

Places: Journal of the Movie "Viva Maria") an ironic diary that displeased the creators of that cinematic extravaganza. In each of its vignettes, the traveller turned transitory actor transmits the captivating and repugnant ambivalence of a landscape with "puddles of urine reflecting the stars". But most eloquent of all is the title. Thousands of Mexicans participated in scenes of an early twentieth-century revolution and their role consisted of adorning the ground as corpses. Before each shot, the assistant director instructed: "Dead bodies: places please!" This is the function we Mexicans perform, not only in the cinema, but in the representation of reality we call "democracy".

Do we have a vocation for being extras or does history edge us into that vicarious role? The fact is that every year Mexico presents the world's largest concentration of living dead on the Zombie Walk.

According to the terms of our film workers' union, anyone who has a speaking part qualifies as an "actor". Extras have no voice. In big-budget cinema, Mexicans are castaways, beggars of the future and heralds of death. They are there, but have no influence. If more are needed, they can be replicated by computer: "doubles of doubles".

Our electoral situation is not much different. Until our politics creates citizens, we will not be protagonists.

"Show me / your face that I may see at last / my true face, that of another / my face forever the face of us all," wrote Octavio Paz.[1] Democracy begins when the extras speak.

The mid-term election of June 7, 2015, ratified the P.R.I.'s supremacy. The antihero of politics that lost power after seventy-one years of exercising and abusing it, returned after twelve years of inefficiency from the conservative National Action Party (P.A.N.). No-one was unaware of the P.R.I.'s pedigree of corruption, but its rule seemed preferable. Like an abusive and authoritarian father who nevertheless provides some benefits to his children, the old "single party" seemed preferable to being orphaned.

This was also possible because of a lack of alternatives. One of the greatest tragedies a society can suffer is the loss of expectations. This particular Mexican moment is defined by its sorrows, but also by the absence of solutions. In the year 1976, when there was only one candidate for the presidency, it seemed like everything would be better when parties proliferated. Today we have ten and none of them represents a civic choice. For them, democracy belongs to the industry of conflict. They decide the amount of their resources and do not submit to any sort of supervision by citizens whatsoever. Between "ordinary expenses" and support of the campaigns, Mexican political parties received 5,100,000,000 pesos in 2015. This ever-increasing plunder is disputed at every election. The cycle is not broken; it perpetuates itself with interchangeable slogans.

The future does not depend on the established parties, but on those who have never had a voice: extras, doubles, the disappeared, Mexicans.

Translated by Anne McLean

LILY SINGS LIKE A LITTLE BIRD

Diego Enrique Osorno

I – Honeyed words

My dad died before I finished high school. That's how the family was torn apart. Mum and my brother moved in with my grandparents, and I moved in with one of Mum's sisters, because that's what Dad had decided. He didn't trust my granddad because he didn't respect his granddaughters.

One day my aunt started telling tales about a witchdoctor who'd told her I'd stolen a gold chain and a bunch of other stuff. A load of nonsense. I think what she really wanted was me to move out of her house, and was making up excuses. Faced with that, I told one of Dad's sisters what was going on with me and Mum's family, and she decided to let me move in with her.

By that time I'd already started university. I was nineteen years old and was quite far into my degree in tourism at the Universidad Tecnológica del Centro de Veracruz, but I had to work. I had a job in a shoe shop which doubled as a boutique selling clothes and accessories. One Saturday I'm given half an hour's lunch break. I go to the city park and in the distance I spot a guy, a young man. He seemed nice, well dressed, and he kept looking at me. He was actually staring, until he came and threw away an empty can near where I was, I think he did it on purpose, and he says, Hello, what's your name? We got chatting. He told me his name was Alex, that

he was from Querétaro, he was twenty-five years old and he was
here because he was waiting for a friend with whom he was going
to look for employees to work with him in Puebla. Then he said,
What do you do? I said I was working and studying, and that I was
running late, so this is where it all ends, I have to get back to work,
they're expecting me. He asked for my phone number. I stupidly
give it to him, and he gives me his, although I was honest and said,
I won't have any credit to reply to your messages. He then pulled
out a 100-peso banknote and I said, I will never accept one cent
from you. If you really want to top up my phone, you can go and
do it yourself. And then he topped up my phone and called me, sent
me texts. In his texts he said that he liked me and so many things.
One day I'd had it up to here with him sending me those messages
and I said, If you really want a serious relationship with me, why
don't you come and ask permission from my family? It didn't take
him long to say yes, right off the bat he came all the way to my
house to speak to my aunt, the one I was living with. And well,
my aunt gave her permission for us to be officially boyfriend and
girlfriend, because she saw him as a grown-up and he seemed like
a responsible and a well-mannered person.

   He was tall, slim and dark, and his eyes looked olive green
sometimes – I think he wore contacts. He had straight hair and
a fringe, he dressed in tight-fitting clothes, usually fuchsia or black
shirts, but patterned, and skinny bellbottoms, and pointy shoes or
white trainers. That's how he dressed. He drove a white Bora that
looked like the latest model. That's the car he came in to see my
family. I remember I felt under a lot of pressure because the day
he came to speak to my aunt he said, The thing is, I really want you
to marry me. I like you a lot.

   And we'd only just met!

   I don't know what happened to me in that moment and I said,

You know what? We're through, I still need to finish my degree.
So he got angry and took off in his car. I told my aunt what had
happened and she says, Lily, you're such a silly girl, that boy obviously loves you, he's grown-up and responsible. He'd told my aunt
that he supported his sister's son and that from time to time he
helped his family, since he had seven apartments in Puebla which
he rented out, and was going for fifteen and then fifty apartments.
He wanted to show off with my family and he'd succeeded, so I
change my mind and send him a text: I want to see you, forgive me
and all the rest. He says, O.K., right now I'm on my way to Puebla,
but I'll come and see you soon.

So he used to come and see me, we would go out for lunch or
dinner. He always seemed like a respectful person. He'd propose
I stay with him at a hotel and I'd say I wasn't into that, and he'd
say O.K., if you don't want to, that's fine by me, I respect you. Until
one day I sent him a message saying I had to move to another town
in Veracruz to do an internship. He was furious and said, You can
keep your studies and your school, let's see if they give you love
and happiness like I do. Then he told me that if we were going
to break up, we needed to do it properly. We arranged to meet in
Córdoba, Veracruz, at the park. I was very sad and he was trying
to convince me: Come with me, you're going to be alright, if you
want I can support you by paying your university tuition. I don't
know what kind of honeyed words came out of his mouth, because
he had a gift for persuasion, you can't imagine.

So eventually after much insistence he convinces me and takes
me to Puebla. We left that afternoon. I warned him that I'd come
back the following day and that he was going to respect me, but he
didn't care; when we arrived to Puebla he did what he wanted with
me and the next day he said, So? Are you leaving? And I said No,
well not anymore, what's the point now? And so I had to stay with

him. The first few days he treated me nice, we'd go out shopping and for a stroll like a normal couple.

II – Prince of Persia

Early on, living with him in Puebla, he would suddenly start telling me about a friend of his whose wives were sex workers and earned a lot of money, up to 20,000 pesos a week. Another day he said, If you worked for me, you'd earn a lot of money, then he started speaking to me about a female friend of his who had a son and was very poor; he'd helped her by explaining how prostitution worked. According to him, his friend started working and within a year she'd bought a big two-storey house in León, Guanajuato, as well as a brand new van straight from the agency. He told me a lot of things which I wasn't even interested in, that he'd had girlfriends in the United States, from Spain, from Honduras, from Ecuador, from the Dominican Republic, and even from Kenya, Africa, that's the name of a place, isn't it? I used to get really annoyed when he said that.

One day he put it to me directly: Would you work for me as a sex worker? I immediately asked what the hell was wrong with him, and was he crazy. After that, he asked me the same thing every single day. Then he would become even more insistent when he came home drunk. He called me a twat, a crazy bitch, a cow; he said that a woman who refuses to help her husband was worth shit and that I had to give my life for him, just as he would give his for me.

And now I can see that because I always refused, one day he decided to change his tactics and invite me to the cinema. I was very excited because it was the first time I went to the cinema in my life. We went to Cholula, Puebla. I remember he said, I'm going to take you to the cinema so that at least you can say your first husband took you to the cinema. We watched the film "The Prince of Persia". On the way back we went to a restaurant and there he said, Petal, you're very pretty, but I can't be with you anymore. He started saying that his first option for a bride had been the Fair Queen of Loma Bonita, Oaxaca; his second option had been a girl from Acapulco; and his third option had been me, but because I didn't want to help him, he was going to have to leave me.

He kept talking for a long time and eventually said: I'm going to give you three options: the first is that I give you 300,000 pesos and you go and finish your degree, but you and me are done for good; the second option is that I'll be sending you a thousand pesos a week as well as clothes and food with my employees, but it's over between us; and the third option is that you stay and work as a sex worker for me.

He'd put me in a difficult position, so I say to him: I'm not going to give you an answer here, let's go home and we can talk there. And it was the same thing again, he intimidated me, belittled me, said, Your dad is no longer alive, your family doesn't love you, and anyway, if you go back, where will go? You don't even have a house. All this hurt because he was right. If I went back to my family, well, they weren't going to accept me anymore or see me with the same eyes.

Well, unfortunately and after he kept insisting, I agreed to his last proposal. He was in a chipper mood and even took me to the village to see my dad's grave before I started working for him. On the way he said I was not to tell anyone that I was going to be a sex worker from now on. By then he was no longer my boyfriend. I didn't have a dad, but I had a pimp.

III – *The detective who introduced me to Lily*

I was a dentist first and then as a mature student I did a degree in Law. At the time I needed to do a project for a foundation, because I was studying a class on community development, and they asked you to collaborate with one. Someone said to me, There's La Roca, a charity that helps boys and girls. When I met with them, they told me they needed a legislation analysis and a comparative report on the issue of human trafficking, but then they realised it existed already. Anyway, I started getting involved and I ended up investigating the case of a girl who was disappeared, and we found her! That's how it all started.

In the case of Lily, when she realises she was not the only girl being taken for a ride by the same guy, and that this guy used the same modus operandi and had several girlfriends and wives, then it's like her heart sees the light and she realises what's going on.

But at first Lily didn't see herself as a victim of human trafficking. She protected that guy. The day she decided to sing, she did so like a little bird. I remember she was in the shelter for about two months and didn't speak at all, not one word. When she finally did we couldn't keep her quiet.

IV – *Travelling to La Merced*

The girl who taught me the ropes and told me how much I needed to charge – I'd already met her as the wife of a friend of the Pimp. They'd both taken me to the doctor to be given a bunch of injections, and in the end, the Pimp said, If you get pregnant, you're going to have to have an abortion.

Then the Pimp dropped us both off at the station so we could catch a bus to Mexico City. On the way we sat at the back and she started explaining the whole shebang. Things like how much I needed to charge for the different positions. When we got to Mexico

City, we took the subway towards La Merced. She had a room there at Hotel Necaxa. I remember it was room 206. There we got changed, got ready, and then she took me first to the Hotel Las Cruces.

When I was interviewed by the receptionist, he asks me, What year were you born? I said '91. He said he didn't believe I was of legal age, even though I had ID. The girl kept begging the blessed receptionist, but he refused, so she got in touch with another girl. She sent her a text message. The other girl was in the alleyway of Santo Tomás, known as La Pasarela (The Catwalk). We went to that alley and I stayed with the other girl. We went into the fleabag apartments there and met with the madam, a woman people called La Pancha. She was really evil, she had the face of a witch. In any case, she accepted me, because the other girl advised me to say I'd already worked before in Tijuana.

Then it was time for us to put on the platforms and I didn't want to put them on. I felt ashamed because I'd seen girls on the street at the Hotel Las Cruces. I remember I kept looking at them thinking, Is that what I'm going to look like? I can't believe it. Then, one of the girls yelled at me. I had to put the platforms on and I stood at the entrance, because the girls who arrived – the ones who were new – stood at the door, and that way the men were around us and, well, they looked at us. If they saw a new girl, everyone was going to want to go in with her. I am snapped up by the first guy and we go in, then the second and so on. I didn't know anything and I didn't think to throw out the bits of tissue I'd used with the other two guys – yuck – and one of the girls who'd been there longer yells at me and says, Get rid of the tissues from the two guys you banged! I was nearly in tears, but I couldn't cry because we were being watched, and if they saw someone like that they'd yell at her.

In fact, La Pancha very often yelled at the girl who was there with me, because she was like my teacher or manager. She yelled at her if I chewed gum, if I didn't walk around the street, if I spoke on the phone, or if I didn't do the client checks properly. To go into the rooms with a client, the first thing we had to do was check them all over. If they had a mobile phone we switched it off, then they had to pay 60 pesos for the room and 10 pesos for the condom, and then we would go in. When it was all over, I had to see the client back to the door.

V – About the falcons

I'll tell you how these bastards work. They analyse the environment. Like when a falcon is going to catch its prey, they analyse their whole surroundings: where she lives, who her family is, where she develops, where she studies. Once he's analysed it all, he goes after her and catches his prey.

There are all sorts of cases: a girl from Guatemala who, if I show you her photos on Facebook, you'll be like, Wow, she's stunning. And how did she get here? When she was underage, they put her to sleep and they bring her all the way to Toluca. In her village in Guatemala, they say, Take these pills for dizziness, and she wakes up in Toluca. All she wanted was to be an event hostess and she went somewhere with a friend who said, Come with me, let's go and get the uniforms. And then this happens. We still don't understand, how can an underage girl cross the border asleep and the authorities not notice?

VI – The unknown ages

The Pimp had told me that there would be a raid at La Merced soon and that when this happened, if I was asked, I needed to say I didn't have a pimp. In all truth I had to tell my pimp everything. I told him when I was going to work and when I finished working.

I also had to tell him how much money I'd earned. Per day I had to earn between 3,000 or 4,000 pesos to cover the quota. He demanded I give him 20,000 pesos per week. The first week I only gave him 15,000 pesos and the second 18,000.

All my work mates had pimps, but we were all forbidden from saying we did. If we spoke about them, strange things happened. I once received a text message from him saying, Get back to work, for fuck's sake. One day I mentioned this and the other girls had received similar texts from their pimps exactly when we were speaking about them.

Almost none of us rebelled. Well, on one occasion I flew into a rage because I had my period and I was being forced to work with a sponge in. I kicked up a row and the Pimp had to send in another girl to pay La Pancha so I could leave, because once you were in, you couldn't get back out that easily. That time I went straight to Puebla and when the Pimp arrived he gave me such a scolding. Are you off your head, you need a psychologist, how could you even think to do that. He used very strong language and I kept quiet, I didn't say anything because he was capable of hitting me and what I didn't want was for him to hit me. I'd already suffered enough when I was a child.

While these things were happening, sometimes I'd think to myself, Dear God, why did you give me a person like this for a husband. Alright, may your will be done on my life. I didn't know what to do anymore. I never allowed myself to cry in front of other people, but anytime I was alone all I did was cry and cry. Until one day there was a police raid and I was taken to the Attorney General's office. It was July 24, 2010. I'll never forget.

It was about two o'clock in the afternoon. Just before the police arrived, some people came through to let us know the police were coming, so the youngest girls went away and hid. I was also told to leave, but I stayed. The police arrived, they took us to make a statement, they fed us and then they showed us some photos of some other girls who worked there, and said that someone had burned them alive.

One of the public prosecutors had it in for me. She said I was underage and that I had a pimp. I kept saying no. I was still denying everything. The hours went by and almost all of the girls started to leave and I was the only one left. I had to undergo some medical exams and, guess what? I wasn't nineteen like I thought I was and my papers said. I was at that time underage, according to the exams. They say maybe my mum increased my age when I was a baby, but I don't know. It's a bit strange.

VII – *Tlaxcaltecans*

Anyway, within all that, I think the groups trafficking women aren't that sophisticated, because they're also people with low income backgrounds. Most of them, 80 per cent, are people who were born in Tlaxcala, in villages like Tenancingo, Zacatenco and San Pablo del Monte. I don't know why so many of them are from there. An anthropologist told me that the Tlaxcaltecan indigenous people, when battling against the Aztecs, used to go after the women and kidnap them and take them away. It's an anthropological thing, this situation took place as far back as then and they still do it. And there are villages now where no-one is allowed in. If you go and enter Tenancingo as a reporter, you run the risk of being mobbed.

In our shelters we've already received more than one hundred young girls from all the states of Mexico, from many countries of Central America: Belize, Guatemala, Honduras, El Salvador, also women from Argentina and Cuba. There are different kinds of cases: there are some who were "boyfriended", others who were kidnapped. We've seen all kinds of modalities. From deceit, or the one who was sold as a child (because that's what some of the customs and traditions are like in many villages), or the cases of low income backgrounds, high income backgrounds, the one whose dad had been raping her for years, the young girl who was courted and was dreaming of getting married, even the one who wanted to play with fire and got burned, while they were underage or even of legal age . . . All the possible hypotheses; we've seen them all. But in the stories there's always a Tlaxcaltecan, although often they change identity and pass as being from other places in Mexico.

VIII – One-way mirror

Because I was underage, they sent me to a shelter of the Fundación Camino a Casa (Way Home Foundation). I was really sad because they had allowed the other girls to leave and not me. I was welcomed by some girls who were in the kitchen cooking a meal for me. Then they gave me clothes because I'd arrived with nothing. Next day the directors of the Foundation came to ask me questions. Stubborn as I was, I kept saying I was there because I wanted to be, that no-one was exploiting me or forcing me as they said.

Many days like that went by until I had to go to the Attorney General's office to make a statement. I went to an officer who said to me, You know what? You do have a pimp. I said nothing, but just stared at him. Your pimp's got Lucero and Carolina working as well. (Lucero was the girl who'd brought me from Puebla to Mexico City, the one who had been my supposed teacher. And Carolina was the one who'd taken me to the alley of Santo Tomás, where La Pancha was.) To tell you the truth I was a bit thrown. And the officer kept talking. He said, We're going to make an agreement. That guy you see sitting there is pretending to be a lawyer, but he's not a lawyer. The story is, he wants to help you. He's going to be given a certain amount of money so that you get out and then they're going to take you to the pimps. I want you to help us so we can follow you and arrest your pimp and the lot of them. I said yes and I gave him all the details I could. I was very angry saying, I'll denounce that bastard, this won't be the end of it, I can't believe he was also the pimp of Carolina and Lucero.

Then I went with the officer who was pretending to be a lawyer. He told me he was going to take me to Circunvalación and that Carolina would be there. But, guess what? We arrived and Carolina wasn't there. Instead, there was another girl, and the one the officer was after was Carolina. So he rings Carolina and hands me the phone. I asked after the Pimp and she wouldn't say anything until suddenly the Pimp kind of loses his nerve and snatches the phone off her to say, Goddammit, get yourself to Puebla, can't you see you're being followed. Get into the subway and go straight to the bus station to buy a ticket to Puebla, but don't give your name. As we were speaking he was hiding at Circunvalación with Carolina and could see me being followed by the police. I know this because as soon as we hung up I caught sight of the Pimp rushing off some distance away. I told the police and they went after him, but he dashed into the subway and gave them the slip.

When all the fuss was over, the officer took the girl that Carolina had sent. They did have some difficulties interviewing that girl, because she didn't even know how many days there were in a week and much less how many months in a year. She was very lost. She had studied very little, just a few years of primary school.

In any case, next day that girl said her pimp was calling her. As the phone was ringing I looked at the number and saw it was the same as my pimp's. I got really angry again. She put him on loud-speaker and I was listening to what he was saying to her: Hello baby, remember you have to come to Puebla early, because you need to wash your little clothes and in the afternoon we're going out to buy you some little trousers. Then he asked after the witch. The witch was me, and she said she didn't know where I'd gone to hide. He replied, That bitch must have gone and crawled under a rock, and then he burst out laughing. After that, the officer took the girl to Puebla because she needed to be on time to meet the Pimp so the police could catch him. And that's how they arrested him and brought him to Mexico City. I wasn't able to see him in person because they said it was dangerous, but they put him behind a one-way mirror and I recognised him immediately.

Only then did I find out that the Pimp was not called Alex Guzmán Herrera and that he wasn't from Querétaro, nor was he twenty-five years old. His name is Arturo Galindo Martínez, he's 35 and he's from San Pablo del Monte, Tlaxcala.

IX – A Mexican thing

It's been five years since this happened and if you go to La Merced today, the girls are still in the alleys. Along Circunvalación and the street leading to Arcos de Belén. They're still standing there. It's not about criminalising women, because prostitution is not illegal, but they're still standing there. And all of them, including the older ones, are victims of sexual exploitation. Even if there are some who'll say that's not true, but prostitution protects, promotes and encourages human trafficking. That's the problem.

And the idea that it's the police who're protecting these networks is simply not true. These networks are also protected by authorities in areas such as judicial, administrative, health, urban development and a long list. They've been working in the neighbourhood for thirty years. There are some who say – and they're not joking – that the girls at La Merced are now part of the cultural heritage of Mexico City. They say it for real. They say it's "picturesque" and folkloric that these girls are there. That it's a Mexican thing.

But this has nothing to do with culture. It's a business. A girl like Lily earned 3,000 to 4,000 pesos per day, at least 20,000 pesos per week. Her pimp had another four girls, so he earned some 400,000 pesos per month. This is, of course, a very considerable amount of money.

La Merced is the biggest brothel in Latin America. There are very many women at La Merced. In the halls of the Attorney General's office, word is that there are about five thousand in total. If that's true, business would be worth around 400 million pesos a month. That's why I say it has nothing to do with culture.

X – God as a psychologist

Lily is pretty and nubile. There's a twinkle in her eye and her body is dark, as robust and stoic as a bird when not in flight. Her voice emits a solemn rage when she tells me her story, when she sings it.

"These days, as you were telling me your story, I've been able to see you are strong, Lily. Did you go to therapy or what did you do?" I ask her.

"No, I didn't need any therapy, I never went to a psychologist. My only psychologist was God."

XI – The escape

When Lily told you she didn't see a psychologist after what happened it's because the service we offer at the Foundation is based on the spiritual aspect. The girls can't be forced to undergo psychotherapy, but what we do instead is encourage them to get involved in what we do, in the spiritual part, which is to have a personal relationship with God. God has an opinion, something to say, God is there to listen, God is there to heal you, to look after you, to protect you, to reintegrate you, to do everything, but how will you discover this? By having a personal relationship with Him, not through any person. It's you and Him.

Meeting with God strengthens your spirit so that what happened to you doesn't happen again, so that you don't have that weakness of character and then someone comes and it's easy to trick you into something due to a particular need or circumstance. What did you do to end up in that situation? I'm not justifying the evil that the pimps produce, their actions are wrongful and incorrect, but in a way the girls also put themselves in a vulnerable position where they can become victims of those guys and, well, that's the work on which our service guidelines are based.

Lots of people criticise us for what we do with the girls. They say we're too religious, that we're far right and things like that, but we know what we're doing and we're helping a lot of girls like Lily escape from the human trafficking networks in Mexico, not just physically, but also spiritually.

XII – Sabaneta Vieja, Sabaneta Chica

When I was a little girl we lived in a remote *ranchería* called Sabaneta Vieja, and if you wanted to go to a city you had to walk half an hour to Sabaneta Chica, where you could catch a bus to Tres Valles, the larger village in the area. My nicest memory of my whole life is when my dad used to take me to school when I was little. He always carried my backpack and I was the happiest girl. A dad is the best thing that can happen to a girl in her life.

Translated by Jennifer Adcock

THE WRECK OF THE TANGERINES

Emiliano Ruiz Parra

ON THE EVENING OF Monday October 22, 2007, Alfredo de la Cruz watched a news report about accidents on oil rigs in the Campeche Sound. Only a few days earlier, the television said, a worker had died when a barge caught fire. Alfredo, known for the past decade as Pensamiento, or Thinker, went to bed feeling confident that such an accident would never happen to him.

Workers in the maintenance department would often gather to talk or watch television in the cabin of José Ramón Granadillo, one of the engineers. That moment of conversation was the reward for twelve hours of intense labour on the Usumacinta self-elevating platform, which only a few days earlier had located itself 18 kilometres north of the coast of Tabasco, in the Gulf of México's Campeche Sound, to attach itself to the wells known as KAB–101 and KAB–121.

After watching the news, Pensamiento felt like going to bed. When he was at sea he often saw his wife, his children, grandchildren and even his one-year-old great-grandson in his dreams. Neither he nor any of the seventy-three workers on the Usumacinta imagined that within a few hours they would be shipwrecked.

Granadillo had warned them that Cold Front 4 was approaching the Gulf of Mexico. At Pemex, Mexico's state-owned oil company, and at the Port Authority, it was not usual practice to vacate oil rigs because of a cold front. Only hurricanes were deemed to merit the evacuation of the 18,000 sea-based workers.

On the Usumacinta – owned by Perforadora Central, which was sub-contracted by Pemex – workers did twelve-hour shifts for fourteen days at a time, with fourteen days on dry land (although some of the temporary workers clocked up as many as thirty-eight consecutive days at sea). Known as A.D.s, or assistant drillers, they worked from either 7.00 a.m. to 7.00 p.m. or 7.00 p.m. to 7.00 a.m. Specialised workers, including mechanics and electricians, had to be available around the clock even after they had finished their shift.

The Usumacinta had a housing block with shared rooms for workers and private rooms for officers, a helipad, a canteen that served four shifts and a system to make saltwater drinkable. Once a week, a ship supplied it with frozen food that the cook, María del Carmen Aguilar, prepared and seasoned.

The platform navigated around the Gulf's waters until it settled somewhere and became a floating island servicing the oil platforms. On Thursday, October 18, it had reached KAB–101 to finish drilling on one of its three wells, and by Sunday 21 it had rolled out the cantilever deck that allows the drilling to take place. But at first it had run into some unexpected difficulties as it tried to anchor itself, because the seabed did not match the charts, so divers and tug boats had wasted three days making adjustments.

At 9.00 a.m. on Tuesday 23, the Usumacinta was hit by the cold front. Sergio Córdoba, nicknamed El Negro, felt the oscillating motion, the soft tremor caused by the slap of waves and the metallic sound of the steel chocks scraping against the platform's legs.

Granadillo and El Negro rushed to the radio room. There was no doubting it, the cold front was blowing in with the strength of a category 1 hurricane: the equipment registered gusts of wind of up to 136 k.p.h. The maintenance manager told his men to stay off the deck and to gather in the workrooms.

Shortly after 11.00 a.m., a welder called Guadalupe Momenthey shouted: "There's a hydrogen sulphide leak in the well's retention area!"

Soon the smell of rotten egg filled the housing block. El Negro saw white-yellowish smoke streaming out of the well like a jet of compressed air.

Pensamiento worried that hydrogen sulphide, a gas heavier than air, might concentrate below the platform, where it could blow it to pieces with a single spark. He also knew that even the briefest of exposures to hydrogen sulphide could be lethal. Everyone else aboard the Usumacinta knew this too.

Chaos followed Momenthey's cry of alarm. The workers dropped their tools and ran to the helipad, the platform's designated safe zone in case of a leak or a fire. El Negro and his assistant, Rigoberto Mendoza, shut down the platform's energy supply and strapped enormous oxygen tanks, known as autonomous breathing systems, onto their backs. El Negro noticed two of the workers obstructing the exit from the housing block.

"Let the others out, don't just stand there, remember Piper Alpha!" he shouted. On Piper Alpha, a platform in the North Sea, sixty-two workers had suffocated inside the housing block.

The workers felt the wind's fury. A few minutes later the screams and cries began.

"We'll die!" one of the men shouted.

Another complained about his autonomous breathing system: "This tank's empty, the cascade has no flow!"

After the power shutdown, the automatic re-filling system for the tanks, known as the cascade, had been rendered inoperative.

Leaking oil was now spreading into the workrooms, the housing block and the lifeboats. The Usumacinta's crew gathered on the helipad. The workers lay on the ground or knelt, clinging to the mesh spread over the surface to absorb the shock of landing helicopters.

The leaking oil and gas caused a crisis that lasted for almost three hours. The helipad became a stage for cries and imprecations. From the platform's third level, where the superintendents were gathered, came some faintly reassuring news: "Help is on its way."

Around 1.30 p.m., the two most senior people on the platform, Pemex Superintendent Miguel Ángel Solís and Perforadora Central's Guillermo Porter – both would die on lifeboat number two – ordered the storm valve to be shut, the last resort in trying to contain the leak. A team of six workers with oxygen tanks on their backs risked their lives to stem the flow of gas and oil gushing out of the seabed. It took them half an hour to complete an operation that required them to hang off the platform, in 136 k.p.h. winds, to cut the risers. They discovered that the retractable cantilever had damaged the wellhead.

The team was successful in closing the valve. They had completed the task by 2.00 p.m., offering the workers on the Usumacinta some relief. Those who were lying down or kneeling stood up, gave thanks to God for the strong winds blowing away the stench of rotten eggs, and got back to work. El Negro and Rigoberto set themselves to wiping the oil off the auxiliary equipment. But the calm would last for less than two hours.

"Hey, Negro, is this normal?" asked Corporal Nicolás González when he saw a gas exhalation emanating from the well.

"No, it isn't, call the Old Man," he replied. The Old Man, El Viejo, was 73-year old Guillermo Porter.

A few minutes later desperation had taken over the platform again. Just before 3.30 p.m., a second leak on Well 121 was discovered.

"Negro, we can't control it, that was the last valve," Granadillo said.

A certainty swept over the superintendents, the engineers, the platform captain, the A.D.s, the mechanics and electricians, the cooks and the waiters: after the storm valve was shut, there would be no other safety resort on the Usumacinta.

Beneath them the sea raged, waves rose eight metres from the surface, the wind blew at 130 k.p.h.

Workers piled onto the helipad again: in the chaos that ensued the oxygen tanks got mixed up and the cries of alarm began, some accurate, others not.

"I can't swim!" cried the cook.

"It's on fire! It's on fire!" a worker shouted out, mistakenly.

The *Morrison Tide*, a support ship, appeared in the distance, on its way to rescue them. Pensamiento considered the difficulties. A helicopter would not be able to land – the winds would toss it around like a mosquito. The ship would not be successful either because it might be smashed against the platform's legs. To head out to the sea on the bright orange lifeboats, known as the tangerines, was no guarantee of survival: just like the rescue boat, they might crash against the platform's legs as soon as they dropped into the water. But to stay on the platform meant to die like rats.

The time for thinking came to an end when the wind changed direction and started blowing the gas towards the helipad. The workers were terrified. One of them threatened to jump into the sea. The Pemex Superintendent gave the order to abandon the platform.

Tangerine number one

El Negro had already piloted lifeboat number one. Two months earlier he had done some training, and during the routine security drills he was always the one at the tiller. But those training exercises were always carried out in calm waters. If the sea was rough, the drills were postponed until the surface was as smooth as a mirror.

This was not the case on Tuesday, October 23, when the cold front blew in with 130 k.p.h. winds and eight-metre high waves. Sergio made sure that the procedures in the platform's security manual were being followed: the group boarded in an orderly manner, the workers alternating between starboard and port to balance the weight. There were forty-one of them. The platform engineer, Éder Ortega, contacted lifeboat number two over the radio and confirmed: they had everyone, there was nobody left on the Usumacinta.

El Negro ordered assistant mechanic Juan Gabriel Rodríguez to release the winch and the tangerine dropped ten metres in a few seconds. Upon hitting the water it turned a few times on its axis and was left facing the wells. A wave pushed it beneath the plat-form. It narrowly avoided crashing against one of the platform's legs. El Negro remembered he had to swing the tiller 180° to port and 180° to starboard to keep the boat moving straight ahead. The wind-blown oil had covered the vessel's windscreen and diminished the pilot's line of sight.

Water was trickling in from the stern and winding its way between the crew's feet. Within a few minutes, the trickle had turned into a puddle. The passengers pulled up their feet to avoid getting their boots wet.

"There's more water coming in than going out!" someone shouted.

El Negro saw the *Morrison Tide*.

"They're coming for us, stay calm, the ship's right there. You keep pumping the water out and the lifeboat will get us through."

The sight of the rescue boat, at times obscured by the waves, at others glimpsed riding high on a crest, cheered the lifeboat's passengers. Juan Gabriel Rodríguez, who was now second in command, opened the hatch to wait for a rope from the boat. At the second attempt Juan Gabriel got hold of the rope and tied it to the hauling hook. But the excitement lasted only for the few seconds it took for a mountain of water to swell up and slam into the lifeboat. Juan Gabriel was left with one end of the rope in his hands while the other was whipped into the air.

The wave burst into the lifeboat and the water rose as high as the passengers' knees.

"We'll drown here!"

"Let's get outta here, we won't make it alive!"

The group decided to abandon the tangerine just as minutes earlier they had decided to leave the platform. Every desperate decision was an attempt to increase their chances of survival. Outside the lifeboat waited the ocean's fury. They knew very little about the sea. They were experts in welding, operating cranes and engines, drilling, preparing concrete and feeding a legion of workers. For them, the sea was simply another layer separating the oil from the platform. Some could not swim. Others had been given the title of Captain but had no naval training. In Ciudad del Carmen they called them "Platformers".

Order had given way to desperation. The need to escape was urgent. Once outside, the workers climbed onto one of the tangerine's ledges and held on to an aluminium rail. El Negro cut the engine before exiting through the hatch. The *Morrison Tide* was nearby, closer with every minute, and was trying unsuccessfully to get another rope over to them.

The sea hurled itself at the rescue ship with a wave that swept the deck and washed two of its crewmembers overboard. A third crewmember died instantly when he was thrown against the tug's winch. The *Morrison Tide* now had to take care of its own endangered sailors.

Another wall of water crashed into the tangerine. No matter how hard the workers tried to grip the aluminium rail, the water pushed them away from the lifeboat. El Negro felt himself being thrown about by a monstrous wave. The smack of water that tore his grip from the rail had also opened his mouth, shot up through his nostrils and sent him tumbling. Once back on the surface he saw the lifeboat in the distance, upturned, the propeller facing the sky and its top facing the bottom of the ocean, and he decided against swimming towards it.

When he lost sight of the rescue boat he took off his boots and resigned himself to spending a long time in the water. He located a few other colleagues and fourteen of the shipwrecked workers linked arms and legs in a star shape. He told them that the boat would rescue the largest group. But the waves dispersed them. El Negro felt two of his colleagues grabbing his shoulders and he was able to pull them along for a few metres, until he realised he had to shake them off or else they would drag him under.

Francisco Abreu, a tall and well-built 47-year-old worker, swam around the group. On the platform, he was one of the most serene, but amid the waves his panic made him swim around in circles, incessantly, resting only for a few seconds at a time whenever his colleagues begged him to stop.

Night fell. El Negro looked at his watch and worried that he would not be on the platform to take a call from his wife, which he was expecting at seven in the evening. Saltwater hindered his eyesight. In the distance he saw three bursts of light and thought it might be three rescue boats. He estimated that, even if none of those boats rescued them, they might reach dry land by noon on Wednesday.

The sound of a helicopter propeller reanimated the group, now down to six.

"They're coming to get us, there's three boats and a chopper!" he said.

Except that the helicopter never came down. Winds of over 100 k.p.h. threw it off-balance. It would point its searchlight at the group of survivors, stay with them for a moment, and then fly off.

A ship approached. It was the *Far Scotia*, which had a larger draft than the *Morrison Tide*. It threw out ropes and ladders. El Negro tried to grab them twice but the wind blew them away. With his body battling the tides and the furious winds, he and his two hangers-on kicked their way towards the ship. When they were only a few arm-strokes away a wave lifted the *Far Scotia* and pushed the three men beneath it. El Negro looked up and saw the keel above his head like a guillotine about to slice him in half. Over the next few seconds his life rushed before his eyes. He thought of God.

Rather than landing hard, the ship fell through the air as gently as a sheet of paper. The same wave that had shoved them beneath the ship had also pushed them away from the spot where the *Far Scotia* landed.

Minutes later a rope was once again thrown in their direction, and Jorge Arturo caught it in the air. El Negro held on and the ship's crew pulled them onto the deck, where they were greeted with a blanket and a cup of hot chocolate. El Negro looked at his watch: it was 9.05 p.m. Over the following hour, eleven out of the fourteen workers who had gathered after being swept off the tangerine by the first wave were lifted to safety.

Francisco Abreu, the well-built and panic-stricken worker, held on to the rope and was being hauled up. A metre before reaching the deck he stretched out his arm so that the rescuer could give him a final pull, but he was a few centimetres short. As if struck by lightning, his arm still outstretched, he fell backwards into the sea. The Usumacinta's medic and crane operator did not reach the deck either.

"Three of your colleagues didn't make it," one of the rescuers told them. "One big guy in an orange overall was three of four rungs away but he just fell back with his arm outstretched. The other one was wearing a white shirt. He just raised his head and lifted his arm but didn't do anything else, he just stayed there. The third caught the rope but fell into the water again and we think he was caught by the propellers."

A C.B. radio interrupted: "We've just pulled out a body, his I.D. says it's someone called Allende Alcudia Olán," a rescuer said from another ship.

His son, Allende Alcudia Sánchez, was one of the eleven survivors. Out at sea, he had twice swum out to get his father when the waves separated him from the rest of the group. At the third attempt his father raised his arm and waved as if to say farewell.

Tangerine number two

The second lifeboat landed in the sea and bounced softly. Pensamiento started the engine and began to navigate. The north wind had spread the leaking oil over the lifeboat's surface, so he left the window open and his safety belt unfastened. As the Usumacinta's Head Mechanic, he was at the tiller.

He had been nicknamed Thinker a few years back when he was operating a crane with extreme caution to move a load.

"What do we do?" his workers asked while he took his time.

"Wait, I'm thinking!" he replied.

On the evening of Tuesday, October 23, at the helm of the tangerine, Pensamiento was thinking again: he had to get away from the platform as soon as possible and avoid a lethal collision with the platform's legs. But he was not sure about steering towards the coast. He preferred to stay near the Usumacinta, and within sight of the rescue ship that was manoeuvring to get close.

The lifeboat was succumbing to the sea's fury. The wind and the waves tossed it skywards and then welcomed it back to the watery mayhem with a kick. Inside it reeked of rotten eggs. The gas that had leaked into the boat for hours cause the first panic: "We'll suffocate!" one of the platform workers cried. After the screams, six of the workers started throwing up. Pensamiento caught a glimpse of the *Morrison Tide*, busy trying to rescue the first tangerine, and soon lost sight of it.

It was agreed that they should steer a course towards the coast. Pensamiento revved the engine. Rigoberto, who had grown up in a family of fishermen and who had braved hurricanes in fishing vessels, asked to take over. He knew the way to dry land because he was from Emiliano Zapata, a coastal fishermen's colony on the Atasta peninsula, but Pensamiento said no and ordered him to keep an eye on the compass.

Then Rigoberto saw a wave so tall he could not believe his eyes. Tons of water crashed onto the lifeboat and made it disappear under the surface as if the sea had swallowed it in a single gulp. The wave overturned the tangerine, sank it many metres under water and then rolled it over. Pensamiento could just make out a jumble of arms and legs flying up to the roof as soon as they hit the floor. He felt the blows on his body and his head, he fell, he got up, he clung to the edges of the seats. He heard the clank of an oxygen tank someone had foolishly smuggled into the lifeboat hitting the walls and thudding against the bodies.

It was the first of many times that Pensamiento felt himself standing on the brink of death. During those long seconds he lost all certainty that the passengers in his care would make it safely onto dry ground. After its final roll the tangerine was left in the dark and started to rise slowly, but as it rose rivulets of water started trickling into it.

When the lifeboat resurfaced, Pensamiento understood the expression "being up to your neck in water". He found an air pocket and breathed in. Around him he felt the still bodies of his companions, floating face down, arms crossed, their last breaths bubbling out. The tangerine had capsized, the roof pointing towards the ocean floor and the propeller above the surface, like an upturned beetle.

Leopoldo Cuarenta, a mechanic who was on probation on the platform, was able to open the oxygen valves. Straining upwards to get air, he used his feet to feel around the lifeboat's roof, now turned into the floor, trying desperately to find a way out. When he felt the hatch's orifice he dived to the bottom, pulled himself out and then kicked his way upwards.

Upon reaching the surface, Pensamiento saw a score of his colleagues clinging to the side of the lifeboat while others tried to climb onto its upturned hull. He realised then that this was not some dream, he was truly there, lost at sea, with no rescue ships nearby and entirely reliant on his own strength. He remembered he was about to turn sixty, with only six months to go before retiring. He thought of his great-grandson and of the car he had only just taken out of the dealership.

"God, if you can truly make anything happen, please make the winds calm down," he prayed.

He climbed onto the tangerine's hull where many of his colleagues were already waiting. He had not realised that as he tumbled around inside the lifeboat he had suffered a bad cut to his ear, and he was now losing blood and strength from a five-centimetre gash in his scalp.

His boss and friend, José Ramón Granadillo, climbed out of the water without a lifejacket. Pensamiento held out his hand and helped him clamber up. The wind turned their voices into whispers.

"Why did you take off the lifejacket?" Pensamiento asked.

"I had to take it off, it was stopping me from getting out."

His boss was lean and short. When he was inside the tangerine he tried twice to dive into the water and escape through the hatch but the lifejacket kept buoying him up. On his third attempt he rid himself of the lifejacket. Pensamiento and Rigoberto attached Granadillo to the tangerine's outer railing. The lifejackets had torches, whistles and silk cords that could be used to tie people together in the event of a shipwreck.

Walls of water kept crashing into the workers. "Head's up!" was the most common shout over the next few endless hours. Waves swept them off the hull, pulled them under and then spat them back onto the surface.

One of those waves broke the cord by which Granadillo was attached to the lifeboat, and separated him from the group. But the head of maintenance was determined to get back to the boat. Rigoberto pulled him back in and helped him up.

Minutes later, another massive wave swept them off the tangerine. Granadillo swam back again. The water's blow sucked two lifejackets out of the lifeboat and left them floating in the water. Granadillo was three metres away from one of them, and the same distance from the lifeboat. He did not hesitate. He preferred returning to the boat to trying to grab a lifejacket.

The sea swallowed one of the lifejackets in a matter of seconds. The other one floated some three metres away from the group. It was Granadillo's lifejacket. The men watched it bobbing on the surface. They were exhausted, almost silent, saving their energies for the following wave and the next gust of wind. After a while the lifejacket began to drift away until it disappeared.

Granadillo was unable to recover from a third charge by the sea. The wall of water crashed onto the tangerine dispersing the workers in all directions. The water's fury hit the shipwrecked worker, who tried to hold his breath, withstand the water entering his nose and mouth, and swim back to the surface. Pensamiento and Rigoberto saw him recover with difficulty from the wave's battering, attempt a few arm strokes and then give in to the watery desert.

Pensamiento saw seven of his companions depart in that manner. One of Perforadora Central's employees, Carlos Gurrión, tried to tie one of the bodies to the lifeboat's outer railing. He failed. Hours later he too would be defeated by the sea.

It was not the waves that were killing them so much as exhaustion. There was a grimace that preceded the moment of death. Resignation appeared on their purple faces, and behind it the energy they needed to get back to the lifeboat was extinguished.

The sound of helicopter rotors filled them with hope. The sun was setting and Pensamiento counted eleven of his colleagues gathered around the tangerine, some trying to lie down on the hull and others clinging to the outer railing.

At first two Pemex helicopters hovered nearby. The men agreed that Pensamiento should be the first one to be rescued. The wound on his scalp had not stopped bleeding despite the Gulf's saltwater having cleansed and washed over it a thousand times. The mere thought of being rescued gave them the strength to withstand nature's blows. But the helicopters left. The strong winds were blowing them about and prevented them from getting any lower. It was only then that a third helicopter appeared, this one belonging to the Mexican navy, and the only one with a winch to save drowning seamen.

One of the hundreds of waves that hit the lifeboat had swept away the night cook, who now flailed about, lost at sea. A diver attached to the winch was lowered to the sea's surface, where he grabbed the cook by the back and pulled him out of the water. The two men were winched up towards the helicopter.

A few metres before reaching the top, the diver could no longer hold up the weight of the heavy and exhausted man. The night cook, who already appeared to have lost all hope, slipped out of the diver's arms. His colleagues could only see the hole in the water where he fell. The helicopters did not attempt any further rescues.

But they did not leave. Night fell on the choppy sea and the helicopters followed the survivors through the long hours in which life and death battled it out. They would disappear for a few minutes and then return. Their searchlights lit up the drops of rain that seemed to dance to the rhythm of the gusts of wind.

"God, Lord, if you can really do anything, please make the winds calm down," Pensamiento begged again.

The searchlight beams were becoming fainter. The saltwater had damaged the survivors' eyesight. The currents had dispersed the torches and whistles in the lifejackets a long time ago. After every wave the men tried to scramble back to the lifeboat. There were screams in the night, and almost no visibility.

"Pensamiento!"

"Rigo!"

"Cuarenta!"

"I'm here!"

"I'm here!"

"I'm here!"

Pensamiento climbed onto the hull and heard a "knock knock knock". He used his knuckles to reply: "Knock knock knock." He put his uninjured ear against the hull but could hear no voices, only knocking from inside the tangerine. There were survivors within the storm-battered lifeboat.

Inside, Maribel Bolaños, an employee with the Commissary Services company, Servicios de Comisariato, would spend almost twelve hours in the dark. Water reached her shoulders and the largest waves left her completely submerged. She heard three of her colleagues' dying words:

"I can't swim . . ." the cook said.

"I just can't go on, I'm too tired . . ." sobbed a worker some time later. "I have no strength left . . ."

"No-one's coming to rescue us," the third one lamented. His breathing turned into sobbing and then it stopped.

"Don't worry, let's pray, let's ask God to help us," Maribel was just able to say.

After the last of her companions fell silent, Maribel remained inside the fibreglass and saltwater womb, with only corpses to keep her company.

At dawn, through half-shut eyes, Rigoberto saw two lights. It was the lighthouses on the spit of land formed by the rivers San Pedro and San Pablo, the natural border between the states of Tabasco and Campeche. The northern lighthouse marked the beginning of the village of San Pedro in the state of Tabasco, and the southern lighthouse was in Nuevo Campechito, the village closest to his home town of Emiliano Zapata.

"Calm down, I can see the way, I know where we are! Just a little longer and we're there, the river's nearby," Rigoberto said, trying to lift spirits.

In less than an hour the current took them to the shore near Nuevo Campechito. The lifeboat, upturned, battered and broken, washed ashore around 3.00 a.m. Rigoberto let go of the lifeboat's railing and felt the ground beneath his feet.

The navy helicopter landed in a clearing on the beach some 250 metres from where the tangerine had run aground. Twelve survivors were stranded on a beach covered with mangroves. They were trembling, almost completely blinded by the saltwater and made deaf by the battering. They embraced one another to keep warm, mouth to ear and chest to shoulder. They thanked God for keeping them alive and prayed for those companions who had not made it.

Pensamiento leaned on Rigoberto. He was exhausted. He had forgotten about the wound on his head.

"Just leave me here, I can't carry on," the mechanic implored.

"You didn't survive all that swimming just to die on the beach," the assistant electrician scolded him, and carried him towards the helicopter.

The men decided that only eight of them would get into the helicopter. The other four went back to the lifeboat and tried to turn it over to rescue Maribel. They were able to drag it until it was some three metres away from the beach. They tried to take advantage of a wave to turn it over but they could not push it hard enough, they needed some of the strength they had left out there in the Gulf as they fought the sea's rage.

Rigoberto found a gap and stuck his hand in but pulled it out immediately, instinctively, when he felt a lifeless leg. A second helicopter arrived a few minutes later, and a navy officer told them to get on. A third one would be arriving soon to rescue the sole survivor trapped inside the lifeboat.

The fish

Following the death of twenty-two people – twenty workers from
the Usumacinta platform, and two crew members aboard the
Morrison Tide – Pemex asked Nobel laureate Mario Molina to
head an inquiry. It also commissioned a separate report into
the incident's root causes from American consultancy Battelle. The
Molina inquiry pointed towards various instances of negligence
leading to the workers being stranded in the raging sea: although
people knew in advance how dangerous the cold front might be,
the forecast's quality and precision were inadequate; even when the
cold front acquired the characteristics of a hurricane, the platforms
were not evacuated; no-one took into account that the presence of
other platforms had already modified the seafloor's configuration,
which is why the maps did not match the underwater terrain,
and why the Usumacinta was so unstable; the personnel were not
trained for an emergency, and the rescue ships that got close did
not have the right equipment or appropriately trained crews.

Battelle exonerated Pemex of any fault: the deaths, it said, were
due to decisions taken by the workers: "The decision to open one
or more of the hatches was the root cause of the lifeboats' failure
and the related fatalities," concludes the 900-page report, even
though it admits that the lifeboats' materials were below the basic
standards. "The erroneous expectation that the transfer [from the
lifeboats to the rescue ships] could have been easily carried out
in stormy waters was behind the attempt to execute the transfer
and was ultimately the cause of the resulting deaths," it says in its
turgid and bureaucratic prose. In other words, the fault lay entirely
with the dead, and with the survivors.

Taking the opposite view, the National Commission for Human
Rights (C.N.D.H.) reported violations to the right to life, to
physical integrity, and to judicial safety. It also accused Pemex of

contravening the law by omission, through non-compliance with safety norms, lack of training and equipment, and a shortage of rescue vessels in the area. According to testimonies gathered by the C.N.D.H. for its Recommendation number 014/2009, many of the workers had never taken part in a drill, the autonomous breathing systems were chained up and could therefore not be used, the alarms never sounded, the doors of the housing block were deliberately obstructed, and one of the leaky tangerines had been fixed with silicone patches that fell off with the first wave. Pemex, the C.N.D.H. said, knew about the many complaints by workers but had done nothing to improve the safety flaws.

"We believe that there were serious violations of the human rights of the twenty-two people who lost their lives on October 23, 2007, in the Campeche Sound, as well as the sixty-eight people who were hurt, because Pemex's officials allowed the Usumacinta platform to operate under conditions that did not guarantee the complete safety and safeguard the lives of the workers." Despite the C.N.D.H.'s accusation, not a single Pemex official was ever prosecuted for the omissions leading to the accident. Nor was anyone fired.

*   *   *

After the accident, Pensamiento noticed he was turning into a fish. His skin became hard and scaly. The regular ministrations of intravenous saline became an ordeal for the doctors, who not only struggled to find his veins but had difficulty inserting the catheter needle.

On the night of Wednesday, October 24, at Ciudad del Carmen's public hospital, he had to wait in A&E for a bed to become available. That did not happen until Friday 26.

The five-centimetre gash in his scalp had become infected, and he had to remain in hospital for fourteen days. He was left with only the lobe of his right ear, and he got used to letting the right leg of his eyeglasses rest against the white bandage. Although a test revealed he had lost 50 per cent of his hearing in his right ear, the doctors told him he could go back to work.

After his skin grew scaly, Pensamiento then seemed to be shedding it, like a snake. Waking up every morning he noticed the small piles of scales at the foot of the bed. A new layer of thin skin emerged beneath the old hide he sloughed off over the next few days.

Even after he shed his fish skin, Pensamiento's soul still bore the scars from the shipwreck. One of his greatest pleasures used to be falling asleep and enjoying his dreams, often featuring his family or replaying a pleasant moment experienced that day. Now the fury of the sea had invaded that once impregnable territory with images of lagoons, sinking platforms, corpses and waves. One night in November, as he drove to Mérida, Pensamiento was alarmed to see a fish the size of a man crossing the road, walking upright on its tail.

Translated by Ángel Gurría-Quintana

THE HOURS OF EXTERMINATION

The disappearance of the forty-three
students in Iguala, Guerrero

Anabel Hernández

The events narrated here have been reconstructed by the author
based on eyewitness accounts, video footage taken by the students
during the attack, the testimony given by the surviving student
Fernando Marín to the author in an interview in July 2015 and
the reconstruction of events that the Tlachinollan Human Rights
Centre organised with the survivors in the place where the attacks
had occurred.

On the night of September 26, 2016, the town of Iguala, about
three hours from Mexico's capital, was transformed into a living
hell. More than a hundred students from the Raúl Isidro Burgos
Normal Rural Teachers College in the municipality of Ayotzinapa,
who were travelling through the town on five buses, were attacked
with gunfire for several hours. Three students were murdered, more
than ten wounded. And forty-three disappeared, their whereabouts
still unknown.

The students, most of them the children of poor rural families,
had gone to the outskirts of the town to hijack a few buses, which
was common practice among students in Mexico's public colleges;
typically there is no violence, and the vehicles are later returned.

On this particular day, these young people wanted to use the buses to travel to Mexico City to join the annual march commemorating the massacre that had taken place on October 2, 1968, in Tlatelolco in which other students had died. Forty-six years later, they would be the ones massacred by officials of the state. Members of the Federal Police, State Police and Municipal Police participated in the attack with the complicity of the 27th infantry battalion.

The student Fernando Marín is lying on the ground by the Estrella de Oro bus number 1568 in his own blood, like his other classmates from the Isidro Burgos Rural Teachers College. The bullet wound he received minutes earlier has almost destroyed his right forearm and the torn tendons are little white strips coming out of his body. The wound is still warm and it does not yet hurt too badly. His breathing is rapid and irregular, at the age of twenty he is in absolutely no doubt that he is going to die.

It is around 10.30 on the night of September 26, 2014, and Juan N. Alvarez street in Iguala, Guerrero, is deserted despite being just metres from the city centre. Traders and their customers have holed themselves up behind the metal curtains of their businesses which they closed the moment the gunfire began. Those who can, run to other streets.

Terrified residents, including old people, adults and children, have thrown themselves face down on the floor of their homes. They are trembling and it seems to them that the walls are made not of brick but of paper. The same bullets that are being aimed at the students could come through the wall and injure them too. Some of them in the darkness behind the windows dare to peer out occasionally.

"Know what? Now you're fucked for sure!" an officer from the state police spits at Fernando Marín in a tone more like a bark than a shout.

"Kill him once and for all. He's injured, just kill him once and for all," one of the nearby policeman encourages him. At that moment, Fernando, whose friends nicknamed him Carrillas, feels the cold metal of the gun on his temple just above his left ear. Yes, they are going to kill me tonight, he says to himself over and over.

Armed civil, municipal and state police at the corner of Juan N. Alvarez and the ring road have trapped the three buses carrying students from the Ayotzinapa teachers college. A few blocks further back the federal police are diverting traffic and onlookers. They want to carry out the operation without witnesses.

As though in a miracle the policeman removes the gun from Carrillas's head and steps aside. Instead of shooting he calls for an ambulance to come and fetch the wounded student. The emergency workers do not want to get close because they are afraid the students at the other end of the street might shoot.

"How are my friends going to shoot if we haven't got guns, we haven't got anything?" thinks Carrillas.

The last thing he sees as he is lifted into the ambulance is his fellow students from the third Estrella de Oro bus number 1568 being kept down on the ground by the Guerrero state and municipal police. Since that night he has not seen them again, nor has anyone else. They were all "disappeared", they make up a part of the group of forty-three so-called *normalistas* – from the local name for a teachers college – of whom nothing was heard again. Carrillas is the only survivor from that bus and he carries the weight in his chest like a stone.

"Maybe it was God who made them not take me or who knows? I don't know what came over the policeman, really I have no idea. I'm the only one," he reports painfully some months later.

Carrillas was not usually much of a believer but he is in no doubt that it was a higher power that saved him on that fatal night.

If the last moments of every life tick towards a final destiny, the clock started ticking for the students of Ayotzinapa the moment Carrillas and his fellow students left their college for Iguala to commandeer some buses to use in their traditional protests. They were heading straight into an ambush.

5.59 p.m. – Departure from Ayotzinapa

Fernando Marín is enrolled at the Isidro Burgos Rural Teachers College in 2013, as his cousins and siblings before him. It is nearly 5.15 in the afternoon of Friday September 26, 2014, and he meets his friend Bernardo Flores Alcaraz a.k.a. Cochiloco at the college's modest sports grounds. Both are second-year students with particular positions of responsibility within the college. Carrillas is in charge of order and discipline; Cochiloco's brief is "the struggle", his task is to get hold of the buses and petrol for the college. They are great friends, inseparable.

Bernardo invites him to go on a "boteo" – to collect some funds – and to commandeer a few buses for travelling to the march on October 2 in Mexico City. A request from his best friend is not something Carrillas can refuse.

Along with some hundred other students, the great majority of them freshmen, Cochiloco and Carrillas board the Estrella de Oro buses 1568 and 1531 which they have stolen days earlier in Chilpancingo, the Guerrero state capital, a city located just an hour and a half from Iguala.

From the moment the two buses leave the college every level of government is notified via the Centre for Control, Command,

Communications and Computing (C4) in Chilpancingo, according to information card number 02370 of Guerrero's Ministry of Public Security, a document to which we have had access. The government is on the alert.

The buses are full, Fernando Benitez recalls. "Our first-years were on their phones, talking perhaps to their mum, to their siblings or girlfriends . . . we were all in good spirits."

They have been on the road nearly three hours when bus number 1531 stops in Huitzuco, in the Rancho del Cura district. Bus 1568, in which Carrillas and Cochiloco are both travelling, continues on its way and stops at the Iguala-Puente de Ixtla toll booth, fifteen minutes from Iguala.

The strategy is set. They are to take as many buses on the highway as they can. They need twenty altogether and on the preceding days they have only managed to commandeer eight. They must have all the buses by the end of September at the latest so that students from other rural teachers colleges can gather in Ayotzinapa and travel together to Mexico City to take part in the traditional October 2 protest, a protest which is held year in, year out, to honour the students massacred by the Mexican army in Tlaltelolco in 1968. Never would they have imagined that they would be the ones being massacred today.

7.30 p.m. – The first police action

Carrillas and Cochiloco are at the tollbooth and soon patrols arrive from the Federal Police (the police institution of the federal government in Mexico) and from the Ministry of Public Security of Guerrero (the police institution of the government of Guerrero). At the same time a red motorcycle appears with just one passenger who is not in any uniform.

In the course of the investigations carried out by the office of the

Attorney General of the Republic (P.G.R.) into the disappearance of the forty-three students, Colonel Pérez Rodríguez, the commander of the 27th Infantry Battalion located in Iguala, revealed that there is a group within the Mexican army called the Intelligence Gathering Authority (O.B.I.) that wears civilian clothes and carries out covert operations. He said that on the night of September 26 he sent one of these men to the tollbooth to keep an eye on the students.

Inexplicably, as part of the state cover-up, the Attorney General's office never investigated any military operations that took place that night.

"The motorcycle started to patrol around, it was circling right round where we were," recalls Carrillas.

After the motorcycle another civilian vehicle shows up and it also starts circling, very obviously keeping an eye on the *normalistas*.

Seeing all this activity, Carrillas thinks they will not be able to get hold of more buses today. They are just about to abort the mission and return to Ayotzinapa when they receive an unexpected call from the students in the bus that stopped in Rancho del Cura to alert them that some of those who had managed to commandeer one are trapped inside Iguala's central bus station.

The two buses set off, each from their respective positions, at great speed, to rescue their classmates. They meet on the way and enter Iguala.

9.16 p.m. – Central Bus Station

When they arrive at the bus station most of the *normalistas* have their faces covered with their T-shirts or pieces of cloth. The security cameras confirm that none of them are armed. Rescuing their classmates proves to be simple and Bernardo Flores, who was in charge of the plan to hijack buses, suggests they take advantage of the opportunity to take three buses and they choose three at random and the hundred students divide up between the five vehicles. Nobody keeps a record of who is going in which bus because of the need to get away as quickly as possible.

The Estrella Roja bus and the Estrella de Oro 1531 leave the central bus station by one exit and manage to get onto a quick route towards Ayotzinapa. Two Costa Line buses and the Estrella de Oro 1568, which is carrying Carrillas and Cochiloco, make a mistake and exit onto Galeana street in the centre of Iguala where they get stuck in traffic in front of hundreds of witnesses and surrounded by Iguala's municipal police.

"The strange thing is that they leave the terminal immediately after arriving, in a matter of ten minutes, and the municipal police are already outside. From this we can conclude that the police were already following them. They could hardly have put an operation together in ten minutes, could they?" explained Vidulfo Rosales in an interview. He is a lawyer with the Tlachinollan Human Rights Centre who has for years been speaking out against state repression of the students of the Raúl Isidro Burgos Rural Teachers College.[1]

Some of the students travelling in the three buses get out at the central square to clear space so they can get through the traffic. The municipal police officers point their guns at them to force them to leave the vehicles.

"We're students, why are you pointing your guns at us? Why do we have to get out?" second-year student Ángel de la Cruz shouts at the officers from the first bus in this convoy. By throwing stones they manage to make the patrol cars part and stop blocking their way.

The first gunshots on Bandera Nacional and Galeana streets are heard in the main square. The noise makes the people who are in the centre of town stampede in different directions unsure whether what they are hearing are fireworks or bullets. In the event nobody is injured.

9.30 p.m. – The first attack

The traders and customers at the corner where Juan N. Alvarez street meets Emiliano Zapata street, a block from the central square, are not aware of what is happening until they see a young man with his face covered by a scarf standing in the middle of the road looking all around him. He is wearing jeans and a shirt torn at the back as though he has been involved in a brawl. He is visibly upset.

At that moment a dark Suburban S.U.V. arrives, and a patrol car. Four or five armed men in civilian clothes with faces uncovered get out of the Suburban. The witnesses notice that they all have very short, military-style haircuts.

"What I thought was that they were soldiers, they were giving the people really nasty looks, one was bearded," reports one of the people who witnessed the event.

The patrol car is carrying six policemen in black, with bullet-proof vests and riot gear. "Hey – stop, assholes!" a policeman shouts at one of the guys from the Suburban. Then a new round of gunfire begins.

A witness records the sound on their telephone. You can hear more than fourteen sharp gunshots with a brief gap between them.

"They're going, they're going!" says a woman amid the commotion. It turns out nobody has been hurt but there are three cars with bullet-holes. Some of the men from the Suburban run after the young man with the covered face and another leaves with the vehicle. They head towards the ring road. The police officers are following them. At that moment the buses in which the *normalistas* are travelling with their faces covered drive right in front of the witnesses.

After this incident a navy blue Focus without licence plates appears and a guy gets out who also looks military and suspiciously collects up the spent bullet cases that were left at the scene. What organised crime group does that? None. Up till now no authority has investigated what happened on that corner as a part of the failings in the investigations carried out by the P.G.R.

"The stalls were all closed because there were several explosions that took place there in the main square," recalls second-year student Ángel de la Cruz, who was travelling in the first bus.

"How do we get out to Chilpo [Chilpancingo]?" one of the students, desperate at being unable to leave, asks a passer-by. The person in question indicates that if they keep going straight ahead that will take them to the ring road and from there keep going straight and it will take them to the state capital.

9.40 p.m. – Trapped

The three buses are just about to make it out onto the ring road when the Iguala municipal police position a patrol car across the middle of the road in front of the first bus and get out, and at least three more patrol cars block the rear-guard of the convoy. The students could have pushed the car aside with the bus but they do not want to hurt anyone.

"... from that point on we couldn't go any further," says Carrillas.

Five students get out of the first bus to move the patrol car, Ángel among them. "We were about to push it when just then they started shooting at us," he reports. The normalistas are caught in the crossfire. The municipal police, the state police, people in civilian dress and undercover military are all there when the shots aimed directly at the buses begin. At that moment terror breaks out, with witnesses including local residents and customers in the restaurants and food stalls and the Aurrera store. The chicken and tacos stands and the little grocery stores immediately close their metal shutters to shield their customers.

"They've killed one, they've killed one!" shout the students in the first bus when they see first-year Aldo Gutiérrez flat on the tarmac having convulsions while blood bubbles from his head. Jonathan Maldonado is shot in the hand and instantly loses several fingers.

"Get out!" shouts another and the students get out and take refuge between the first and second bus. Aldo is still on the ground waving his arms in the air. The students in the third bus are isolated, alone.

There is more than half an hour of shooting. Inside the stores people are crying, as are the students on the street.

The *normalistas* from the first buses who have cellphones start calling their classmates who are in Ayotzinapa, at the teachers college, calling for reinforcements.

"Call an ambulance, call an ambulance!" shout the students, terrified.

Julio César Mondragón, another freshman, is the first to start recording images of the attack on his phone. Hours later he will be found tortured, murdered and flayed not far from here.

Local residents and traders witnessing the events remark that the students were not only shot at by uniformed municipal police officers but also by people in civilian clothing. On the *normalistas'* side not a single shot is fired, they are unarmed.

One of the police vans has an attachment for a machine gun and from there it fires off rounds indiscriminately, as witnessed by one terrified resident. None of the municipal police patrol cars has this attachment.

The sound of the police officers' R15s echo along the street. Moments later more powerful bursts are heard, from more powerful, higher-calibre weapons. The residents who were standing at their windows now throw themselves to the floor.

"We're unarmed! Don't shoot!" the boys cry.

On the third bus Carrillas can see clearly that his attackers include municipal and state police. He can easily make out the logos on the backs of the uniforms. The municipal police are in their regular uniform and the state ones are in riot gear with the state police lettering on the backs of theirs. They are firing bursts at the tyres and windows of the third bus. Almost all the firepower is concentrated there.

"The police were trying to kill us all," he would recall months later.

Despite Fernando Marín's testimony, Guerrero's Minister for Public Security, Lieutenant Leonardo Vázquez Pérez, declared to the office of the Attorney General (P.G.R.) that his officers did not go out that night because their numbers were too low and that supposedly they remained behind to protect their barracks.

Inside the third bus the *normalistas* throw themselves into the narrow gangway to save their lives. Carrillas thinks if he does not do something soon they will all be massacred, so he takes the fire extinguisher and gets out of the bus to try and drive back the police officers shooting at him. Despite the shower of bullets he manages to hurl it at the police, when the fire extinguisher explodes one of the shots hits him in the arm and he falls to the ground. He manages to get himself back up onto the bus but he leaves a pool of blood behind him.

"There was a thought going through my head that I was past saving. I thought if I got it from them in the arm, then they're really going to kill my classmates now . . ."

Carrillas suggests to his friend Cochiloco that he call David Flores, a.k.a. La Parca, who is the college's general secretary and who stayed behind in Ayotzinapa. A terrified first-year, Ángel Hernández Martínez, a.k.a. El Botas, makes him a kind of tourniquet to stop his arm bleeding.

When he sees his friend losing blood, Cochiloco decides to surrender. "You know what? We've got to give in because they've already shot Carrillas, he won't be able to go with us anymore, he can't help us," he says to the driver of Estrella de Oro 1568 and asks him to get out and try to negotiate with the police.

When he steps out and identifies himself as the driver the police shout at him contemptuously: "We don't care who you are! You're one of them. You're just like them . . . you're an Ayotzinapo too."

At that moment the police start getting all the students down off the bus with their hands behind their necks and move them to the left-hand pavement. They lie them face-down on the ground in a kind of alleyway that serves as the garage of one of the houses. Carrillas notices that the people getting them onto the ground are the same state and municipal police, approximately twenty of them. One of these police officers says he is going to kill him and puts the cold barrel of his gun to the back of his neck.

Ángel de la Cruz who is on the other side of the road in the first bus manages with his fellow students to see the police getting those from the third bus out but they can see no more than this because the police blind them with the headlamps of their patrol cars and the lights they are carrying.

Cochiloco does not want to throw himself to the ground. "You know what? I'm not going to lie down," he says to one of the uniformed men who hits him roughly on the temple with the butt of his gun flecking the wall with blood. The man overpowers him and throws him to the ground with the others.

When they see their leader down none of the *normalistas* protests or resists, they no longer try to shout or to escape despite not being tied up.

El Botas, one of the younger students, can no longer contain his panic and starts to cry. "What are we going to do? Why are they doing this?" he says through his tears to Carrillas. "Take it easy, my friend, our guys will be here any moment to get us out of this. Don't worry, don't give up," he replies to give him some hope even though he has none himself.

On the ground Carrillas is writhing with the pain. As he lies there they kick him in the ribs and the face. Later, he reports, more police arrive. At that moment, fortunately for him, the ambulance arrives and takes him to the Iguala general hospital.

More ambulances arrive from the ring road to take away the two wounded students and a third who has had an asthma attack. Up till this moment the decision has not yet been taken to exterminate the *normalistas*.

10.30 a.m. – The Federal Police

A man who lives in the adjoining streets comes out of his house and heads towards Juan N. Alvarez street where the attack is taking place. His brother placed an emergency call to him asking for help as he was in one of the food stalls when the shooting began. When he reaches the junction of Juan N. Alvarez with Revolución street he runs right into a federal police roadblock.

The federal police units do not have their light bars on but they are only a few metres away and he can clearly make out the logos of the units stationed in a V formation and the insignia on their uniforms. The federal police are armed.

Desperate to rescue his brother he circles the adjoining streets but he is also unable to take Juan N. Alvarez because the roads that flow into it have also been closed by patrol cars. The whole section of the outskirts of town where the attack against the students is happening has been locked down. He cannot get any closer and calls his brother who comes out of a house he managed to run to when the shooting started and where he has been allowed to take refuge. His brother tells him that he saw buses going past and civilian vehicles firing at the buses.

At approximately 10.30 p.m. the federal police are present at another attack on the students on the Iguala-Chilpancingo highway close to the Palacio de Justicia. They stop an Estrella Roja bus carrying *normalistas* who have managed to get out of the centre of Iguala and are headed for Chilpancingo. This vehicle was never covered in the expert report by the Guerero Attorney General.

"The federal police officers get them in their sights, they try to shoot them, they call a halt, they come down, they throw stones at them, there's a confrontation with the officers and they [the *normalistas*] run for the hills," reports lawyer Vidulfo Rosales in an interview. Rosales has managed to reconstruct events with the surviving students.

Some metres ahead the twenty or so students travelling in Estrella de Oro 1531 are removed from the bus. Since then nobody has known their whereabouts, they make up a part of the forty-three students who have disappeared. All that was left in that place were rocks and blood-stained clothes.

"The fourth Estrella de Oro bus is surrounded by municipal police, and with the federal police behind them as back-up," said Rosales, based on the reconstruction of events.

Months after the massacre the head of the intelligence squad of the 27th Battalion declared to the office of the Attorney General (P.G.R.) that he had been present, supposedly only as an observer, when supposedly the municipal police removed the students from Estrella de Oro 1531 close to the Palacio de Justicia but he omitted to mention that the Federal Police were there too.

According to official documents at least two federal police officers have been identified as having been active that night: Luis Antonio Dorantes Macías, commander of the Federal Police base in Iguala and N.C.O. Victor Manuel Colmenares. Dorantes resigned from the federal police days after the event while Colmenares was transferred to another base of the federal police.

12.00 a.m. – The final attack

The witnesses from Juan N. Alvarez street can see that the students have been kept on the ground for more than half an hour. The video recorded by one local resident shows the patrol cars at 11.11 p.m., then the street empties: state police, municipal police and people not in uniform all leave. The students from the third bus vanish from the street with them but nobody can clearly see which vehicles they were taken away in.

Minutes later a Chevy appears as well as a white Urban van carrying students. They are the *normalista* students who received the calls asking for help but they have arrived too late. The survivors from the first and second buses meet them and tell them what has happened, journalists are gradually arriving while the students do their best to preserve the crime scene and gather up the spent shells from the guns.

Although the place is just metres from the 27th Infantry Battalion, the Federal Police base and the Combined Operations Base of the Attorney General of the Republic, no representative of authority – not one – comes to protect them.

Still in shock, the *Ayotzinapos*, as they are called today, improvise a press conference. A journalist there to cover the story recognises among the other journalists somebody who works for the federal government's Centre for Intelligence and National Security (C.I.S.E.N.), and he also sees people from the army infiltrated there wearing civilian clothes. He has no doubt who they are as he knows them well from another context.

C.I.S.E.N. documents obtained after the attack confirm that owing to earlier links to guerrilla fighters the Ayotzinapa teachers college is monitored permanently.[2] Four hundred metres from the Palace of Justice where the other group of students was disappeared is a house that serves as C.I.S.E.N.'s Iguala headquarters.

The students are giving statements about what has happened to the journalists on the corner of Juan N. Alvarez with the ring road when their words are interrupted by a hail of bullets. An armed group in dark-coloured clothing gets out of civilian vehicles.

They shoot first into the air then aim their fire directly into the human mass. There is a stampede, bullets whistling everywhere. Journalists and students equally are targets.

The armed unit advances towards the people who are running away. Not content with dispersing the crowds they follow them on a blatant hunting-spree and enter the adjoining street. At this moment two students are stretched out on the tarmac breathing their last. They are Julio César Ramírez and Daniel Solís, who managed to cry out "Help!" while the shot went through his back. The other students scatter at a run. In their flight one student heroically saves the life of a reporter, throwing himself on top of her so she does not take any of the bullets.

12.50 a.m. – "Help us, please, they're killing us!"
"Help, they're killing us! Help!" shout the students as they run terrified down Juan N. Alvarez towards the ring road. Behind them comes the sound of the machine-gun fire, sharp, constant, pitiless.

Nobody opens the door to them, a local woman looking out the window does not have the courage, her eyes are filled with terror and her heart with guilt. There is nothing more she can do, she has her grandchildren in the house and she fears that if she opens the door whoever is murdering the students will also kill her and her family.

In the desolate night it starts to rain. Some of the students are wounded. Among them is Omar García, head of the students' organising committee (C.O.P.I.) who came from Ayotzinapa to save his friends and fell into the same trap. He and his classmates are carrying the body of Edgar Vargas who has been shot in the mouth and is losing blood. From their windows some of the residents shout to them that the Cristina Hospital is just a little further up and they go there.

Others desperately knock at the doors of nearby houses and a few more jump the fences to save their lives.

Witnesses from parallel streets who hear the gunfire see a dark Suburban circling like a glass bubble out of which military-style men emerge, in civilian dress, and they too are hunting *normalistas*. The disappearance of some of the forty-three students happened around this time. The hunt is taking place and no authority prevents it.

A group of eight students crouch down and hide between the cars on a street perpendicular to Juan N. Alvarez and in the distance they see their fellow student Julio César Mondragón, the one who had been recording the attack on his mobile. At that moment somebody finally opens the door to a house and lets them in, they gesture to Julio César but he does not see them and keeps running.

At the same moment as this final attack Captain José Martínez Crespo's squadron is driving around Iguala, coming through Juan N. Alvarez street. From a distance one of the reporters can clearly see him and his men get out of their military vehicle and kick the bodies of Daniel Solís and Julio César Raímez. According to the autopsies at least one of them was still alive but they did not help them. Like criminals they continue on their way to the Cristina Hospital where Omar García is with his wounded fellow student.

They knock on the door and cock their guns as they enter. The platoon checks through the whole hospital and gathers together all the *normalistas*, including the young man who is wounded, in the waiting room. They photograph them and search them to check that they are not armed.

"You'd better have the balls to face up to things now, the way you do when you're pulling those fucking stunts of yours," says one of the soldiers threateningly.

Omar thinks to himself, "Right now the army is going to do whatever it wants to us. We won't get the chance to so much as object . . ."

"Give me your real names, I don't want you to give me fake names because if you give me a fake name they'll never find you," Captain Martínez Crespo warns them. Omar and his fellow students do not know up till this point that forty-three of the *normalistas* have already been disappeared.

The students beg for medical assistance for their friend because the hospital are unwilling to give him any, the soldiers tell them they have called the municipal police to come for them and they leave the hospital to return to the corner where the abandoned bodies are. It is not until 2.40 a.m. that a platoon corporal calls the Guerrero Attorney General to report the discovery of the already lifeless bodies.

After the tragic night when the sun comes up the *normalistas* realise that several of their fellow students have disappeared and they present their formal accusation to the Guerrero government whose own police force took part in the disappearance.

* * *

It is after 9.00 in the morning on September 27 when Infantry
Lieutenant Jorge Ortiz Canales reports to the state prosecutor's
office the discovery of a male body in a red polo shirt, black jeans
and white trainers with black and grey trim, abandoned on the
Petroleum Industry road, where the facilities of the Iguala C4 are
located from which all levels of government – federal, state and
municipal – were monitoring the *normalistas*. This is Julio César
Mondragón, who displays clear signs of torture and as an indica-
tion of the brutality of the hours of extermination he has a
fractured skull and his face has been flayed.

Three students and three civilians were murdered in the Iguala
massacre. At least twenty-nine people received gunshot wounds,
among them at least ten students. And forty-three *normalistas*
were disappeared. During the dark hours of hunting, fear and
devastation in Iguala while the Mexican state attacked, killed
and disappeared the *normalistas* there were eight families who
that night opened the doors of their houses and managed to save
the lives of at least sixty students, thanks to which it is possible to
recount what happened that night in Iguala, Guerrero, Mexico.

Translated by Daniel Hahn

I'M THE GUILTY ONE

Diego Enrique Osorno

ON FRIDAY JUNE 5, 2009, Roberto Zavala Trujillo and his wife Martha Dolores Lemas Campuzano were unsure about whether to circumcise their baby boy, Santiago, or not. In the state of Sonora it is usual to circumcise boys for hygienic reasons or to prevent illnesses. But Roberto was not entirely convinced and had asked for time off work to accompany his wife to a talk about it by a Mexican Social Security Institute (I.M.S.S.) doctor. Roberto had begun work at six that morning. At eight, he took off the mask, overall, gloves and safety glasses that he wore for the maintenance department of P.P.G. Industries,[1] surrounded by giant tanks filled with sulphuric acid and bubbling vats.

At nine o clock sharp, before the sun had begun to warm up the day in Hermosillo, Roberto parked his Chevy outside his house. His wife and child had only just got up. The idea was to leave Santiago in the nearby A.B.C. nursery, where he had been enrolled for more than a year. But when they got to the nursery, they realised that breakfast had already been served there, and so Roberto decided to take Santiago to have a bite to eat, while his wife kept the appointment with the doctor. The doctor explained the arguments for and against circumcising the baby, while Roberto and Santiago drank orange juice and ate cakes in the car. After the meeting, the three of them returned home. Roberto had to get back to work, and Martha had to start hers at a call centre. Around midday they left and headed for the A.B.C. nursery. Roberto got out of his car and took his son to the main entrance, then returned to take his wife to work.

Although his shift finished at 2.00 p.m., Roberto decided to stay a while longer to attend one of the reflection meetings often held to improve productivity and create a good working atmosphere. Shortly before 3.00 p.m., Roberto hurried out of the factory. As he was walking towards his car, he saw a plume of smoke in the sunny sky above the city.

"Look over there. What can be on fire?" he said to a workmate.

After getting into his car, Roberto had a strange foreboding and changed his routine. The clothes he wore for work were often impregnated with chemical smells and traces, so he usually went home, had a shower and then went to collect his son from the A.B.C. nursery on the western edge of Hermosillo. That afternoon, he headed straight for the nursery. As he drew nearer, he gradually realised that this was where the smoke was coming from.

When he was still a couple of kilometres away, he ran into a noisy traffic jam; all the access roads were blocked by patrol cars, their lights flashing. Bewildered, Roberto decided to try to avoid the queues of traffic, and drove in the opposite direction along an avenue that also led to the nursery. When he arrived, he parked his Chevy at a nearby tyre repair garage. The first thing he saw was that the smoke was rising from a Sonora government warehouse. He felt relieved, as he thought this must be where the fire had broken out, and that the children from the nursery would be safe and sound in a neighbouring house.

However, when he went round the corner to the nursery's main entrance, he came upon a scene of chaos. An old pick-up truck was rammed into the wall of the warehouse. The driver had collapsed at the wheel, and was enveloped in a cloud of smoke where the vehicle had hit the building, making a hole like an emergency exit that the nursery had never previously had. Roberto ran towards the accident, and grasped the shoulders of one of the nursery teachers who was shouting unintelligibly, her face raised to the sky.

"Where is Santiago, Santiago Zavala?" he demanded.

"Some of the children are over there, in that house," the teacher responded, pointing to a dwelling some 100 metres away. On the ground between the two buildings were about twenty children crying desperately, while assistants and strangers tried to comfort them. Roberto ran to the house, looked closely at the children inside, but could not see his son among the group of those saved from the fire.

"Where is Santiago?" he asked the next teacher he ran into.

"I don't know. I don't know what happened."

Without a second thought, Roberto went into the nursery, where flames were still raging. He walked through the smoke, trying to find the room he had left his son in a few hours earlier, but he could not see a thing. After wandering around for five minutes, he emerged again. He ran into the teacher he had met first. She was more frantic than ever.

"Look, stay calm, but which room is Santiago Zavala in?"

"In B–1."

"Where's that?"

"At the back, near the washroom."

Roberto forced his way into the building once more, and headed for what until that morning had been room B–1. The closer he got, the thicker the smoke became. Reaching the room, Roberto had to start to crawl, feeling with his hands to try to identify his son in the choking air. He could not stand this for long, and so left the nursery. He took off his shirt and soaked it in a bucket a neighbour had brought to help in the rescue attempts. Wrapping the wet shirt round his mouth, he went in again.

By now, there were more people searching in the darkness. The rescue team, made up of both firefighters and locals, came across a ceiling light, backpacks and mattresses, but no children. In another of the rooms, a shadow with a voice said that the remaining children were being taken out from the end class.

Leaving the nursery a third time, Roberto saw with horror that two state policemen were on guard outside, machine guns at the ready.

"What happened here?" he asked them.

"No idea."

"So why are you pointing your gun like that?"

"I've no idea what happened."

There were several children laid out on the verge opposite the nursery. A group of sweating paramedics was trying to revive them with mouth-to-mouth respiration. Torn between hope and fear, Roberto went over to see if Santiago was among them. However, none of them was his son, who that day was exactly two years, one month and ten days old. A policeman patted him on the shoulder and told him to go to the C.I.M.A., a nearby private hospital where most of the injured children had been taken.

Roberto climbed back into his Chevy, and then began the blasts of his horn, the stops and starts, the curses from car window to window, shortcuts through out-of-the way neighbourhoods. On his way he went to pick up his wife, but she was not at her work-place. Martha had learnt about what had happened and had gone to search for Santiago herself.

Roberto was one of the first parents to reach the emergency department of the C.I.M.A. hospital. The receptionist had still not realised that a tragedy was unfolding in the city, and reacted in the off-hand manner typical of overworked hospital staff.

"Hey, say something! I'm looking for a boy, Santiago de Jesús Zavala, from the A.B.C. nursery," Roberto shouted.

"Ah, yes: carry on down that way."

Another member of the hospital staff confirmed that the intensive care rooms were crammed with children from the nursery who had burns and damage to their internal organs. For the moment he could not give any further details. Shortly afterwards, Martha and other parents arrived. The hospital director came over and told them as calmly as possible that some of the children had died, and others were in a critical condition.

At 5.00 p.m. Roberto decided to go and search for his son in other hospitals. He went to the D.I.F. (Integral Family Development Clinic) where at seven that evening he was allowed in to see a baby who had not previously been identified. When Roberto entered, he saw a small child wrapped in so many bandages that only its face was visible. He asked what blood type the child was, and the doctor said it was A positive. This meant he could not be Santiago, who was O negative.

Over the next few hours, Roberto visited all the city hospitals. The last he had to visit was the I.S.S.S.T.E. (Institute for Security and Social Services for Public Sector Workers), where it had just been reported that there was another male child survivor who had not yet been identified by his parents.

When he reached the hospital reception, Roberto saw a T-shirt that reminded him of one Santiago used to wear. That day, in order to help identify the children, some of their clothes were hung up in the entrances to the Hermosillo hospitals. When he saw the little T-shirt, Roberto's hope of finding his son was rekindled. It was his last chance to find him alive.

A nurse took him to the intensive care room and he came to a halt in front of a cot. In it was a child with red, blistered skin and a rudimentary breathing apparatus covering its face. Roberto studied him for a minute with weary eyes and said: "Yes, that's my son." Soon afterwards, his sister Jessica came in to take a look at the child as well.

"Are you sure it's him, Roberto?"

"Yes, Jessica. Take a good look. It's him, but his face is burnt."

Then Martha came in.

"It's not him," Roberto's wife said categorically.

"Yes it is, Martha."

The couple's doubts were resolved when they learned the patient's blood group: it was not that of Santiago.

The last place they had to visit was the Forensic Institute. In the entrance to the morgue, a grim-faced employee showed them several photographs of the children inside. One of them was their son Santiago.

After offering his condolences, the employee took them to an office where the Sonora public prosecutor, Abel Murrieta, was waiting, together with the archbishop of Hermosillo, José Ulises Macías. Taking Martha by the hand, the prelate began to talk about how she must be resigned to the death. Roberto himself had passed from sadness to fury.

"Don't say a word," he told the archbishop.

"But my son ..."

"No, don't say a thing. Not a word. Quiet!"

"But my son, you must understand that ..."

"Don't you understand when I say you should be quiet?"

The archbishop didn't say another word.

"How many children are dead?" said Roberto, this time addressing the public prosecutor.

"I can't tell you. It's confidential."

"How the fuck can it be confidential?"

Roberto insisted so much that a few minutes later the state official told him: twelve.

By now it was midnight, and in reality the number of dead children was much higher than publicly acknowledged. In the midst of all the confusion, the authorities appeared to be trying to limit the impact the fire might have on the change in the state government, due to take place within a month.

That night, Roberto and Martha did not return home. They were devastated, and Roberto's mother convinced them to sleep at her house. The following afternoon, while their son's body was taken to a local funeral parlour and a vigil held, before it was carried to a niche in the Iglesia de Fátima, Roberto decided to return home to pick up some clothes. When he reached 30 Calle Moctezuma in the Perisur neighbourhood, he broke down. He got out of his car, opened the gate and approached the front door. Plucking up his courage, he went in.

He sat for a while among some of Santiago's things: an Apache tricycle, a yellow toy Tonka dumper truck, Batman costumes, a high chair, posters on the walls, toys from the film "Cars" and a T-shirt of the Chivas of Guadalajara football team. An overwhelming feeling of solitude.

A few minutes later, Roberto exploded. He began kicking things and punching the walls. He grasped at shadows. Santiago's birth had meant a radical change in his life, and the boy's death heralded another one. Later on, Roberto admitted he was terrified at all the crazy ideas that went through his mind that Saturday, June 6, as he stared at the cot where his boy used to sleep before dying in one of the worst tragedies in the recent history of Mexico.

At nine in the morning of Monday, June 8, Roberto Zavala went to the prosecutor's imposing office. Abel Murrieta received him straight away. Some officials had been ordered by the governor of Sonora, Eduardo Bours, to attend the families of the forty-nine dead children. His critics felt this was done in order to try to reduce the tragedy's inevitable impact on the state authorities, who were responsible for the warehouse where the fire had started. Roberto asked him who was to blame for the fire. The official answered that he did not know, but asked Roberto to trust him that they would investigate the matter properly.

"How the fuck do you expect us to trust you – tell me how?" Roberto protested.

The official assured him that in the next few hours three independent experts would arrive, so that the inquiry into the fire would be completely transparent. Roberto went back home and shut himself in with his wife Martha.

On Wednesday, June 10, a small group of genuine social leaders, as well as agents from the P.R.I. and the P.A.N. political parties – who it was assumed by many, were both seeking to manipulate the tragedy for electoral purposes – called a demonstration. More than twenty parents and relatives responded to the call, but not Roberto and Martha. They felt they could not yet go out into the street.

However, a subsequent press conference given by the prosecutor Murrieta enraged Roberto so much it convinced him he had to do something. Murrieta announced to local, national and international journalists who had come to cover the event that the independent experts had concluded that the fire had been caused by a cooler, the name given in Sonora to air conditioning machines. Moreover, in an interview with the journalist Carmen Aristegui, governor Bours Castelo had been forced to admit that Marcia Matilde Altagracia Gómez del Campo Tonella, one of the shareholders of the nursery run as a franchise from the I.M.S.S., was a cousin of his and of Margarita Zavala, the wife of Mexican president Felipe Calderón. He also admitted that two high-level officials in his administration were shareholders in the burnt-out nursery, together with their wives. Later on, investigations by the newspapers *Milenio* and *El Universal* revealed that the I.M.S.S.-franchised nursery continued to operate despite failing to meet basic safety requirements and that the contract had been renewed at the start of President Calderón's term of office by means of a communiqué signed on December 29, 2006 by the then director of Social Security, Juan Molinar Horcasitas.

"Fuck the lot of them. Now we are going on the march," Roberto told Martha one night after they had seen the news coverage of the tragedy on T.V.

The second protest march over the fire at the A.B.C. nursery took place on Saturday, June 13. Close to ten thousand people marched from the ruined nursery premises to the doors of the Sonora governmental palace.

As he was walking in silence through the streets of Hermosillo with a photograph of his son in his hands and across his burnt shoulders, Roberto thought and thought about who was to blame for what had happened at the nursery. The media had exposed evidence of negligence by the influential nursery owners, by the I.M.S.S., the state government agency that rented the adjacent warehouse where the fire had started, and the municipal health and safety department that had given permission for the nursery to remain open despite having a flammable tarpaulin under the corrugated iron roof and having no proper emergency exit. "We're all to blame for this damned tragedy," Roberto told himself.

When they reached Plaza Zaragoza, some of the parents began to shout their demands. Martha told the crowd she wanted justice for Santiago's death, then passed the microphone to Roberto, who had not intended to say anything in public, but now accepted the situation. He did not even know how to handle a microphone properly. Once he had a firm hold on it, he began speaking in a quiet voice, as if giving a class.

"Neither the I.M.S.S.," he began, "nor the owners of the nursery, nor the person who rented the warehouse from the state finance department have accepted their share of the blame, but there is one person who will accept it and is carrying the burden of it: and that is me."

"It's not you, it's those corrupt people who are guilty!" someone in the crowd contradicted him.

"Yes, it's those corrupt people . . . but I am the main one responsible, because I am an honest person who has a job, who has to fulfil his working hours, who pays into Social Security for giving me the chance to send my boy to that nursery, where I was told they had adopted all the proper safety measures. I am guilty for trusting them, for paying my taxes, I am guilty for going to vote. I am guilty for the death of my son."

At this, Plaza Zaragoza exploded with shouts for and against what Roberto was saying. Roberto paused in these calm reflections and began to speak more loudly, then to shout angrily:

"Señor Governor, here is one of the guilty people you're looking for! Come and get me! I'm waiting for you! I've had enough! You make fools of all of us too often! Telling us everything is fine, when we know that Mexico is a load of crap! Everything that's in the news: corruption, drug trafficking. You're making fools of us! I'm guilty for letting you do so!"

*   *   *

Early in the 1980s, when Roberto was four, his father was transferred from Hermosillo to the federal highway police in Guadalajara.

The Zavala Trujillo family grew with the addition of Jessica, Roberto's only sister. Three years later, Roberto was transferred to Ciudad Guzmán to patrol the main road between there and Guadalajara. In 1992, when war was raging between the gunmen of the Arellano Félix brothers and those of Joaquín (El Chapo) Guzmán, Roberto's father was shot in the back as he tried to intercept a drug traffickers' convoy on the highway. He survived, but lost the use of his legs. In recognition of his bravery, he was promoted from captain to deputy commander.

A few weeks later, the Zavala Trujillo family returned to Hermosillo. His father started doing office work in the federal highway police headquarters, and Roberto's mother went back to the post of administrative secretary where she had first met her husband.

These constant moves led to Roberto having problems at school, where his classmates looked on him suspiciously simply for being new. On their return to Hermosillo, his parents enrolled him in a school in the tough neighbourhood of Las Isabeles, where during his first weeks, fist fights were a daily occurrence. Later on, he attended Escuela Técnica No. 6, where school life was calmer.

After finishing secondary school, Roberto went to Colegio de Bachilleres Norte, but he was only there until the fourth semester, when he had to leave because of bad marks. He began to work, starting in La Macedonia, one of the oldest pizzerias in Hermosillo in Colonia Granjas, famous not only for its pizzas but also for its Slush Puppies with sweet flavourings that were both delicious and very welcome in the city's hot summers. In a few hours, he learnt how to ride a motorbike and the next day he was out on the streets delivering pizzas and spaghetti dishes. Although accidents were common among his delivery colleagues, Roberto never had one.

From La Macedonia he went to work in a travel agency as a

messenger boy. He soon realised how tough life would be if he continued working so hard for such slender pay packets. With his parents' support at the age of eighteen he went back to his pre-university studies, this time enrolling in a private pre-university college called Preparatoria Regional del Noreste, where he had to start at the beginning. One of the teachers observed that Roberto was a "twisted tree", lacking discipline when it came to work, but always ready to rebel in class. One day, the teacher confronted Roberto.

"What is it you want?"

"The thing is, I don't agree with the way things are done."

At that age, Roberto saw himself as an anarchist, because he was always against the rules. His anarchist influence was more musical than political or literary. He listened to Spanish groups like Ska-P, Sin Dios and Reincidentes. Although these groups were rarely played on the commercial radio stations, Roberto could hear them on La Bemba radio station in Hermosillo, a radio with which years later he would once again have a special link. After hearing the anarchist bands on this community radio, Roberto began searching for more of this kind of music on the internet, on YouTube and special music downloads.

The teacher responded:

"So you're against the system, are you?"

"Yes, that's right."

"You want to change things, do you?"

"Yes, I'd really like that: to live in a country that's different."

"Well then, get inside the system. Once you're in there, change it. If you're outside, you'll never be able to bring about any change, you'll just be shouting your head off. If you really want to do something, get inside the system, react to it, and once you have the means, you'll be able to really change things."

This conversation marked Roberto. He was still a rebel, but he did the work and had found a part-time job at Domino's Pizza, starting as a delivery boy, until a few months later he had risen to become the manager of a branch in Hermosillo's Zona Satélite. In those years, Roberto had a shaved head, wore dark-coloured clothes, steel-tipped boots, and had padlocks and other metal objects dangling from his belt, although he never liked piercings. The relationship with his heroic federal policeman father was difficult: and one of the reasons was the clothes Roberto wore. His mother used to tell him: "If you dress like normal people, I'll buy you a car." But Roberto never got that car: his clothes were a code that said: "I won't be tamed."

The person who could tame him was Martha, an old friend from college days whom he met again sometime later. They got together, and because he was in love, Roberto occasionally used to wear light-coloured shirts and didn't wear his steel-tipped boots every day. When she was about to finish college, Martha told him she was pregnant.

Roberto asked her to marry him. His parents had just moved home, leaving the other house empty. Eventually, Roberto and Martha moved in to await the birth of their child. Roberto then left his job at Domino's where he only earned 1,700 pesos a fortnight, even though he was in charge of a branch. Fortunately he found a better one earning twice as much in Henkel, a chemical company that produced cleaning fluids for Ford. Roberto was put in charge of changing filters, cleaning out tanks and checking the pressure of the assembly line.

Their first child was born on October 21, 2005, in a private clinic. Seeing how big the baby was, the doctor joked: "When he leaves here tomorrow he'll go straight to kindergarten." A few hours later, the baby caught a fever, and died only days later of heart failure. Neither Roberto nor Martha like to talk about Daniel Guadalupe, the name they gave their first child.

The next year, in 2006, Henkel lost its contract with Ford and had to close its plant at Hermosillo. P.P.G. Industries, the company the car manufacturers had decided to award the contract to, kept Roberto on. A few days later, Martha told him she was pregnant again. With the settlement cheque from Henkel, Roberto bought his wife a medical insurance plan and paid for the birth of his son at the Licona clinic. There, a gynaecologist checked his wife's health every month and they gave her ultrasound tests to see how the child was growing in its mother's womb. "We're going to make sure he's looked after like a rich baby," Roberto told his wife.

On April 26, 2007, Santiago de Jesús Zavala Lemas was born, without complications. After one night in the clinic, Martha and the baby arrived at the house in Colonia Perisur where the couple had set up a cot beside their bed and painted the walls of the room in bright colours. They put toys, nappies and clothes on special, easy-to-reach shelves. The birth of Santiago led Roberto to decide to study at the University of Sonora in the evenings, so that he would be in a better economic situation for his son. Following the first five months when Santiago constantly woke up in the early hours, Roberto began classes. His days started at five in the morning, when he opened his eyes to get ready and set off for work. At the end of his shift at two in the afternoon, he would go straight to college. His day ended when it was growing dark and he came back to his wife and son at home.

But a short time later, the family finances began to suffer. The house the Zavala Trujillo family lived in belonged to Roberto's parents. They paid the mortgage every month to the bank, but suddenly were unable to do so when an illness left Roberto's father, who by now was a commander in the federal police in Nayarit, unable to work. Roberto went to the bank on his parents' behalf, and promised to cover the arrears with his credit allowance from the government housing agency. In the end, the bank accepted, and when the money began to be deducted from his wages, Roberto decided to suspend his studies.

In order to supplement the family economy, Martha took a job in a call centre, and the couple began to look for a good place to leave Santiago when they were both at work. At first, they left their son with Martha's sister until a friend recommended Martha enrol Santiago at the A.B.C. nursery, which was close to their home. Although doubtful at first, Roberto finally accepted the idea. He was reassured because the nursery was highly recommended, and besides, their boy would not have to go there very often, because Martha only worked at weekends, so that from Monday to Thursday he would not need to attend. In order not to lose his place, Roberto used to take Santiago to the nursery for three hours, three times a week. Friday was the only day Santiago spent the whole day at the nursery, where another 200 children were registered.

When he left work on Fridays, Roberto picked Santiago up, and since his mother was not at home they spent the afternoon together. If they stayed at home, Roberto would put on music from groups like Basket Case, Green Day or The Offspring. There was also the possibility of watching the Discovery Kids T.V. channel. If they went out, their favourite excursion was to the city zoo. The first time they went there, it was not the lions, the monkeys or the giraffes that fascinated Santiago, but the crows. As soon as they reached their cage, Santiago became agitated and gestured to his father for him to show as much excitement at the sight of the birds as he did. That night, Roberto told his wife Martha that Santiago might in fact be little Damien, the friend of crows.

Sharing his life with Santiago changed Roberto radically. Before his son was born, it was not uncommon for him to start a fight on the slightest pretext. But Santiago roused a previously unknown protective instinct in his father. Roberto began to try to get into fewer scrapes, not to argue with other drivers, and he even began to study closely the safety regulations of the products he had to handle in his job for P.P.G. Industries.

*   *   *

Following the march when Roberto declared himself to be the guilty one, the parents began to talk about the need to organise to prevent the death of their children going unpunished. The Emiliana de Zubeldía square, smelling of hot-dogs and opposite the university quarter, was turned into the place where relatives of the dead children and other inhabitants of the city spontaneously built an altar in honour of the small victims. After several days of debates, in which up to forty parent couples took part, the Movimiento Ciudadano por la Justicia 5 de Junio was created. Not all the parents wanted to join. Four couples decided to try to forget completely what had happened and left it to God to take care of the investigations and the dispensing of justice. Others preferred to enter into talks about compensation from the authorities, in exchange for not protesting.

On the fifth of every month, those parents who are part of the movement carry out some kind of protest. These can be marches or meetings, or citizen trials of the nursery owners or the implicated officials. These demonstrations often seem like spiritual pilgrimages. They walk along in silence, with mothers and relatives at the front pushing their dead children's empty pushchairs, followed by a group of relatives carrying photographs of the victims from the nursery as if they were carrying lit torches in their hands. Drum-beats mark the rhythm for the crowd dripping with sweat, and occasionally the recorded voice of one of the nursery children is heard from a cell-phone. Songs like "Pin Pon es un muñeco" can suddenly ring out in protest.

As with other parents, Roberto Zavala's views about things in Mexico changed with the death of his son. Before, when Roberto saw on the news that there was a demonstration in Oaxaca or in the capital, he would say to his wife: "Stupid people doing all that for nothing. This is Mexico, they'll never get anywhere like that, we'll always be screwed". He never imagined he would be making a protest speech to a crowd of 20,000 people. Santiago's death removed any sense of shame at seeming ridiculous, or fear of repri-sals. After several months of comradeship and struggle alongside the other parents in the Movimiento por la Justicia, Roberto began to have fresh dreams and a little hope. One of them is that once they have succeeded in seeing all those responsible for the deaths of their children sent to prison, and in pushing through a reform of the current national nursery system, the Movement will continue to exist, to help other people whose rights have also been trampled on. Roberto would like the Movimiento Ciudadano por la Justicia 5 de Junio still to be in existence in fifty years' time, led by com-pletely new people, youngsters not even born when the A.B.C. nursery tragedy took place.

*   *   *

One Saturday evening in March 2010, Roberto was watching Diego, his sister Jessica's son, as he played with the daughter of Julio César Márquez and other children, in the yard of the Paulo Freire pre-university college. They were holding a baby shower attended by most of the parents from the Movimiento. The parents felt a sense of satisfaction. After nine months, their efforts had led the Supreme Court to appoint a group of judges to investigate the case. In their preliminary report, these judges concluded there had been grave violations of individual guarantees among the most senior officials of the I.M.S.S. as well as the state and municipal authorities. They also declared illegal the system of franchising that governed the A.B.C. nursery and a further 1,400 nurseries run by the Social Security ministry.

Roberto was leaning against a small fountain as he observed his nephew Diego, who despite being the youngest and smallest among the group of children was the one who took the lead. When he saw Diego, Roberto could not help recalling with that sense of sadness that comes and goes in waves how his younger sister's small son would come and mess up the toys Santiago was trying to line up on the floor while the two were playing together. In spite of the good news in his life, it was inevitable that Roberto should be gripped by these feelings of passion and despair, this constant effort to try to overcome things.

By now, in addition to the preliminary report by the Supreme Court in their favour, the group of parents had won the support of thousands of people throughout Mexico. Solidarity meetings had been held in the capital, in Monterrey, Guanajuato, Villahermosa, Guadalajara and Tijuana. Nationally respected journalists such as Katia D'Artigues, León Krauze, Ricardo Rocha, Olivia Zerón and Epigmenio Ibarra, among others, were closely following their campaign. The prominent activist Daniel Gershenson, known for his attempts to get collective action onto the statute books had become an active member of the group, taking part in public events and using Twitter to organise support for the parents. In Sonora, Mari G. Escalante, the owner of the college where the baby shower was being held, was one of the people who had joined the parents' movement with the greatest enthusiasm, together with Claudia Díaz Symonds, Professor Rubén Duarte, the journalist Silvia Nuñez, and the lawyer Lorenzo Ramos.

Most important of all, Roberto was living a moment of great personal hope. The baby shower was in honour of his wife Martha, who was about to give birth to a girl, the third in the family. She was born later that month, on March 29, 2010, in San José hospital, and was called Ana Victoria Zavala Lemas. Roberto was happy, but still had an open wound. He was thinking of a date in the near future: April 26, 2010, when his son would have been three. Together with his wife Martha, Roberto was planning a special event to honour Santiago. This consisted in placing a huge photograph of his dead son on an advertising hoarding on the busy Rodríguez boulevard close to some I.M.S.S. offices and only a few metres away from ex-governor Eduardo Bours's private office. Together with the photograph, Roberto and Martha were going to ask for the following message to appear: "Corruption did not allow me to reach my third birthday this April 26. Santiago de Jesús Lemas. April 26, 2007–June 5, 2009. JUSTICE!"

On April 30, 2010, during celebrations for the Day of the Child, the then president Felipe Calderón Hinojosa met parents who had lost their children in the fire at the A.B.C. nursery but who were not part of the Movimiento. At the end of their meeting, there was no announcement of any commitment to bring justice in a case in which there are 49 dead children and no official or other person in jail. The only thing to come out of the event was a photograph of the president with the relatives.

That day, Roberto was in Mexico City, with other parents who the previous afternoon had met Arturo Zaldívar Lelo de Larrea, the head of the Supreme Court considering the case, which was

to be put to the full panel of the highest court in the land that summer. When the news from the presidential palace was confirmed,
Abraham Fraijo, father of the victim Emilia, wrote on his Twitter
account, "I feel so sorry for the families who have been made
fools of by the president," and Julio César Márquez, father of
another little victim of the fire, wrote: "I'll never call you president
again. Aren't you ashamed of yourself? You have destroyed what
little faith many Mexicans had left with your cowardly excuses."
Roberto is not on Twitter, but his comments about President
Calderón were no less harsh than those of his colleagues.

On May 6, 2010, a day after the most recent protest by the
Movement in Hermosillo's Plaza Zaragoza (a citizens' trial of
the officials they considered responsible for the fire) Roberto went
to the Hotel Kino to meet the photographer Rodrigo Vázquez, who
he had agreed to allow to take his photograph. When he arrived,
the photographer from the capital was studying some images he
had shot a few hours earlier in the warehouse belonging to the
finance department of the Sonora state government, where the fire
that spread to the adjacent A.B.C. nursery had started. Accompanied
by a local photographer, Jorge Moreno, they had succeeded in
avoiding the two patrol cars still guarding the burnt-out building
and had managed to take a series of photographs inside. Roberto
sat next to the computer and looked at the photos for a while
without showing any great emotion. At one point in the slide
show of images, he said: "That's the damned *cooler*," pointing at
a shapeless heap of burnt metal.

A few minutes later, Roberto and the photographer left the
hotel. They visited Roberto's former home, where he had lived with
his son Santiago and where his cot and some toys still remained.
After the photo shoot, they left for the site of the A.B.C. nursery.
While Rodrigo was taking advantage of the afternoon light to

take more photos outside, Roberto sat opposite and stared at the warehouse where the makeshift nursery had once been. Unlike some of those in Sonora, to him, the place where his son and 48 other children perished is not a shrine. What Roberto wants above all is for this dreadful building to be completely demolished as quickly as possible, and something beautiful put in its place.

Translated by Nick Caistor

II

IMPACT

ANAMORPHOSIS OF A VICTIM[1]

Sergio González Rodríguez

IN ANY LEGAL SYSTEM a victim is usually one of the individuals present or caught up in an act of violence. Their existence becomes part of a police and judicial inquiry that will decide their role in the conflict and assess the damage inflicted.[2] Legally speaking, the victim is part of an edifice of Law that is characterised by a vertical, linear design symbolised by the scales held by the goddess Themis, a cornucopia or the image of the pyramid of Law.[3] Within this imaginary construct, victims aspire to be seen and recognised as individuals who acquire a physical presence in their spatial-temporal relationship with the realm of the Law.

Victims know they stand outside a vast, labyrinthine building that, nonetheless, is nearby. And that they are defenceless, like the peasant in Franz Kafka's parable, "Before the Law",[4] a victim of an injustice who finds himself outside the edifice of Law where a doorkeeper prevents him from entering and wastes his time in a rambling conversation that only triggers endless exasperating questions and answers. The victim listens to the doorkeeper: "If you are so drawn to it, just try to go in despite my veto. But take note: I am powerful. And I am only the least of the doorkeepers. From hall to hall there is one doorkeeper after another, each more powerful than the last. The third doorkeeper is already so terrible that even I cannot bear to look at him." Years go by and the victim ages.

Now dying, he has one last question: "How is it that for all these many years no-one but myself has ever begged for admittance?" The doorkeeper replies: "No-one else could ever be admitted here, since this gate was made only for you. I am going to shut it."

Given that their access to justice is blocked, victims can only be certain of one thing: that they hover on the periphery of the law. They can never be sure they will receive a hearing and their very identity as individuals connects them to a pattern that links them to people who share the same predicament. The conforming and conformity of victims makes it probable that they will end up as mere statistics alongside others in some official compilation.

The path followed by victims forces them to emphasise their only feature that can challenge the homogeneity the law represents and enforces: the extreme experience of violence, the non-transferable specificity of their bodies and their consciousness at the moment they become the victims of a crime, abuse or atrocity. The distortion of the everyday stability of individual life by an act of violence, denominated here the anamorphosis of the victim,[5] contrasts starkly with the symmetry of the law and institutions responsible for upholding their rights through their mechanisms, measures and procedures. It denotes and describes the direct experience of hurt, damage, danger, risk or other circumstance that infringes their human rights.

The difference between what victims have experienced and the legal system at hand highlights two realities in conflict: the first is lived as an anamorphosis, that is, an image, representation or memory that may be blurred and confused or sharp and precise, depending on when or where it is evoked; the second reveals a tendency to be symmetrical. A threshold stands between both at a point where the political arena functions as a hinge or axis in a permanently virtual conflict: a wound, trace or fissure that, inasmuch as all supporting institutions fail, widens exponentially and never closes. Devastated in this way, victims disintegrate. Disintegration brings back their experience of the original trauma and continual inscription in the anamorphosis of the irrational and a-rational, horror and panic at being obliged to relive the unspeakable. The chaos of a moment extended forever.

Victim status can only be overcome via a symbolic exchange in respect of death. And even then victims reappear as anamorphoses of their own memories: torn apart, distorted, inscribed in an anomalous representation of the familiar, where the self becomes other, alienated, remote and strange, and emotions are engulfed by the atrocity and cruelty inflicted by others. In a fateful move, the world is imposed as anamorphosis, alternating between norm and anomaly. Victims are trapped in the middle with their catastrophic experiences on the threshold of the very worst imaginable.

Victims usually appear as part of a judicial investigation that confers an identity encompassing their experience on the frontier between life and death and an institutional review focusing on the incident and probable outcomes. The incident is integrated into the logic of a time-line with an urgent need to retrace steps (the antecedents) and clarify the truth about what has happened. And although victims are located outside the judicial order, their existence in the world harbours the possibility that they may be incorporated into a logic of documentation and judicial inquiry, where the human element will probably be the written word and perhaps later a statistic that in turn will swell columns of data in registers of criminal convictions.

Rather than understanding the victims solely from the perspective of their appearance in a chronological account, that translates them into grains of sand in the great clock of shared existence, or as a notch on a time-line, if one evaluates them on the basis of their reality in the flesh, of their presence in a given space and transformation into a trajectory within a three-dimensional ambit (or four-dimensional if the conceptual sphere is added), and of their humanity amid a host of morphological, geographical and transgeographical features (taking into account telecommunications and the intangible territory of cyberspace), any conclusions might offer better insights into the individuals and their mutation into victims. If victims are set in a tangible space, become space, then individual bodies will stand out from the social body in a cultural topography and critically focused spatial perspective.

A cartography of victims re-sites damage, injury and insult. A body is a person. Life in its extreme defencelessness before a power that subjects and annihilates it: bare life.[6] To better appreciate the anamorphosis of victims, one must consider examples that illuminate the influence of space and the new cartography of the battlefields suffered by so many at a civilian level in a variety of localities and situations.

The body/person of Adriana Ruiz:[7] a model and sports organiser in the city of Tijuana, mother of one child and breadwinner for the rest of her family. She was active in the area of public relations. As part of her work, she advertised herself on social networks: she spread her image and professional experience around. She participated in the occasional beauty competition and advertising campaign. The company that contracted her as an organiser belonged to a local power group. One Saturday she was kidnapped by armed delinquents in the doorway of her own house. The family reported her kidnapping. The media broadcast the news. They put pressure on the authorities. Four days later the police announced they had found the victim's body and arrested those responsible for the murder. The young woman's body had been half-buried a metre down on a rubbish tip in Colonia Altiplano on the city outskirts.

Beheaded. There was evidence of torture: they had extracted her toenails and severed a toe from each foot. Those in the dock confessed: the head of their criminal gang had ordered them to kidnap, interrogate, torture and behead the victim, as a warning "to everyone else". The criminal gang believed she was an informer, since she had been accused of being one by other women close to the gang. The police found the victim's mobile phone in the assassins' possession: they had taken photos of her decapitation. The authorities underlined the links between victim and killers, which the families denied. The press attacked the police's haste in arresting those responsible and the various contradictions and omissions in the official communiqué. The police responded by saying that it had dismantled a criminal gang that was very active in the city. It had already been alleged in the media that the head of police was protecting one criminal gang in order to favour another.

With its five million inhabitants, Tijuana is part of the trans-national urban space that comprises Rosarito, Tecate and San Diego in the U.S.A., and represents a huge asymmetry in respect of the frontier with the United States: it developed in a valley and now sprawls across tableland and over hills, canyons, ravines, streams and canals. The dominant feature is one of rugged folds. Adriana Ruíz's life criss-crossed with organised crime which controls a good slice of the urban terrain through its illegal business activity. The impact of media (press, radio, television channels) and transmedia (the internet, social networks) is one way of establishing connections within the community that flatten the territory's ruggedness and triggers simultaneous, ubiquitous, immediate reactions from institutional agencies. The rigid bureaucracy of institutions is challenged by the a-legal backlash fired by lack of trust at the level of public opinion. A victim's murder is a repeated occurrence: first in reality and later, as sensationalist news items powered by what only interrupted by road-blocking tactics used by criminal gangs in their struggle to coerce the authorities. The victim and his brothers' business was involved with organised crime: dealing with new and used cars is a common way to launder illegally acquired money. Once the victim was implicated in that illegal flow, his position became extremely high risk.

Body/person of Daniel Arriaga:[9] he came from Córdoba, Veracruz, now lives in the state of Mexico and has a daughter who is studying in Europe. He manages and analyses civil intelligence operations in Mexico. His experience and honest approach are recognised by his civilian and military colleagues and by U.S., European and Israeli intelligence agencies. The dismantling of intelligence departments in Mexico from 2000 to 2010 and their reconfiguration around the Secretaría de Seguridad Pública (S.S.P.) (the Ministry for Public Safety) in the frontline war against drug trafficking from 2007, meant that he was gradually relieved of his responsibilities despite that experience and honesty. In the course of his duties, he uncovered various acts of corruption, negligence and criminal omission on the part of police and civil servants at the highest level in the S.S.P.. He decided to reveal what he had found and wrote a letter to the president of the Republic. The reply was silence. One day, there was a knock on his door. When he opened up, he found a suitcase full of money on his doorstep. He took it to the office of the individual he suspected had sent it: someone higher in the chain of command. He handed the suitcase over to the man who threatened him with two options: either he should accept the money or resign and keep quiet, otherwise he and his family would be killed. The civil servant offered his resignation. He went on to work as an independent intelligence consultant for federal state governments.

The corruption in state security and intelligence departments is something that militates against any improvement in the situation in Mexico. As a result they are dysfunctional throughout the country. Because of his track record and qualities a civil servant like Daniel Arriaga represents an obstacle in the a-legal rise of the new public security arrangements: he went from the centre of intelligence activities to institutions on the periphery, while anomalies have only multiplied in the state apparatus for police control and surveillance. Institutional degeneration is complete, and is far from being addressed and corrected: the S.S.P. is a body that was tainted from the start. Now marginalised, the writing is on the wall for this civil servant.

Body/victim Elías Castillo:[10] a political journalist who has invested money in a range of enterprises; he lives in the Port of Veracruz facing the Gulf of Mexico. He is well known in local political circles and one day was kidnapped in the street. He was taken to an unknown safe house where a permanently hooded figure conversed with him for days on end. Family and friends negotiated a ransom. The kidnappers knew the victim's every routine act as a result of their surveillance and interception of his emails and post. Apart from a ransom sum, they demanded he handed over the house where he lived. The victim replied that it was mortgaged: if he gave them the contract of purchase, they would only acquire debt. News of the kidnapping hit the newspapers. Family and friends found the ransom money. The kidnappers freed him. A hooded individual told the victim: "We're only letting you go because we have the same friends in political circles." The victim knows they could kidnap him again and is considering leaving the city.

The spaces occupied by criminals can no longer be distinguished from those inhabited by the political class. Organised crime's knowledge of an individual's field of activity and property that it can exploit means potential victims are subject to systematically planned searches and attacks that expand centrifugally. The lack of demarcation between what is legal and illegal covers the trails of those who resort to crime. Or to politics. Victims are conscious of a reduction in the space for living their lives that correlates with the growing expansion of the space for criminals. Where the latter predominate, any division between the public and the private vanishes. The victim assumes the status of hunted prey. Or of a person enjoying the provisional freedom granted by organised crime.

Body/person of Jesús Torrijos:[11] after midnight, several soldiers entered his house in Ciudad Juárez, Chihuaha, without a search or arrest warrant: they ransacked the house, stole money and took him prisoner. His wife made representations to the Chihuahua State Commission for Human Rights and handed over video images taken by a mobile phone of all the damage caused by the military. The army declared that the arrest took place three days after it actually happened: they reported that the soldiers approached Torrijos in the street and saw him throw a bag of marijuana onto the ground. They arrested him on the spot. Torrijos was accused of "crimes against public health" and "possession with a view to sale". The incoherencies in the army's version of events became obvious in court. Three months later the victim was released. The judge failed to instigate an inquiry into the soldiers' possible criminal acts: abuse of authority, theft, assault and torture. The relevant public prosecutor similarly turned a blind eye and didn't investigate those responsible.

The violation of victims' rights and guarantees on the part of the military opens up a dimension of a-legality and convergence with organised crime. The legal order disappears as a real presence for victims who now find themselves trapped between the extreme violence of the armed forces and organised crime. The abolition of legality undermines the civil status of citizens. Judicial oversights by the authorities themselves means that the law is sidelined and justice is not obtained. The rule of law becomes the rule of crime.

Body/person of Eliud Naranjo, thirty-three years of age, municipal policeman:[12] he was arrested at 8.45 a.m. by some twenty policemen and soldiers who forced their way into his dwelling in Huimanguillo, Tabasco, in the south of the country. The security forces beat him up in front of his family. They blindfolded and drove him in an unidentified vehicle to an unknown destination. They tortured him until he agreed to confess that he worked for organised crime. The police reports state that he was arrested in "*flagrancia*" at a checkpoint near Cárdenas. In their "Narrative account of the facts" the police state that they saw him following a police convoy "suspiciously" and that, after his arrest, Naranjo "spontaneously" confessed to working as an informer for criminals. Naranjo insisted he was forced to sign his statement by means of torture. Naranjo impugned the charges formulated against him: he alleged he was arbitrarily arrested and then tortured until a false confession was forced out of him. Nonetheless, he remained in prison until his appeal was resolved.

The authorities contrive a "narrative" that re-casts what has happened after the events have taken place in order to cover up the way the rights of individuals have been violated. Such re-casting is a repeated *modus operandi* in which the authorities intervene in premeditated actions agreed by the police, their hierarchy and the prosecutors responsible for bringing charges. Ignoring any respect for the principle of a due process, the judge involved will stick rigidly to protocols and leave out of account substantial matters of impartiality, justice and freedom. The edifice of the Law becomes a minefield for the victims the second they cross its threshold.

Body/person of José Barrerra:[13] originally from Durango, in the north of the country, he owned a glassworks in an outlying district of Ciudad Juárez. He started his business in 1995 and could afford a better house and higher standard of living than his neighbours. He attracted around him relatives who had come to the frontier to look for work. One morning, delinquents entered his premises. They had been extorting money from him but on this occasion the victim refused to hand any over. They shot him and then repeated the exercise in a nearby store and stationery shop. When she heard the shots, his wife ran from her house to the adjacent store. By the time she reached her husband he was dead. The police claimed the victim's body and took over a day to hand it back to the family: the murder of individuals always tends to be seen as a proof of links with organised crime that includes the victim. His six young children, wife and family had no choice but to leave Ciudad Juárez after they had shut down the glassworks.

The barrios of Ciudad Juárez are the domain of criminal gangs who charge everyone for right of movement and abode: in exchange for money the police accept and protect such a regime that functions as an illegal government. Exploitation of traffic, locality and illicit business activities establishes the rules of co-existence in poor barrios on that frontier. The citizenry participates in a society that works normally on the surface though in reality it is a quasi-prison, where avenues and streets can only be used with relative peace of mind during the day. At night, only police and criminals walk out in the open. It is extremely risky for ordinary citizens to show their faces. Private space as such has ceased to exist: criminals can intrude at any time; there are no walls, barriers or boundaries to their activities: what is private is one more corridor for the pursuit of their illicit endeavours: they jump over, destroy and drill walls, doors and barbed wire fences. The illicit devours the licit, since the legal economy has been sucked into the illegal, underground economy. The domain of organised crime at war with government, urban territory is now transformed into a zone of daily warfare on a par with low-intensity conflict.

The body/person of Rodolfo Nájera:[14] a policeman in Lerdo, Coahuila. He appeared on social media in front of a screen. Los Zetas had filmed him on video: two masked men with assault rifles were guarding him. The victim was on his knees, with his hands tied behind his back, his face had obviously been hit and was swollen around his right eye. His ear on the same side was half severed. A voice, out of frame, was interrogating him in an impersonal tone. The victim confessed that he worked for drug dealers who are rivals to Los Zetas: el Pirata, el Delta. His interrogator compelled him to inform on the criminal and police networks he belonged to. The victim related episodes that had taken place in the city of Torreón, Coahuila, in the north of the country on the frontier with Texas: a group of assassins attacked bars and private parties murdering and injuring dozens of people. After each massacre, the murderers returned to the prison where they were incarcerated. The victim claimed that the woman directing that penal institution endorsed and protected their criminal acts. In the video images, the victim reappeared in another location. The exchange was resumed. The voice asked if the victim's people preferred to kill innocent people because they were incapable of standing up to Los Zetas. The victim replied: "*Sí, señor.*" The voice persisted: "They cannot defeat us." The victim agreed: "No." The guards separated out. A shot was heard. The victim fell forward. The following day when the video was transmitted on social networks, the authorities took the prison director and assassins into custody.

Police are in the hands of the highest criminal bidder. Gangs are a supra-institutional power that roams everywhere, crossing prison

walls whenever necessary. Investigations into criminal acts tend
to be subsumed by organised crime itself, thus destroying the
conventional parameters of institutions and it imposes its own
Law of Retaliation or distributive justice: *lex talionis*. Cruelty and
lack of respect for human rights is their norm, and the space of
what is legal is rolled back by what is not. Videos broadcast the
panic of victims and the arrogance of gangs, and transmedia space
multiplies the aggressive potential of organised crime by fusing
media and transmedia into a single abject panorama. Viewers are
fed a perverse, distorted, formless vision from the viewpoint of the
victim's defencelessness: anamorphosis and the indescribable. The
space of culture is turned upside down.

Body/person of José Antonio Elena, 16,[15] living in Nogales,
Sonora, on the frontier with Arizona. He was shot down at a city
crossroads adjacent to the frontier boundary. The U.S. Border
Patrol stated that the youth, along with three other individuals,
were bringing packets of marijuana into the U.S.A. When they
were spotted, they ran to find refuge in their own country. From
behind the wall separating the frontier on the U.S. side, a Border
Patrol agent shot at the victim eight times, twice in the head, four
times in the thorax, the other bullets were embedded in the wall of
a nearby medical consultancy. A Border Patrol spokesman alleged
that the youth threw stones at the Border Patrol agents to distract
them and one of the latter counter-attacked. He went on to affirm:
"When a person, an agent, thinks that his life, or the lives of another
agent or person are in danger" – read, a United States citizen –
"there is no boundary, the frontier is erased."

The frontier boundary is subject to the logic of war. On a battlefield a U.S. soldier or police agent is duty-bound to defend his
country and its way of life, according to the Code of Behaviour of
the U.S. armed forces.[16] Given that the U.S. government is inclined

to believe that drug trafficking is a crime comparable to terrorism, a terrorist lacks any guarantees as regards his person, being considered an active combatant that falls outside the status of those protected by the Geneva Convention.[17] The mere assumption on the part of a U.S. soldier or agent that U.S. national security is under threat is enough to permit him to take the necessary action in the full knowledge the outcome will be endorsed by the U.S. government. Consequently, criteria are enforced that are expressed in the assertion: *Inter arma silent leges*: "In times of war, the law keeps silent."[18] Submission, devastation, extermination.

From the perspective of the battlefield, reality intervenes in military actions with its strengths, tensions, incidents, features, factors and opportunities. In contemporary military thinking two concepts encapsulate the crux: friction, that describes the resistance in reality against whatever may have been pre-planned, and fog, that refers to the ambiguity and uncertain knowledge operatives must assume in a battle situation. In fact, war operatives speak of the "fog and friction" of war.[19] The anamorphosis of the victims arises from the foggy, fractious situation that reflects the experience of the threshold between war and non-war. On the battlefield, nature, the species itself, is a virtual victim.[20] The planet is implicated in a bellicose situation that is endlessly extending: space, air, sea, land and cyberspace.

To explain the meaning of anamorphosis, one can imagine the victim in a situation that is split into two phases: firstly, normal reality fractures as a result of a traumatic event that, in the cases described, stems from interventions in their lives by a criminal agent or an act of war; secondly, victims begin to see what is happening from a distorted perspective that includes themselves: they are no longer what they were before the advent of criminals or war, though their memories prefer to indicate otherwise. Every criminal or bellicose incident in which a victim is inscribed, represents an anamorphosis. The victim's object of desire is the restoration of normality. It is impossible for victims to enjoy the oblique gaze that allows an ordinary observer to enjoy an anamorphosis in a painting or drawing:[21] they would have to be outside the frame. The victim is already an anamorphosis in the flesh. Any desire to restore normal time and space expresses the contrary: speechlessness, the edge of the void, the nothingness that gradually arises from the extreme distortion which they experience before they die (even though death may be deferred or delayed by contingency or inertia).

If we compare a victim's experience to the classic example of an anamorphosis, "The Ambassadors" (1533) by Hans Holbein the Younger,[22] the victim would be in the skull represented next to the feet of those portrayed, which in the painting represents death's supremacy over worldly vanity. In the case of videoed or filmed murders and atrocities, the victim's anamorphosis unfolds as a potential variant of scopophilia: the compulsive, pleasurable contemplation of something that is perceived to be sinister. In such a process, the victim of what is anomalous evaporates in the observer's fantasy, morbid fascination or fixation. Everyday normality is restored through the enjoyment, self-absorption or panic of the other, the subsequent observer who always remains outside the frame.

For the executioner, the anamorphosis is something invisible, since the acts of cruelty and transgression he commits are his objective world: the incarnation of darkness. From his point of view, the victim is devoid of value, an object he can subject to vile acts driven by his desire for supremacy. The theatricality of the abuse and torture he inflicts leaves out of account any objective that is not the victim's depredation, annihilation or imprisonment. He is a figure of anamorphosis incapable of seeing himself as such. The only human or necessary trait the executioner is afforded is his anonymity. A face without a name, behind a mask or hood, he seeks refuge in distortion and wants to be erased and nullified. He constantly fears he will be discovered and punished.

Whilst victims sink into the anamorphosis represented by the violence employed against them, executioners attempt to become invisible as individuals and to stay alive and function as exterminators; both are linked by that intersection which momentarily leads their respective destinies and trajectories to meet on a tragic axis.

Criminal groups involved in drug trafficking and the exploitation of other criminal industries have two strategic advantages over the armed forces that are fighting them and, of course, over their potential victims:

1) a first-hand understanding of the territories they are occupying based on their knowledge and activities: they plan or project their activities and simultaneously steamroll or set out to steamroll the area where they are operating;

2) they develop networks of war through telecommunications and contacts with customers or community employees to improve their logistic and tactical operations. Organised crime implies a variant of fourth-generation war (4GW): "it uses all available (political, economic, social and military) networks to persuade those taking decisions for the enemy that their strategic objectives are unattainable, or else too costly in respect of any gains that might be generated."[23]

The outcome from the two advantages reformulates the idea of the space and territories in the path or under the domain or control of criminal gangs that become protean, acquire various abnormal forms, for example, the implementation of control over entrances and exits to some localities. Criminal gangs have recourse to working methods organised with the utmost flexibility: they interrupt linear or established traffic or else alternate it with ever-changing alternatives via unusual paths or breaches, including the tactical model of swarming: a diffuse multiplicity of semi-autonomous small units that are mutually coordinated and operate with coherent synergies.[24] The direct consequence of this type of operation creates a malleable space that affects the territory and localities under their influence, to the point that the conventional map is transformed in its ends, goals and aims, for example, when they set up tactical divisions that isolate and protect the criminal gangs in the event of possible attacks by the armed forces, and that draw support from their human and media networks and webs of clients and employees.[25]

The battlefield is a medium transformed by the operations it experiences, is flexible "almost liquid" matter that remains subject to contingencies and suspended in terms of its conventional state.[26] It oscillates between repose and continuous movement, where unstable expansion is the order of the day.

That order also modifies usual habits within the community: individuals, the potential victims, have three options: to join a criminal gang either provisionally or for good; to be marginalised; and, finally, to go into exile. Drug-trafficking wars tend to produce hundreds of thousands of exiles in flight from criminal rule. And if everyday space is distorted by crime, so is its organisation and temporary management: as well as surging over walls, frontiers, boundaries, entrances and exits, the groups or bands fragment and act simultaneously and in diverse directions, just as they lack linear chronology: they are unpredictable, dispersed, unstable and are favoured by asymmetries, synchronisation and chaos.[27]

Criminal gangs operate by surprise and that increases the fear factor for probable victims: rumour-mongering, shock tactics and the noise generated about themselves join in a communications loop that proliferates and is constantly repeated.[28] Anticipation of fear as a psychological element is part of an arsenal boosted by the bungling of the armed forces pursuing them. The net immediate effect, especially if the armed forces show no respect for the rights of individuals, is the population's rejection of constituted power and legality and that transforms them into virtual adherents of organised crime.

The flattening of space and territories becomes hugely sophisticated: criminal gangs burst upon the scene, bring a new smoothness to the terrain, even in rural fastnesses, by linking strategic sites through their own means of communication,[29] show contempt for the boundaries between the legal and the illegal and destroy real and symbolic divides between public and private. For example, a series of commandos often carry out operations to block the flow of traffic in cities: they occupy crossroads or entrances/exits simultaneously or in succession, steal cars and burn them there, invite the armed forces to react and relish the subsequent shootouts. They then flee, leaving in their wake vandalised property, debris, victims and fear. They paralyse metropolitan areas where thousands and even millions live in Guadalajara, Nuevo Laredo, Torreón, Matamoros, Veracruz, Reynosa etc. Communities are suddenly plunged into a flattening process of homogenisation.

A situation of war is a mandate for total dispossession. The alienating experience means victims confront situations full of risk and anomalous or traumatic incidents. As the flattening homogeneity imposed by criminals or the armed forces is established and becomes the norm, reality is rapidly reduced to its most elemental features. And the human aspect of individuals is reified inasmuch as it is useful or useless in the pursuit of criminal acts, or collateral damage for the army. The lives of individuals subject to criminal control or the fight against crime tend to empty out and be filled by the strictures, rules and whims of criminals. Without that emptying out, it would be impossible to generate the anamorphosis of victims who, from their first direct or indirect contact with the influence of crime or the state, are aware that they are under threat. All of which stokes inner fear: a secret passage opens up in symbolic terms linking reality and subjectivity.

Faced by the threat of violence and power that bulldozes all boundaries and lacks any restraint, individuals fall prey to extreme changes: ideas of time and space are subjected to a perverse or inverted regime that spawns a horrible structure that subverts all known values and establishes a reality of adjacent spaces, controlled and guarded by organised crime or the armed forces. People are exposed to agoraphobia (danger from the outside) or claustrophobia (the threat from within). Citizens lack any security or certainty in relation to themselves, and live only a prolonged experience of uncertainty: a climate of fog and friction.

While the battlefield allows it, individuals are invisible, and once they become invisible and targets, they enter into an anamorphosis that has an additional feature: it communicates a complete lack of moderation. Faced by such excess, individuals see and feel themselves as increasingly defenceless. Excess or the breakdown of conventional order is a factory for the production of monsters and monstrosities.[30]

Criminals in particular create a peculiar kind of excess out of their re-structuring and flattening of space and time: they endow it with their own symbols, contents, myths, images, icons and representations. This gamut of uses appropriates derivations from vernacular culture and mass-media culture: music, radio and film.

And products circulating on social networks: the exaltation of crime, boasting about crimes, glorifying of deeds against the law, memories of lives of crime etc. The excess in the fantasies celebrating the liturgy against the constituted order invades real space with practical outcomes that also project the imperative of homogeneity, flattening and smoothing out, in brief, the reality of limitless crime encompassing a monstrous phantasmagoria: the cruel carnival that inverts the conventional world.

A virtual display of bellicose might ensues enacted through the symbols of the group or region, extravagant appearances and distinguishing features opposed to their rivals, forms and styles characterising each criminal group, which they use to differentiate themselves from ordinary people, like the armed forces pursuing them, which, in contrary mode, elaborate their own style of image and propaganda, or communicative flattening.[31]

Real and symbolic space is invaded by criminal excess that produces figurative symbols (emblems, uniforms, masks, tattoos ...) as well as utilities, artefacts, vehicles, goods, buildings that carry the marks of identity of the different criminal groups. Use value is endowed with an added value: the forms they give, with or without meaning, to their transgressive activities.

Each object produced by the criminals carries the imprint of their foundations, allowing criminal artefacts to meld usefulness and decoration in similar measure. And they trumpet their origins: they are excessive, monstrous, tangible omens, and the very fact that they exist is intimidating. Their immobility is threatening, their movement, lethal. People watch a representation of a statement of anamorphosis being performed before their very eyes.

One example can be found in the design of the four-wheel drive vehicles that criminal gangs use, especially those they transform from a civilian to a bellicose character. They manufacture armour plating, and various low-cost additions and adaptations (ten to fifteen thousand dollars a time) in special workshops.[32] Such freight or general transport trucks or vans are transformed into tanks of war for the purposes of assault or armoured transport to safeguard criminal effectives or goods. The armour-plating comprises the addition of iron parts or steel sheeting with high levels of resistance (level 6, able to withstand bazooka fire) and are complemented by bullet-proof tyres and reinforced glass windows, as well as having recourse to the installation of night-time floodlighting and plat-forms on the top of the vehicle or orifices for pieces of artillery and other firearms. These machines acquire monstrous forms that parody purpose-built war vehicles (tanks, armoured and amphibi-ous vehicles), and endow their artisan-vernacular origins with the idiosyncratic fantasy of the criminal gangs and their symbolism of war, intimidation, ruthlessness, invulnerability and defiance of all norms of coexistence.

Faced by the mere presence of these vehicles, a possible victim grasps that even the armed forces might at times be at a disadvan-tage. Also created for combatting rival groups these vehicles can have facilities for electrocution or anti-pursuit fire-power (they shoot out metal spikes on the road, oil or pepper spray). According to specialists, the vehicles' vulnerability lies in their slowness (40 or 50 k.p.h.), their huge weight, their tyres, and even their appearance that is easily detectable from land or air.

Their optimal use is on flat paths or tracks in rural areas; they are difficult to manoeuvre in urban areas, and that means their existence has symbolic significance rather than any real use. They are devices to intimidate and impact psychologically by com-municating a perception of absolute power on the basis of their sculptural appearance redolent of the might, massive energy and machinery of the industrial era, and the imaginary and graphics of heavy metal and post-apocalypse or horror films.[33] The reduction of reality to the message of the supremacy of the strongest thrusts the victim into the perspective of anamorphosis. The effect of mobility and power that crosses all boundaries in the end provokes panic in communities and, perhaps, in rival groups.

If one examines the shapes of these vehicles, built by diverse criminal gangs, one finds recurrent similarities: the alternating of the symmetrical and the asymmetrical; the phallic suggestiveness of sharp spikes; the trapezoidal; turrets and would-be might in motion; fronts like ghastly masks, dark, rusted surfaces, crude accoutrements. The combination of such forms suggest the realisation of criminal fantasies and the imperative to reduce their bellicose power to an apotropaic effect: the replacement of the real by a faith in a symbolic defence generated by superstition. It is a case of pre-modern thinking that grants certain gestures, rituals, objects or liturgical phrases the ability to avoid, drive away or deter evil or material or non-material threats.

By dint of such beliefs a protective mantle is woven against destructive spirits or demons or against malign actions of a magical nature. The criminal gangs' armour-plated vehicles are giant amulets in motion that, apart from any use value, seek to galvanise the fears they provoke and spread. Aggressive toys that achieve their highest meaning in the overall span of organised crime's operations and domination of space and territory, and in the potential impact on their victims.

On the other side stand the armed forces of the constituted order, where the logic of the strong or terror state rules. The bodies of individuals and their vulnerable perimeters are trapped in between.

Translated by Peter Bush

IN THE DUNGEONS OF THE MEXICAN GOVERNMENT

Torture in the Iguala Case

Anabel Hérnandez

HE DOES NOT KNOW whether it is day or night. He is face-down on the floor, his hands bound tightly, he can feel carpeting against his face. He is certain he is not in some clandestine location, but rather in the Attorney General of the Republic's offices, in the custody of the Federal Ministerial Police from the Criminal Investigation Agency. It is October 15, 2014, and several hours ago he was detained in a restaurant on the Mexico-Toluca highway, where he was eating with a woman and a colleague. He had been accused by the Mexican Government of the disappearance of the forty-three students in Iguala, Guerrero.

Minutes earlier a man wearing a suit had entered the room where he was bound to a chair. He approached slowly and spoke into his ear, saying that he had been sent by the Attorney General of the Republic (P.G.R.), Jesús Murillo Karam, who was personally responsible for solving the case of the *normalistas*.[1] He said he would be able to sort things out before it was "too late".

"You have three minutes to make up your mind," he warned him, but there was nothing to say, he did not know what had happened on the night of September 26 in Iguala. Then a group of seven agents from the Federal Ministerial Police entered the room with blindfolds, pieces of wood and metal shaped like dildos, and lots of black plastic rubbish bags.

"These people will get you to cooperate, I have the Attorney General's permission," the man in the suit said, and ordered them to begin the unspeakable rites that would not end until he had said what the government wanted him to say. The policemen blindfolded him with the dexterity of executioners, they placed him face-down on the floor and bound his hands behind his back.

He is lying face-down and he still does not have any idea what is in store. The minutes drag on forever, each tick of the clock brings new pain. They flip him over, face-up. His body is a puppet they do what they like with. One of them pulls his arms up above his head, so his back is flat against the floor, another sits on his stomach and puts a plastic bag over his head, while another sits on his legs to immobilise him completely until he loses consciousness. For a few seconds he feels nothing at all, no pain, not even life, until they revive him by beating him on the chest.

"One way or another, you're gonna die," one of the agents says. He begs for mercy, but no-one listens. "This is just the beginning."

They flip him over again, pulling his trousers and his underwear down, and, still face-down, they remove the restraints around his ankles and spread his legs to pour water on his testicles while they suffocate him with a plastic bag once more, this time with a sinister addition: he can feel an iron object penetrating his anus, slowly tearing him apart. The pain is indescribable. They rape him while they suffocate him with the plastic bag, while others give his testicles electric shocks, until he faints again.

They revive him once more. Since the blindfold has loosened he can see a man bearing down on his chest, he is sitting on top of him, sweating, he seems nervous and agitated. "The son of a bitch has come around again," one of the P.G.R. agents says. They order him to stand and pull up his trousers, and he realises that he is soaked from head to toe, he feels an intense pain in his anus, his belly button and in his chest, right where his heart is.

The man who ordered the torture, the one who said he was sent by the Attorney General, asks him if he is ready to say what they want him to and he says yes. "I'll do whatever you want, but for the love of God, don't torture me anymore." Then they hand him over to other agents, who take him to fresh torments. His body hurts all over. When they let him use the toilet he realises his rectum is bleeding and there is crusted blood between his legs. He quakes in terror.

After more than twenty-four hours of physical and psychological torture in the early hours of October 17, the P.G.R. obtained the signature of Sidronio Casarrubias Salgado on a confession falsified by the P.G.R., in which the government accuses him of being the leader of the so-called Guerreros Unidos cartel, and of authorising the murder and cremation of the forty-three students from Ayotzinapa in a dump in the municipality of Cocula, Guerrero. According to the documents signed after his brutal torture, his brother Mario Casarrubias Salgado ran the criminal organisation known as Guerreros Unidos, which included the mayor of Iguala, José Luis Abarca, his wife, María de los Ángeles Pineda Villa and members of the Iguala police force. In addition, the government of Mexico required him to state that members of the criminal group Los Rojos were travelling in the buses with the students that night, and that, with Abarca's blessing, Gildardo López Astudillo, a.k.a. El Gil, had attacked the buses with the local police, to prevent Los Rojos from invading Iguala.

His testimony was used by the Mexican government to accuse the criminal organisation called Guerreros Unidos and the mayor of Iguala, José Luis Abarca, of the attack on and disappearance of the forty-three *normalistas*, in order to placate the multitudes of protesters raising their united voices on the streets throughout Mexico: "It was the government!"

Casarrubias was not the only defendant who was tortured in this case. It has been proved that at least thirty-one others who were detained were beaten, suffocated and sexually molested, with electric shocks to the genitals and penetration, threats of rape against their families and, in some cases, consummation of these threats. All this to get them to incriminate themselves, implicate others and sign statements that were fabricated by the P.G.R.

The government of Mexico falsified statements and created the so-called "historical truth" that claims the students were murdered and cremated in a dump near Iguala, their ashes disposed of in a river.

The fact is that nearly two years after the disappearance of the *normalistas* the Attorney General of the Republic does not have a single piece of expert or scientific proof that the students were cremated at that dump. The P.G.R. had reached its highly suspect conclusion before the investigation started: "[the students] appear to have been completely cremated, which would make it impossible to identify them if their remains are eventually found," read the first pages of the documents obtained through this journalist's investigation. To this day the government of Mexico has been unable to clarify how and why it knew the forty-three *normalistas* were supposedly cremated. And the only verifiable evidence that one of the disappeared students, Alejandro Mora, was cremated appears to have been planted by the P.G.R. itself in a river near the dump.

The "historical truth" has been disproved by the investigation undertaken by the author of this article in the months following these events. It has been disproved by expert opinions confirming that the forty-three students were never cremated at the dump. And it has been disproved by the investigation of the Interdisciplinary Group of Independent Experts (G.I.E.I.), which the Inter-American Commission on Human Rights sent to Mexico in response to requests by the parents of the students to uncover the truth.

President Enrique Peña Nieto's government has no real interest in resolving the case, it simply created scapegoats in an attempt to heal the suppurating wound that has exposed the abuse of power and the travesty of justice in Mexico to the rest of the world.

As a result of this journalistic investigation, special proceedings initiated by five committees from the United Nations, and the final report of the G.I.E.I. presented in April 2016, it has been documented that at least thirty-three key detainees who were used by the government to fabricate the historical truth were brutally tortured by the Mexican government. According to documents and testimonies that have been obtained, government offices were converted into dungeons where members of the Army, Navy and Federal Ministerial Police played the role of torturers.

Based on medical reports produced by the Navy, Army and P.G.R, as well as on direct testimony, the author of this investigative article was the first to expose the systematic use of torture by the Mexican government to "resolve" this case in the Mexican magazine *Proceso* in December 2014.

As a result of this investigation, five bodies of the United Nations began to investigate these serious violations of human rights: the Working Group on Arbitrary Detention; the Working Group on Enforced or Involuntary Disappearances; the Special Rapporteur on the Independence of Judges and Lawyers; the Special Rapporteur on Torture and Other Cruel, Inhuman or Degrading Treatment or Punishment; and the Special Rapporteur on Extrajudicial, Summary, or Arbitrary Executions. The rapporteurs began special proceedings based on the "serious" accusations of "arbitrary detention, torture, and cruel, inhuman, and degrading treatment" made by thirteen detainees in the Ayotzinapa case: Cassarubias Salgado, Marco Antonio Ríos Berber, Raúl Nuñez Salgado, Agustín García Reyes, Jonathan Osorio Cortes, Patricio Reyes Landa and Carlos Canto Salgado, all of whom were detained and accused of supposedly belonging to the Guerreros Unidos, and of participating in the attack and disappearance of the *normalistas*. The U.N. also initiated proceedings due to the torture of Verónica Bahena Cruz, Santiago Mazón Cedillo, Héctor Aguilar Ávalos, Alejandro Lara García, Edgar Magdaleno Cruz Navarro y Jesús Parra Arroyo, all members of the local police forces in Iguala and Cocula, accused of participating in the attack and disappearance of the *normalistas*.

In addition to the thirteen detainees named by the U.N., the author received denouncements from a further ten: Iguala policemen Honorio Antúnez and David Cruz Hernández, as well as alleged members of the Guerreros Unidos Gildardo López Astudillo, Felipe Rodríguez Salgado, Eury Flores, Luis Alberto José Gaspar, Francisco Javier Lozano, Napoleón Martínez Gaspar and the brothers Miguel Ángel and Osvaldo Ríos Sánchez.

In its first report, presented in September 2015, the G.I.E.I., composed of the investigators Carlos Beristain, Ángela Buitrago, Claudia Paz, Alejandro Valencia and Francisco Cox, stated that of eighty detainees 80 per cent bore signs of abuse. The final report of their investigation, published on April 24, 2016, confirmed that in at least seventeen cases the torture was indisputable, ten of which are different from those documented either by this journalist or by the U.N.: Miguel Ángel Landa Bahena, alleged member of the Guerreros Unidos, and members of the Cocula police force César Yáñez Castro, Roberto Pedrote Nava, Oscar Veleros Segura, Julio

César Mateos Rosales, Alejandro Aceves Rosales, Alberto Aceves Serrano and César Nava González. And, from Iguala, Edgar Vieyra and Alejandro Mota Román.

Among their tormentors the thirty victims included members of the Federal Police, the Federal Ministerial Police, the Army, and the Navy, with the likely complicity of the Attorney General of the Republic, Jesús Murillo Karam; the director of the Criminal Investigation Agency, Tomás Zerón; and the head of the Assistant Attorney General's Office for Special Investigations on Organised Crime (S.E.I.D.O.), Gustavo Salas Chávez. These three were responsible for the investigation to locate the students and bring the guilty parties to justice, but instead of doing so they altered the course of the investigation, fabricated testimonies, and even planted evidence.

The disappearance of the forty-three *normalista* students from the Raúl Isidro Burgos Rural Teachers College, Guerrero on September 26, 2014, exposes the grim reality of how the Mexican government treats its citizens: disappearances, death, corruption, impunity; and the systematic use of torture by law-enforcement agencies and the Attorney General of the Republic to imprison innocents and protect the guilty. The crimes committed that night remain unsolved due to a vow of silence that the Mexican government does not wish to break. Perpetrators maintain their silence to protect one another and witnesses remain silent out of fear. This silence prevents the discovery of the whereabouts of the young men.

Although Mexico has suffered more than 25,000 unaccountable disappearances over the course of the past eight years, the case of these forty-three students is not just another one for the pile. The difference between this and the other cases is not just the profile of the victims: young men from the poorest of the poor, with families who bravely organised to fight to discover the truth and the whereabouts of the young men. The difference is that it is the only large-scale case in which there is clear evidence that the attack and operation to disappear the students was undertaken by the Mexican government: the Mexican Army, the Federal Police, the state police, and some of the local police from Iguala took part in an operation coordinated by the Centre of Command, Control, Communications and Computing (C4) which is run by the military and controls the security cameras throughout the city, whose critical video footage from that night was edited or erased.

As time has passed the victims of events on September 26 and 27, 2014, have multiplied: more than one hundred students from Ayotzinapa were attacked, of whom forty-three disappeared. Six civilians murdered: Daniel Solís, Julio César Rodríguez, Julio César Mondragón, Blanca Montiel, David Josué García and Víctor Manuel Lugo, the first three of whom were *normalistas*. The Avispones football team, whose bus was confused with that of the *normalistas*, was shot at, and more than twenty people were wounded by bullets. Not to mention the dozens of detainees who were accused without proof of a crime they maintained they did not commit; to this day this group remains the least visible of all these victims.

The shocking stories of the victims of the Mexican government's dungeons provide brutal, incontrovertible proof that when the forces of law and order are trained to inflict pain on every inch of a body they are worse than hyenas with their prey.

The Attorney General's bribes

In the minutes following Sidronio Casarrubias's rape and torture he was taken to the chief of the Criminal Investigation Agency, Tomás Zerón, who was located in the same office building, to speak with a woman, allegedly the one he was with when he was detained in the restaurant hours earlier. The police chief ordered him to speak with her.

The woman's name was Dulce and she was not the woman he had been with. She was trembling with fear and crying, and told him that she had been tortured. He never saw her again and has no idea of her whereabouts.

In front of Zerón the police who had tortured him warned him not to discuss what had just taken place. "Or else you know what we can do to you and your family; think of your children, your wife and your parents."

In the offices of S.E.I.D.O. in the early hours of October 17, an agent from the Public Ministry drew up his statement. "All you do is sign and put your fingerprint on it," he said.

On the same day that the P.G.R. fabricated Casarrubias's testimony Attorney General Murillo Karam and Zerón gave a press conference where they announced his arrest. "This will help us resolve the deaths of six people in Iguala as well as the disappearance of the forty-three students from the Teachers College in Ayotzinapa," the Attorney General confirmed.

Days later Sidronio Casarrubias was incarcerated in the maximum security prison C.E.F.E.R.E.S.O. No. 1, known as El Altiplano. His wounds still had not healed and his trials were not yet over.

During his first thirty days in prison he was visited three times by employees of the P.G.R. who pressured him to confirm the confession he had made under torture before the judge. One of these visits was from Murillo Karam himself.

"I'm the Attorney General of the Republic, Murillo Karam," he said, sitting in one of the prison offices, smoking nervously.

"I know you were tortured and I'd like you to tell me whether you could recognise the voices of the people who tortured you, because the men who did that to you are criminals, too. Were you raped as well?" the public servant enquired.

"Yes."

The Attorney General proceeded to offer Casarrubias 66,000,000 pesos if he would tell him where the students were; he reiterated that he had no idea.

"I'll lock you up for eighty years in solitary, you'll never leave prison, I know you're not guilty … I can see that you don't want to help yourself, I know that you don't have any money and that you'll need the best lawyers out there but it looks like you're not going to be able to afford a single one," the Attorney General said, and he stormed out.

On February 25, Sidronio Casarrubias told a judge about the offer of this bribe. And suddenly, on February 27, 2015, Peña Nieto stripped Murillo Karam of his office. In February and July of 2015 the United Nations sent the Mexican government two letters signed by five rapporteurs from the U.N., calling attention to the "serious" accusations of "arbitrary detentions, torture and cruel, inhumane and degrading treatment" of detainees in the Ayotzinapa case.

"We wish to express our serious concern about the detention, torture (including rape), and the denial of rights experienced by Mr. Casarrubias Salgado," states the letter dated February 25, signed by Mads Andenas, President-Rapporteur of the Working Group on Arbitrary Detention; Ariel Dulitzky, President-Rapporteur of the Working Group on Enforced or Involuntary Disappearances; Gabriela Knaul, Special Rapporteur on the Independence of Judges and Lawyers; Christof Heyns, Special Rapporteur on Extrajudicial, Summary, or Arbitrary Executions; and Juan E. Méndez, the Special Rapporteur on Torture and Other Cruel, Inhuman or Degrading

Treatment or Punishment. "We are also seriously concerned about allegations that torture and mistreatment were used in order to extract forced and falsified confessions. We fear that the use of these methods is not an isolated case, and that the investigation into the disappearance of the forty-three students from Iguala could also be based on information gathered through torture," they added.

Incoherent and outlandish confessions under torture

In the P.G.R.'s dossier on the case of the disappeared students twenty-five people signed confessions stating they knew about or had participated in the disappearance. But all contain serious contradictions, stories that vary wildly including those that purport to have confessed to abducting and killing the students. The only thing these declarations have in common is the torture and pattern of injuries that were inflicted, according to the medical records that were available.

Of the twenty-five witnesses ten are local policemen from Cocula, there are three policemen and a fireman from Iguala, and eleven alleged members of Guerreros Unidos. Among these confessions there are eight alleged murderers who gave statements on when and how they killed the students. But these confessions specify four completely different locations (and methods) describing how the crime took place: in Pueblo Viejo; La Parota hills; a ranch in Loma de Coyotes; and a dump in Cocula.

Marco Antonio Ríos Berber, Martín Alejandro Macedo Barrera, Luis Alberto José Gaspar and Honorio Antúnez were detained on October 3 and 4, 2014 by the Ministerial Police of Guerrero in a joint operation with the Federal Police and the Army, carried out in Iguala as a result of the events of September 26. According to police, all suspects were apprehended in the streets. These were the first alleged members of the Guerreros Unidos to be arrested.

In their official statements made on October 5, Ríos Berber and Macedo Barrera confirm their participation in the attack on the students in detail. Macedo Barrera said that when the students arrived in Iguala they were armed, and that he and others began firing at the *normalistas* immediately, that some of them died on the spot and that they took seventeen of the students in private vehicles to a safe house in Loma de los Coyotes where they killed them and burned fifteen of them in a pit, but that they did not burn two of them.

"They [the students] became violent when they were abducted and to keep them from making trouble it was decided to kill them, I think they used a digger to bury them on the ranch we keep," Macedo Barrera is alleged to have confessed. "I took part, killing two of the Ayotzinapans with a bullet to the head, and those two we didn't burn."

On the contrary, Ríos Berber said that it was the Iguala police who took twenty students to their headquarters and that a criminal called El Choky took three of the *normalistas* away in a black Mustang. According to his signed statement he witnessed the murders of the three students on a hill in Pueblo Viejo, and he himself dug the pit where they were tossed, doused in diesel and burned, and that afterwards fourteen more students were taken away in a white pick-up, that ten were killed and the four others were bound and beaten, after which Choky killed them.

The government says that these two statements led them to hidden graves in Pueblo Viejo, where twenty-eight bodies were found, but subsequent D.N.A. analysis proved these were not the bodies of the students.

Ríos Berber told the United Nations how he had been detained without an arrest warrant and taken to the offices of Attorney General in Guerrero, where he was threatened, stripped, and tortured. "A number of times he was nearly suffocated as he was tortured . . ." The following day he was transferred to the offices of the P.G.R. where he signed his statement under duress.

He was sitting on a bench

Luis Alberto José Gaspar was eighteen when he was arrested. He testified in court that he was a bricklayer's apprentice who was responsible for his wife, his child and two siblings, providing their food, shelter and education. He noted that on October 2, 2014 he was sitting on a bench opposite a school when he was arrested.

"As regards the crimes I've been accused of, I had nothing whatsoever to do with them, I'm a good man, a hard worker, I'm innocent of these crimes . . ." he said in desperation before a judge on November 25, 2014.

He related how he had been detained by a patrol of six vehicles from the Ministerial Police, who said he looked "suspicious", and was taken away.

They asked him where he had been on September 26, and he replied he had been at home. That was when the beatings started and they put a bag over his head to suffocate him, then they told him he was a member of the Guerreros Unidos but he protested he did not belong to any such organisation and that he had evidence to prove he was a bricklayer. "We don't care about your evidence," they told him. Then they took him to the Attorney General's office in Chilpancingo to make his statement.

"Since it was the middle of the night when they moved me, they blindfolded me, they took me somewhere isolated, then they stripped me, they tied me up, then they put tape around my head, and said I'd better tell them what I knew about the students, I said how could I tell them if I didn't know anything about the students and they said how could I not know anything if I was from Iguala, and they spent four hours pouring water over my head and hitting me in the ribs and on the head . . ."

When they took him to make his statement he told what had just happened to him but he was ignored and they ordered him to sign a statement, which no lawyer was allowed to review beforehand. Initially he refused to sign but the police threatened to take him back to the place where he had been beaten if he did not. "I signed those papers out of fear," he told the judge.

The following night he was taken to Mexico City by plane. When he arrived at S.E.I.D.O. they told him that he had to make his confession but he refused because he still had no idea what he stood accused of.

How to dig your own grave

On October 8, the Federal Ministerial Police detained the brothers Miguel Ángel and Osvaldo Ríos Sánchez in Cuernavaca, Morelos, also for allegedly appearing suspicious. According to police they were carrying drugs and weapons, and that after reading them their rights they immediately confessed to being members of the Guerreros Unidos, to selling drugs, and to knowing that the *normalistas* had been murdered and buried in a place called La Parota near Iguala.

They were not delivered to the offices of the P.G.R. in Mexico City until October 9, due to alleged car trouble. Miguel Ángel had more than ten injuries and Osvaldo had fourteen. At 6.30 a.m. on October 9 they were both transported by helicopter by members of the Navy from Mexico City to a national highway between Iguala and Teloloapan, and from there they were taken to a place called La Parota in Army vehicles.

Viridiana Ramírez, Miguel Ángel's wife, confirmed that her husband and her brother-in-law were beaten and tortured by the police for hours. When they were being transferred in the Navy helicopter they told her husband that they were going to toss him out en route and that no-one would be any the wiser, ordering him to confess to the disappearance and murder of the students.

Her husband told her that when they arrived in La Parota the members of the Navy made them dig a pit and told them it would be their final resting place. "They wanted them to sign a statement they had brought with them," she said. They threw Osvaldo into the grave they had made him dig and shot at him, grazing his ear, and when he tried to get up they shot near his hand. The nightmare continued: plastic bags and electric shocks. Eventually they signed the statement.

Disturbingly, just days later, on October 23, members of the Union of Villages and Organisations from the State of Guerrero found nine hidden graves near La Parota, with human remains and traces of blood, along with shoes, backpacks, and pencils.

They tied him to a dentist's chair

Honorio Antúnez was a policeman in Iguala. He was in the Army for twenty years and when he retired he went to work for the local police. On September 26 he did not go to work because he was on a training course. On October 3, 2014 when he attended roll call a group of operatives from the Federal Ministerial Police arrived and took him away.

"You're a member of the local police force and you're a fucking dead man," the Federal Police told him.

They put him in a white vehicle and took him to a place where a variety of vehicles were parked, including a double-axle long-bed with the words Mobile Medical Dental Unit. He said that two men appeared whom he had seen at the state police headquarters on

September 27, one of whom was the Attorney General of Guerrero, Iñaki Blanco.

They interrogated him about the mayor, José Luis Abarca, and his wife, as well as where the *normalistas* could be found, but he answered that he did not know.

"You know where they're buried!" they shouted at him, between insults.

The Federal Police took him, still handcuffed, into the medical unit and put him in the patient's chair. They tied him up and tortured him, insisting that he tell them where the *normalistas* were buried.

"Nobody knows you're here, if you die while we're torturing you it won't matter," they told him.

"After putting plastic bags over my head they put a rag over my face, covering my eyes, my nose, and my mouth, and they began pouring water on my face so I'd inhale the water through my nose and my mouth when they hit my stomach," he told the judge during his first court hearing.

Then the Federal Ministerial Police took him out of the truck and handed him over to members of the National Gendarmerie Division of the Federal Police along the highway to Chilpancingo at the Rancho del Cura junction.

"On the way to Tepecoacuilco they pulled off the highway into the brush, where they began torturing me again, beating me in the stomach and asking me about the *normalista* kids." Then they took him to Chilpancingo.

That night he gave them his statement. They began telling him the names of local police "Since I didn't say anything and I didn't answer the questions they were asking me they took me to another office and showed me photographs . . ." He says that they showed him photos of colleagues he knew only by sight and asked him whether they were part of the Guerreros Unidos; he said he did not know.

"I disavow the statement they forced me to sign in Chilpancingo; I disavow it because it was made under torture," he told the judge. Honorio's statement, falsified and signed under duress, was used by the P.G.R. to detain more than twenty members of the police forces in Iguala and Cocula, who were accused of attacking and abducting the students.

Cries in the dungeons

The Federal Minsterial Police blindfold her, take her into an office and tie her to a chair, then they threaten to take her house and rape her family. They hit her in the ribs, kick her legs, and administer electric shocks. Verónica Bahena, a member of the Iguala police force, is so afraid she wets herself and the police torturing her begin to taunt and insult her.

Her screams join the screams of ten other members of the force who were detained with her on October 14, 2014 at a military ground where they were training.

According to testimony gathered from relatives of these police the torture took place in the offices of the P.G.R., conducted by heavyset men dressed in black wearing hoods over their heads to protect their identity. While they were being similarly abused, each member of this group of police was interrogated about the disappearance of the students and the Guerreros Unidos.

"Why'd you kill them?" A punch. "Why'd you abduct them?" Another punch, knocking them to the floor, even into semi-consciousness.

Sue Martínez has been married to policeman Héctor Ávalos for thirteen years; they live in a house made of cardboard and sheet metal in a poor neighborhood on the outskirts of Iguala. Her husband had been in the Army; he did not enjoy it but it was the only way of getting ahead and earning money for the family where they lived. She confirmed that he was off-duty on September 26, and official documents verify that he was on leave. He was a patrol driver.

On September 26, when the attack and abduction of the students took place, he was at home all day, and as the 27th was his son's birthday they went to McDonald's. At approximately 8.40 in the evening they returned home and did not leave again until the following day.

After he was arrested she waited four endless days before seeing him again in a jail in the state of Nayarit.

"When I saw my husband he was desperate, he thought he was going to die there they had beaten him so badly." He said he had passed out twice from the beatings inflicted by the P.G.R., and that they had revived him by kicking him. In tears, Sue told how, after the beatings in the offices, her husband and the others were taken out into the hallway and left there.

"They wanted them to take the blame. They kept asking them where the students were."

She related how her husband had told them he had no idea because he was not working that day. "You'll take the blame anyway," they answered.

Laura Martínez, the wife of Alejandro Lara, confirmed that her husband was also off-duty on the 26th, and that they had been together all day, "he accompanied me wherever I went, on his day off he always kept me company and I kept him company, too." She said that day they went to pay an instalment on a gold necklace they had pawned because they needed money and that at nine in the evening (around the time of the attack on the students) they were at their daughter's basketball practice, far from the centre of town. She also noted that she had gathered numerous character references because her husband had never had problems with anyone and that the people who were at the basketball practice went to corroborate the fact that he had been there with them.

After he was detained many days passed before she was able to see him. When they met, Alejandro Lara broke down in tears, he could hardly speak as he told her what he had been through.

"The violence likely lasted around four hours, during which Mr Lara would have heard the other people who were detained with him being tortured," note the rapporteurs from the United Nations in a letter dated July 10, 2015.

Lara was one of the first to denounce his torture before the National Commission on Human Rights "against the Federal Police who detained us, beat us and attempted to force us to tell them where the bodies were".

Of the ten police who where detained, eight bore multiple, medically documented injuries, many on the pelvis and thighs, which exhibited burns from electric shocks. When Verónica Bahena was examined she had at least five injuries. According to testimony from her colleagues she bled heavily from her uterus for several days.

We'll rape your daughters

Twenty-five-year-old Patricio Reyes Landa was detained on October 27, 2014, in Apetlaca, Guerrero by members of the Department of the Navy who beat him over the head with a firearm until he bled. Before presenting him to the judicial authorities they took him, along with Jonathan Osorio Cruz y Agustín Reyes García, by helicopter to see someone who was dressed in Navy uniform and stitched up his wound.

In a handwritten letter penned for this report, and in testimony made to the United Nations, he confirmed that inside the military's facilities they were kept seated on the floor for a long time, listening to howls of pain from their colleagues before their turns came.

"Two people dressed in Navy uniform came to get me, they put me in a room and began to tie my hands behind me and then my feet . . . They began giving me electric shocks on my testicles, my anus and my mouth . . . and they put a bag over my face till I couldn't breathe and as soon as I couldn't they began hitting my chest and stomach, this lasted for three hours, telling me that they were going to tell me what they wanted me to say," Patricio says in his grim letter.

While he was being tortured they showed him photos of his family to make him more afraid.

"They asked whether now I was willing to cooperate with them, and that if I refused they would kill my wife and my two daughters, too, but that they'd rape them before they killed them and that they'd shove the barrel of a gun up their ass and that they'd all take turns raping my wife ... and that none of it would matter because I was a nobody."

Before he was detained and his face appeared in the national press as the murderer of the *normalistas* Reyes Landa was a bricklayer in Cocula. He and his family are so poor that they rely on support from a government programme for families in extreme poverty to make ends meet. Although the P.G.R. accused him of taking part in the crime and receiving a sizeable sum for doing so, he does not even own a bicycle. He lives in an adobe shack with his wife, his daughters, his parents and his siblings.

According to analysis of his wounds conducted during the investigation of the G.I.E.I. Reyes Landa sustained over seventy injuries.

Jonathan and Agustín suffered the same fate.

"They tied Jonathan's hands behind his back and suffocated him with a plastic bag, making him lose consciousness three times. They threw ice water on him to revive him. They also gave him electric shocks on his testicles and his anus," Estela, the twenty-year-old's mother stated in an interview. He was arrested with Patricio, who also worked as a bricklayer in Apetlaca.

"He even had crusted blood on his testicles, and they even put a pistol in the other boy's mouth," she said, her voice breaking.

Jonathan dropped out after secondary school because he could not afford to study. He worked as a bricklayer's apprentice and sold tacos in Mexico City where he had relatives. His mother said that when there was no work he would shuck corn or lay fertiliser. He travelled back and forth from Mexico City intermittently. He had no car, no motorcycle, no bike.

"When they arrested them they tied them up and tortured them, and he heard them digging around for something and they said it was a bag that they were going to use on them, it is too awful . . ." she says.

Her son also told her that when they were being transported in the helicopter they were told that "if they pushed one of them out, no-one would ever know". While they were in the helicopter one of the guys from the Navy said, "We'll close the case with these suckers."

Jonathan's mother said that he, too, was offered money to incriminate himself along with friends and acquaintances on his Facebook account.

"He decided not to, because it was bad enough what they were doing to them." He was taken by the P.G.R. to the dump, supposedly to show them how the students had been killed. But when he got there the authorities told him what to say and even marked out the path that he was supposed to take. This farce was recorded on video without his knowledge, according to his testimony before the United Nations. Attorney General Murillo Karam made this video public on November 7, 2014, saying that, thanks to Jonathan's "confession", the death and burning of the *normalistas* had been solved. According to the G.I.E.I.'s research, Jonathan had over ninety-four injuries.

Things fared no better for 23-year-old Agustín Reyes García. He was detained on October 26, 2014 but he was not taken to the public ministry until the following day. He told the United Nations that he, too, had been tortured, first on Navy premises and later in the offices of the Attorney General.

"These members of the military forced him to memorise certain dates and names in order to include them in his subsequent testimony," according to a letter from the five U.N. rapporteurs to the government of Mexico dated July 10, 2015.

"In the days that followed, employees of the P.G.R.'s office would take him to the dump in Cocula to act out how events took place, a number of people coercing him and telling him what he should say," the letter from the United Nations adds. On October 27, he was taken to a place near the San Juan River and forced to show where they had allegedly disposed of the ashes. On April 24, 2016, the G.I.E.I. accused Tomás Zerón himself, head of the Criminal Investigation Agency, of taking Reyes García to make the video that day and his employees of planting a black plastic bag containing the remains of Alexander Mora, the only disappeared student whose death has been confirmed, and thereby changing, thanks to these remains, the course of the entire investigation.

In an interview Agustín's wife confirmed that he told her when he was taken to the river and recorded by the P.G.R., allegedly showing them where the bags of ashes had been dumped, he was guided by employees who told him where to walk and what to do.

The G.I.E.I.'s investigation confirmed that Agustín had over forty wounds.

Twenty-five-year-old Felipe Rodríguez Salgado, alleged boss of Patricio, Jonathan and Agustín, according to the P.G.R., was detained on the afternoon of January 15 in Cocula, though the federal police said they detained him in Morelos. He worked as a bricklayer with the father of his wife, who is a teacher. She confirmed that on the night of September 26 they were with relatives, making it impossible for him to have taken part in the crime of which the P.G.R. accused him. He was also tortured to get him to sign a falsified confession. His body bore more than sixty-four injuries.

In a letter he wrote that, days after being detained, Tomás Zerón came to the federal penitentiary in Nayarit where he was being held.

"He wanted me to take the blame for what happened to the students and sign some documents and testify that I worked for people I didn't even know, and that they paid me and some guy called Sidronio and the former president of Iguala, and that in return he'd give my family money and buy them a house . . . and that I'd get eight years in jail." He confirmed that on February 18, 2015 [Zerón] returned to the prison to reiterate his offer. When he rejected it again he threatened, "Careful, you're passing up a great opportunity and don't you dare tell a soul about this conversation or else things could go very badly for you and your family."

In his letter Felipe says that if anything happens to him or his family it will be the director of the Criminal Investigation Agency's fault.

All four young men signed statements confirming that they killed the forty-three *normalistas* all at once in a dump where they burned their bodies to ash, after which they threw the ashes into a rubbish bag, which they tossed into a river. Although all four were supposedly at the scene of the crime their statements contradict each other to the point that they are completely implausible. The timings are different, as well as how and who brought the *normalistas* to them, and how they killed them and burned their bodies.

In addition to these contradictions, three independent studies undertaken by the National Autonomous University of Mexico (U.N.A.M.), the Argentine Team of Forensic Anthropology and the G.I.E.I. confirm there is no scientific proof of a large fire at the dump or that the forty-three *normalistas* were cremated all at once.

One of the most chilling questions that remain is why, if the students were not murdered and cremated in Cocula, the Mexican government had the burnt remains of one of the *normalistas* in its possession.

Over the past two years the United Nations Special Rapporteur on Torture and Other Cruel, Inhuman and Degrading Treatment and Punishment, Juan Méndez, and Amnesty International have produced reports which denounce the systematic and widespread use of torture throughout law-keeping institutions and the military in Mexico as a means of obtaining falsified confessions.

In Mexico the premises of the military, the P.G.R., the federal police, state police and local police have become replicas of prisons like Abu Ghraib and Guantánamo, whose cruel and inhumane treatment of prisoners shook the world. But it would seem that the cries of victims in Mexico have yet to be heard by the international community.

The use of torture is always evil, but in the investigation into the disappearance of the forty-three students it is worse than that. The Mexican government focused its efforts on detaining citizens and obtaining false confessions from them in order to close the case as well as to avoid investigation into the testimonies, videos and expert advice that show how at least thirty members of the 27th Infantry Battalion actively participated in the attacks and disappearance of the forty-three *normalistas,* as well as at least seven members of the federal police, two of whom were clearly identified by a witness before the National Commission on Human Rights. According to documents obtained during this journalist's investigation, there were at least eighteen spent cartridges from G3 automatic rifles found near at least two of the crime scenes. The Army was the only entity carrying those weapons that night. Some of the cartridges are inscribed with F.C. (*Fábrica de Cartuchos,* or Ammunition Factory) produced by the Department of National Defence.

Translated by Samantha Schnee

THE COUNTRY OF MASS GRAVES

Marcela Turati

THE RESCUER CLIMBED DOWN the shaft towards the accumulated stench at the bottom; rung by rung, he descended 150 metres into the disused mine. The lamp strapped to his helmet lit up the wall of the shaft, picking out silhouettes suspended in the void, caught in the beams, and rocks streaked with blood. At the bottom of the old opening, instead of the ground he found a pool of stagnant water out of which rose a mountain of shapes like the backs of pigs. But they were people. A pile of human remains, somewhere between shiny and dull, with the soapy texture of decomposition. Their faces were marked with the rictus of anguish. All bore the trademark of organised crime: their wrists tied behind their backs, brown tape covering their eyes, their underwear balled up in their mouths or sacks tied around their heads at the moment of torture.

The rescuer spent a week in May down in the pit, in the damp cavern adjoined by straight passageways, through which a chill draught blew. The temperature was 14 degrees. During the day he and his colleagues untangled the bodies, pieced them back together and placed them in white bags, arranging them in a blue plastic tub which other colleagues pulled up from outside with the help of pulleys. Scales of humus covered tattoos, the only remnant of identity those bodies had left among the anonymous mass. There was the body with the dragon, the worshippers of Santa Muerte, those whose skin was marked with the names of the women they loved, the one with a clown with a single tear. One of the bodies belonged to the recently disappeared governor of a prison. Two of the human remains were skeletons, three were mummified, another three were headless.

On Sunday June 6, 2010, the fifty-fifth corpse was extracted from the La Concha mine in Taxco, Guerrero. It was the last.

With this image I began my book *Fuego Cruzado* (Cross Fire), which I wrote in 2010 to document the reality I had to cover as a reporter when, not having chosen it, I had become a war correspondent without leaving my own country.

My aim was to denounce the violence that was happening in Mexico and becoming normalised: the murders and extrajudicial executions, the disappearances, the massacres, the mass displacements caused by fear, the impact on people of all the death and terror since the "war on drugs" was declared in 2006 by president Felipe Calderón, who planned to use the military to combat "the narcos", but whose strategy led to an increase in *unseen* violence.

The unearthing of the mass graves in the city of Taxco, a popular tourist destination, was another feature of our daily dose of terror. Although it seemed like a distant, isolated news item, one difficult to generalise, it summed up the home-grown horror.

No-one imagined that six years later, the discovery of clandestine burials would be a permanent fixture in the news, with daily confirmation that murdering people and hiding their bodies had become a kind of national sport, if not an epidemic.

At that time I equally had no idea that my reporting would lead me to specialise in forensic matters.

From 2008 onwards, I had dedicated myself to writing about the victims of violence who were rendered invisible: official discourse did not mention them, except to blame them for their own deaths because "they were up to something" or because "they were in the wrong place at the wrong time".

Starting that year I began to interview people who were desperate because they did not know the whereabouts of a family member who someone had seen being abducted or simply had not come home, and of whom there was no trace. In the fog of confusion, they did not know who to turn to or how to start the search, and the authorities were not helping either.

I soon discovered that, in various parts of the country, these families had started to meet and set up their own groups with others who were suffering the same tragedy. I attended the workshops where they shared information, learnt their rights, planned actions to make themselves heard. I documented their journeys through the labyrinth full of false doors which the bureaucracy was determined not to investigate. I bore witness to their tireless demands on all state governments to create specialist search and rescue bodies to look for their loved ones, and to put in place laws to criminalise forced disappearance. I accompanied the mothers on their marches, which later became caravans, protest camps or hunger strikes. I wrote about their visits to morgues where they had to look through photographs of skeletons to see if they recognised any features, to cemeteries where they asked for information about unidentified bodies buried in mass graves, to vacant lots widely known as dumping grounds for corpses, and to various government departments where they continually demanded the creation of a national database of unidentified bodies and a national

D.N.A. bank so as to avoid having to leave blood samples every-where they went to denounce the disappearance of their relatives. I met these women every time the discovery of a clandestine grave was announced. They always asked for information about the distinguishing features of the bodies, they wanted to see photo-graphs, they tried to peer into the hole to see if they could recognise any piece of clothing, tooth or tattoo that would allow them to identify a loved one and take them home to bury them.

Over time, wherever bodies were buried in secret, they began to ask the authorities to carry out exhumations and to use search dogs, specialised technology or ultrasound and georadar equip-ment that would allow them to locate where the soil had been disturbed. I later saw them doing these things without permission, clawing at the earth with their own bare hands, digging up bodies themselves.

As this horrific side of the country was revealed, my journalistic work became reporting on corpses, human remains and mass graves.

*   *   *

I had been oblivious to the issue: in all my formal education up until university I had not heard that in Mexico the mass disappear-ance of people was being used as a strategy of war. My only references for that were Chile and Argentina.

During the year 2000, the year of democratic transition when the P.R.I. (Institutional Revolutionary Party) lost the elections after seventy-one years in power, I was a novice reporter assigned to write about street protests. One of my assignments was to cover the demonstration of a group of old women dressed in black: they were mothers of the young people detained and disappeared in the

1970s, during the time known as the "dirty war", who were demanding that archives be declassified so they could discover the whereabouts of their children.

Two years later, the government created a department called F.E.M.O.S.P.P. (Special Prosecutor's Office for Social and Political Movements of the Past), with the mandate to investigate and punish the so-called "past crimes". This body recorded 532 people who had been disappeared in the 1970s and '80s, the majority in the southern state of Guerrero, home to some of the country's poorest areas and a centre of guerrilla activity and poppy cultivation.

The enthusiasm for democracy revived street protests in which these mothers – known as Las Doñas of the Eureka Committee – unleashed their historic war cry: "They were taken alive, we want them alive"; it also provoked the public reappearance of ex-guerrilla fighters who had survived the repression and were demanding the reopening of official files that recorded where their missing comrades were last seen, as well as *campesino* communities which, suspected of being guerrilla sympathisers, had been destroyed and were now beginning to demand the search for and exhumation of their dead.

In 2001, I took part in an exhumation for the first time: that of the historic guerrilla fighter and leader of the Partido de los Pobres, Lucio Cabañas, who was murdered by military officers in 1974 in the turbulent area of the state of Guerrero.

My first forensic article began like this:

They had been digging for 10 hours and reached a depth of 120 centimetres when the forensic scientist Carlos Jácome felt a "historic load" on his shoulders. A skull gradually appeared underneath the brush he was using to remove the soil, followed by a jaw with three teeth and a piece of cloth. It was, apparently, Lucio Cabañas Barrientos, ex-guerrilla fighter buried in secret in the Atoyac cemetery exactly 27 years ago.

In the grave they found no coffin, neither empty nor full of stones as it had been rumoured; earth had simply been piled on top of Cabañas' body. His were human remains and not equine, as people had suspected, thinking that would be the ultimate mockery from a cruel *"campesino*-killing" government.

"It's clearly a human skull," Jácome would confirm during the break that night after families and sympathisers had filed past the remains again and again, shouting *vivas* to the teacher-*comandante* and passionately singing his heroic ballad.

Jácome was the first forensic scientist I met. Back then he was starting to bring together a team of independent forensic anthropologists and had this highly unusual phone message: "If they've been killed and buried, I'll find them," with *cumbia* music playing in the background.

On one occasion when we met for coffee he introduced me to a friend with whom he was talking enthusiastically about the beauty of a pre-hispanic skull she had just found. I felt as if I was listening to a conversation between aliens.

I kept in touch with this interesting character. One day I learnt that he had had to leave the country because there was not enough work in Mexico for people of his profession. He later returned and founded an independent group of forensic scientists, only to be forced to leave again: this time because a government human rights commission had employed him to open an old tomb, but upon arrival he found recent skeletons, and armed men all around, who were narcos, and who did not like the idea of him digging up the bones they were trying to hide.

Mexico was starting to change. We were only just beginning to notice this.

*   *   *

Contrary to what we all hoped for following the arrival of the much-celebrated democracy, the forced disappearance of people was not buried along with the P.R.I. regime. From the beginning of the so-called democratic government I could tell that the problem would continue, but at the time I did not realise its significance. This is how I recorded it in an article:

> A young, unknown woman, not dressed in mourning black, joined the demonstrations held by the Doñas of the Eureka Committee, who since the 1970s have been asking each successive government to investigate the whereabouts of their children. She was holding up a large colour photo of a smiling man in his twenties, dressed in a modern football shirt, which contrasted with the 1970s black-and-white portraits of young people with outdated haircuts and serious expressions carried by the old women.
>
> The name of that new arrival in the limbo of the disappeared was Alejandro Martínez Dueñas, who according to his relatives had been kidnapped in Colima by the Federal Investigative Agency (A.F.I.), tortured and admitted to hospital for the treatment of his wounds. He was being investigated, so the family later learned, for alleged falsification of banknotes. But this was never proven.

Diana Martínez, Alejandro's sister, spent the six years of P.A.N. (National Action Party) president Vicente Fox's government staging occupations, marches and demonstrations, and for a while she lived in a tent she set up outside different government buildings, especially the P.G.R. (the office of the Attorney General of Mexico), which should have been coordinating the search. She stormed the Senate and the Chamber of Deputies, and stood in the way of the president, the attorney general, the governor of Colima and whichever officials had any responsibility in the case, in an attempt to gather information about her brother, whose body was never returned to her.

The disappearances continued even after the P.R.I. was no longer in office.

Those complicit in the political machine that disappeared people through the 1970s and part of the '80s were never in fact called to account. The public prosecutor's office specifically created to punish past crimes did not manage to convict a single person during its five years of existence.[1] The ex-presidents under whose regimes the majority of disappearances took place died of old age in their beds; police and military officers accused of having taken on the job of "cleaning" the country of subversives remained in areas of government related to security or gave up government office (no-one knows how many of them joined the ranks of organised crime).

Impunity set the tone for what was to come. What happened later, starting with the "war on drugs", was the logical consequence of that lack of investigation, that absence of punishment, that recycling of government officials who were experts in getting rid of people, that collusion between criminals and government. There had been several signs of what was to come. For example in Ciudad Juárez, from 1993 onwards, a wave of disappearances of women began – poor, young, pretty women from migrant families, workers at *maquiladoras*;[2] the bodies of only a few of them were found, abandoned on disused land.

One of the most high-profile discoveries occurred in 2001 in "Campo Algodonero", where the bodies of eight women were found. This case gave its name, eight years later, to the first sentence issued by the Comisión Interamericana de los Derechos Humanos (C.I.D.H.), known in English as the Inter-American Commission on Human Rights (I.A.C.H.R.), against the Mexican state for the phenomenon of the femicides, in which it became clear that not investigating missing persons reports is the step prior to those women being found dead. Also in 2009, the same inter-national court convicted Mexico of the forced disappearance of Guerrero community leader Rosendo Radilla, which took place in 1974, when a policy of disappearing people suspected of being linked to guerrilla organisations was in place in Guerrero.

Only a few years after that, the same defence lawyers and citizens who had celebrated the sentence, hoped for an end to the P.R.I. regime, fought for the inclusion in the Constitution of laws protecting human rights, or who had seen international law as a means to make way for change in Mexico, realised that none of these things were effective in dismantling the framework of impun-ity which forcibly disappears people. Those changes did not have the power that had been attributed to them nor had they worked as levers for the desired transformation. The disappearances, there-fore, continued.

(The Mexican government is yet to act on all the recommenda-tions issued with the verdict.)

*   *   *

In 2006 Felipe Calderón became Mexico's second P.A.N. president, and with him came the unsuccessful strategy of the "war on drugs". What primarily drew people's attention then were the serial murders taking place in some cities, some of them massive, other spectacular massacres, which overshadowed the phenomenon of the disappearances, no longer discussed because they were less striking, more silent and less easy to digest given the confusion surrounding them.

One by one, desperate families began to arrive in newspaper offices to see journalists and denounce the disappearance of a loved one, and we started to receive information from organisations wanting us to publish reports on one case or another. Before long, the visits became frequent and these families soon organised with others and founded their own collectives.

At the time it seemed to me symbolic that Norma Ledezma, a mother who had had her baptism of fire as a lawyer searching for her daughter in the era of the femicides, was teaching the next generation of relatives of the disappeared how to fight. The tragic wave of disappearances of women in Ciudad Juárez thus served as a school for other mothers who had lost their children and needed to learn the same skills. But this time there were thousands, not dozens. And the phenomenon was not only on the northern border, it was all across the country.

The disappearances of the twenty-first century are of a different variety than the detained-disappeared cases of the past. The current modus operandi evolved from the practices of the "dirty war" which had police cars or military vehicles taking people to barracks or police stations where they were tied up and interrogated, tortured, before their bodies were thrown into the sea if they were not buried in clandestine cemeteries.

In the current Mexican war, with so many different state and private armed groups, everything is nebulous and blurred. Even though marines, soldiers or municipal, state or federal police are still often responsible for forced disappearances, in the majority of cases those who disappear are intercepted in the street or hunted in their own homes, and taken in vans by unknown armed individuals not wearing uniforms. In the majority of cases no-one calls to demand a ransom.

What follows for all the families seems to be based on the same script: when they go to report what happened to the various Attorney General offices, public prosecutors refuse to open investigations, or they fritter away the most crucial hours before initiating the search, and waste valuable time before asking for information that would help locate the missing person such as images from street C.C.T.V. cameras, mobile phone signals or credit card use.

In recent years, I have heard mothers say that their children could be alive ("They've got them working," some say), but that the authorities do not want to go and "rescue them". I used to think the desire for them to be alive was a reflection of their hope. Few mothers say they are looking for their missing child's remains so they can bury them and have a place to take them a flower, pray for them, place a cross. Most insist that they are still alive but are being held captive.

*   *   *

In April 2011, 47 clandestine burials containing 193 corpses were found in the municipality of San Fernando, Tamaulipas, which is on the way to the border with Texas.

Hundreds of families came from all over the country, wanting to look into the hole to see if they could recognise any trace that might help them find a disappeared relative, or lined up for D.N.A. tests against which the remains would be checked. The discovery of that site with so many bodies announced a silenced tragedy which would later be common in Mexico. At the time, I wrote:

> The stench seeps through the walls of the morgue. It gets into schools, businesses and homes, it impregnates clothes, chokes throats, makes people nauseous, forces them to hold their noses and quicken their step. In the white building where the smell originates there are 71 bodies on the floor, piled on top of one another, waiting their turn for an autopsy. In the car park, a truck like the ones used to transport fruit holds another 74 corpses wrapped in bin bags and sealed with adhesive tape marked with the place where they were found.
>
> Hearses arrive every so often with more recently exhumed bodies. At the last count they numbered 145.
>
> The clandestine cemeteries discovered in the municipality of San Fernando – situated between Reynosa and Matamoros to the north and Cuidad Victoria to the south – reveal the level of decomposition of the narco-war. Each grave is proof of the official covering up of daily abnormality: the roads controlled by criminals, the daily massacres, the under-recording of deaths, the mass disappearances of people, the primitive barbarity of the clashing groups, the forced recruitment of young people for warfare, the complicit indifference of the law and the forced silence of citizens.
>
> (...)
>
> The people arriving at the morgue have to wait in at least four queues which take hours: two to report the disappearance, two to leave blood samples for D.N.A. matching. As people wait in the reception for the expert services office, common complaints can be heard:

"Señorita, can't you give us photos of the bodies?" asks an old farmer.

"No. The passage of time and the conditions of their deaths have made them unrecognisable," answers the receptionist. "We can only tell from descriptions of their clothes, tattoos or chains. That's why we need that information, because even though there are 100 bodies, 400 families have come looking."

"When will we be notified?" asks a frustrated woman who has been waiting for four days.

"Señora, there are a lot of people and we have to send the packets off to be checked."

The office seems like a purgatory full of people with distant expressions, watery eyes, tearstained cheeks. At times there is a silence like at a wake, at others it becomes a self-help community.

It became known not long afterwards that most of the corpses belonged to Mexican and Central American migrants intercepted on their journey to the U.S. border.

In that human "fishing" area, those captured were taken to criminal camps where they were held in the hope that someone would pay for their freedom, or they were put to work in occupations such as contract killing, packing drugs, domestic servitude or sexual slavery. All were tortured; some to death.

The bodies in the graves all had damaged skulls, split into pieces. They were buried using excavators, heavy machinery in plain sight.

In San Fernando, Tamaulipas, travellers were detained over the course of months, and when buses reached their destinations they arrived with more suitcases than passengers: baggage that no-one claimed.

"Why were they killed?" I asked a federal investigator at the scene of the crime.

"All men, young men, of an age to enlist [in the war] are seen as potential enemies. It could be that they're so desperate that they kill them to stop them getting to Matamoros and Reynosa, so they won't be recruited as hitmen for the rival cartel, the Cartel del Golfo, which controls that area."

The madness of the battle to control the routes for human trafficking. They are preventative murders. Clandestine burials to hide the victims. The bodies speak, denounce, condemn.

The scandal over the graves in San Fernando was soon buried by the subsequent commonplace barbarities. Because in Mexico each horror story surpasses the previous one.

The questions remain unanswered: How can it be that no-one did anything? How can it be that the massacre went on for months? Why did the government not warn people that the roads were dangerous? Why did the bus companies act as accomplices keeping a secret? What is going on in this country?

*   *   *

Mass graves are an indicator that allow us to take our country's pulse, because each time one is found, families searching for their loved ones pour in from every direction. The graves help us measure the size of the phenomenon of the disappearances, which official figures estimate at more than twenty-seven thousand in the last ten years. Twenty-seven thousand is a nightmare figure, just like the number of graves found.

Every so often another news item announces that one of these illegal burials has been unearthed.

And Mexico looks increasingly like one enormous mass grave.

In 2013, the National Autonomous University of Mexico set up a degree programme in Forensic Sciences to respond to the emergency due to the scarcity of professionals trained to exhume bodies.

Every so often, families or organisations stage protests – sometimes hunger strikes – demanding the presence of teams of international forensics experts, such as those from Argentina, Peru or Guatemala, and even the F.B.I., to help us dig up our tragedy. An independent group called E.M.A.F. (Equipo Mexicano de Antropología Forense – Mexican Forensic Anthropology Team) was also created.

At the same time, a group of relatives who have searched tirelessly for their children began a training process to become "citizen forensic scientists", because they want to do without the authorities, who not only fail to look for their missing family members but also hinder the searches, and because they want to create their own independent D.N.A. bank that would allow them to cross-reference results with each discovery of bones. In late 2014, a group of relatives began to go every Sunday and do what government offices should be doing, but are not: carrying out searches and exhumations in the hills around Iguala, Guerrero. They have found countless graves and more than 120 bodies.

The example of the Iguala group prompted the formation of other groups of families elsewhere around the country, who call themselves trackers, sleuths, rattlesnakes, or have not yet given themselves names.

Journalists accompany the forensic families and alongside them we learn how to identify hidden graves.

*   *   *

In the task of accompanying victims of violence so as to document and publish about their actions, I always felt out of danger . . . until the families, frustrated by impunity or because the weight of legal investigation falls on their shoulders, began to carry out their own investigations.

They started going into prisons to confront the murderers of their children and ask where they had dumped their remains. Or they followed information that led them to hidden burials: hills hiding bones, lakes with bodies in their depths, pits containing skeletons.

I learnt of families who went as far as entering areas controlled by cartels, forbidden territories, in an attempt to find clues as to the whereabouts of their relatives (several have been killed themselves for investigating).

The families gradually gather information. Dangerous information. And although they notify the police, they receive no help. So they start to organise with others and create their own groups of families who investigate and exhume, who publish on Facebook pictures of the bodies they find to help identify them. They do what the law does not.

One of the first groups of families came together in 2009 in the border city of Tijuana, after the army presented a terrible character to the press: El Pozolero – whose real name is Santiago Meza López – who, within the cartel, was in charge of dissolving bodies with caustic soda, a technique known as making *pozole*, a typical Mexican soup.

With the public presentation of El Pozolero came the confirmation that people who disappeared were not only murdered and buried, they were also subjected to processes that reduce their bodies to fragments such that they lose all identifying characteristics. All their features. Because very often it is impossible to tell if a fragment of bone belonged to a human or an animal.

One day in December 2011 I called Señor Fernando Ocegueda,

a father searching for his disappeared son and founder of the organisation United for the Disappeared, to ask about his findings, and he emailed me a picture. A photo I cannot describe, one that left me speechless.

The image was of the bottom of a cup in which you could see fragments – bones? – the size of teeth.

"How many people have you found?" I asked Ocegueda.

"I can't say how many people, I can only say how many pieces: about 100 pieces of bone, 30 or 40 teeth. I don't know . . . But in the place where we found the pieces of bone and teeth [Santiago Meza] told the authorities that he buried about forty-five or fifty people." It took me hours to write my article. I needed time to assimilate the horror. I was no longer writing about bodies, I was writing about fragments of what was once a person.

*   *   *

That investigation led me to other discoveries. On January 25, 2009, being questioned by the public prosecutor, Santiago Meza gave the following response when asked about his job:

> . . . he said his job was to make *pozole*, in other words, to dissolve bodies in caustic soda.
>
> In the official report it says that Meza López is married, a father, hailing from Guamúchil, Sinaloa, but residing in Tecate, Baja California, 45 years of age, educated up to third grade of primary and employed by Teodoro García Pimentel, a.k.a. El Teo, member of the cartel that dominated Tijuana.
>
> "What is your specific role within the criminal group?"
>
> "My specific role within the organisation is the job of making *pozole*, which means that members of the different

cells of the organisation bring me corpses to be dissolved in a solution made from caustic soda and water."

"How many criminal acts have you participated in on the orders of El Teo?"

"On the direct orders of El Teo I've made *pozole* with about 70 people, but in total it's about 300, because I also received orders from El Mayel (Ismael Higuera Guerrero) and El Efra (Efraín Pérez) to make *pozole* with the bodies."

The statement continues: "I learnt to make *pozole* with a bull's leg which I put in a bucket and put some liquid on it and it dissolved; the bodies they gave me to make *pozole* with were already dead when they arrived, and I put them whole in tanks and covered them with 40 or 50 kilos of powder which I bought in a hardware shop (. . .) a kilo of soda cost me 35 pesos (. . .) some young lads helped me make the *pozole*.

Thus begins the professional career of someone who disappears people. There was no Mexican who was not revolted by the news. But the families with disappeared relatives were devastated, as if mortally wounded. When they found the strength to go to the Attorney General's office, they asked that the man in custody be shown photographs so he would confirm whether he had seen the faces of the people who passed through his "kitchen".

He told them he did not recognise any of them because all his victims were brought to him hooded, already dead.

When they were able to assimilate that news, pick themselves up off the floor, recover from the torture of imagining that their relatives might have been dissolved in a tank of acid, they took the investigations into their own hands. They found some answers.

Then I wrote this report:

When the families of the disappeared learnt of the capture of El Pozolero they went to the building on the piece of common land Ojo de Agua, where it was known that the last bodies had been dissolved. There they placed candles and prayed for the dead.

(...)

Señora Gómez says that with every exhumation, every interview or appointment at the Attorney General's office, she relives the anguish of her son's disappearance, that wound which is "always open, which doesn't heal" because she does not know his whereabouts.

"Every time a new area is found, a new door opens. You hope something might come out of it, something new, and so there you go, searching and searching your whole life. It's remembering things again, spending days and nights thinking, imagining what they did to my son: if they hit him, if they gave him food, if they killed him, if they put him in acid," she says, and is frightened by her own words. "I can't think about that thing with the acid. I imagine they shot him, he fell and that was that; that he didn't suffer much."

In the border city of Tijuana people visit the extermination centres where it is known that numerous people were dissolved in acid. There you can see, if the soil is disturbed, a gelatinous yellowish substance mixed with the mud in which, if you examine it, you can find teeth, pieces of bone, surgical screws or fillings, and if it is stirred it gives off a fetid smell, impossible to rid of, which lingers in your throat, which causes nightmares.

When people learnt what happened there, families went with flowers, candles and holy water; over time, a group of victims, neighbours and artists decided to redefine the place by painting walls, scattering holy water, cleaning up, hanging mandalas.

The authorities took advantage of the figure of El Pozolero: it was the perfect excuse not to investigate the disappearances.

In 2014, for example, representatives of the P.G.R. informed the families belonging to Ocegueda's organisation that due to the use of caustic soda, none of the teeth or fragments of bone found in the areas where Meza López worked were suitable for any process of genetic identification.

That same reasoning was soon being used in other states: "Stop searching, it's likely he was cooked."

"Meza López says it was 300 people. I think it was at least 900," says Ocegueda, the father-investigator, incredulously. "The saddest thing is that when there's a disappearance which coincides with the dates when he was working, they tell the families to not even bother searching because the person is likely to have 'ended up' with Santiago Meza. It's their way to sidestep investigations."

*   *   *

It was increasingly difficult to face up to that horror, which was impossible to digest, much less imagine.

The fate of the disappeared was not only explained by bodies dissolved in acid: I also started to hear stories of people who – after an intense search – bumped into their disappeared relative in the street, but could not take them home because they were drugged up, or enslaved by some drug trafficking cartel or other, watched by other captives, with no way of escape.

Families began to report to the highest levels of government that the disappeared – the great majority of whom are men, many of them migrants – were held in slave labour camps, farms, safe houses or warehouses. And that they were forced to do jobs such as

"falconing" – keeping watch on behalf of criminals – contract killing, harvesting marijuana, installing communication equipment,
collecting extortion money from businesses, digging tunnels to
smuggle drugs into the United States, cleaning safe houses and
feeding the prisoners kept there, or sexual slavery, among many
others.

Most of the disappeared are men of working age (between
nineteen and thirty-five) and many of them are professionals with
specialised jobs, such as the twelve technicians working in the
maintenance and installation of telecommunication antennae, ten
of whom disappeared in Tamaulipas and two in Coahuila.

Initially, this information that the disappeared might not be
dead but working for the cartels was difficult to believe, even for
the organisations supporting the families working together around
disappearances.

Blanca Martínez, from the Fray Juan de Larios Centre for
Human Rights, which covers the Fundem/Fundec organisation
of families founded in 2009 in Coahuila, says that at first those
testimonies seemed like a dream, but later there were clues, for
example: families receive phone calls on significant personal dates,
such as a mother's birthday, an anniversary, and when the phone
rings no-one speaks on the other end.

When this happens, the mothers start speaking despite the
silence, believing that their children are on the other end of the line,
getting in touch even if they cannot speak, because they are being
held captive and want to protect their families.

The bishop of Saltillo, Raúl Vera, who accompanies the families
of victims in his state, also believes that the disappeared serve other
possible purposes: "They might be in concentration camps, where
they're in forced labour. We've heard of people who say 'I escaped'
and that they were in camps where they were being trained to use

weapons. Migrants have told us that they were held in safe houses."

Father Pedro Pantoja, founder of the Casa del Migrante de Saltillo, who has talked to the survivors of that hell, described them: "They arrive emaciated, abused, traumatised because they were forced to 'work'. They can't always speak, and if they do it's with the horror of what they went through in the hotels, warehouses, storerooms where they were held, where they would see the police coming and going. Some were tortured, others seem to have almost entirely lost their personality."

According to Alberto Xicoténcatl, director of the hostel at Casa del Migrante, survivors of that tragedy have come to them: "It's very likely that [the disappeared] are walking among us, off the leash, but watched because they have a job to do."

It has been known to happen. Xicoténcatl says that the few who do "appear" after having been disappeared, give statements that coincide with one another: "They say that they were in safe houses, in the countryside, in barely urbanised areas, together with other detainees and with no permission to talk to one another. They were taken out to work on a daily basis. Some were held there for six months, others a year, in a state of terror because each week they brought everyone together and killed one of them. They were able to escape when there was a navy operation, they managed to run away in the confusion."

Defence lawyer Malú García, from the Chihuahua organisation Nuestras Hijas de Regreso a Casa (Bring Our Daughters Home), says that from 2008 onwards, when the army and the federal police occupied Cuidad Juárez, members of the Los Aztecas gang, seeing the decline in small-scale drug dealing, applied themselves to trafficking women as well. At least 30 women have disappeared and the organisation assumes that as long as the women remain good business, they will be kept alive.

Teresa Ulloa, director in Mexico of the Latin American and Caribbean branch of the Coalition Against the Trafficking in Women, says that in all the regions disputed by drugs traffickers there is evidence of the disappearance of young women who are probably used as sexual slaves by gang leaders or their troops.

It has been difficult to prove this hypothesis. Very few of the disappeared reappear, and when they do, fear causes them to vanish again of their own accord: they get home, tell their families they are O.K., tell them what happened and the very same night they run way, change identity. They can not stay at home for fear of endangering their loved ones; they are sure that their captors will recapture or kill them because they know too much.

No-one wants to speak about that hell. They do not trust anyone.

I met the sister of one of these people who have disappeared and reappeared. After interviewing her, I wrote her testimony in this article:

"My brother disappeared when he was 19. He was working in town, at a carpenter's workshop, and one day some friends got him to go with them to take a truck up into the hills, when they got there with a bit of furniture they were told, 'You lot are going to stay here and work,' and they were given heavy weapons and trucks and told to guard the town. They're under the orders of a *comandante*, among the people, killing. Because they were told to kill. But my brother never killed anyone."

This is the testimony of a young woman from Chihuahua. It is not just another story like all the others whispered in the meetings of families searching for their missing, abducted, kidnapped or disappeared relatives, the stories which say that not all the disappeared are dead, some are alive, in slavery; this story contains facts, names of towns, descriptions of criminals.

"They went into people's houses and just pointed their guns, and raped women. The men were treated very badly, they went two weeks without washing, all they were given to eat was instant noodles, they were armed, made to patrol the town and steal."

"And how do you know this?" I asked.

"My brother told us."

"How?"

"One day he managed to go to a hill and from up there he called our dad to say he was O.K., but that they were treated really badly. Another day he turned up at home . . . he got away while there was a shootout . . . He escaped."

The young woman, even though she keeps her voice low, does not look nervous. It seems she needs to tell her story. She is in a meeting with families from all over the country who are also looking for their relatives. Here she found out that her case was not an isolated one and has promised herself that she will not stop searching for her big brother who came back from hell and described it to her, but had to go back to it, under his own steam, to save his family from being condemned to a slow, cruel, barbaric living hell.

Her brother was forced to go back. It was the last they heard of him. He was probably killed.

The hell she describes is that of a prison without bars, an open jail that has its own ways of preventing escapes: her brother lived only among young men, some recruited by force, others there of their own volition, in an abandoned house outside the town. They took it in turns to keep watch and to check that no unknown men came to shoot them.

Since the municipal police were not armed, the young men patrolled in stolen 4×4s, they did not have any time off, they ate what they could, they were always high on marijuana or cocaine, and their excesses often ended in shootouts and murders among themselves. They were not paid but could not stop working because their captors know their families.

She talked about many young men recruited by force.

Statements tell of farms in inhospitable areas, where they have wire cages "like chicken runs, where they are kept day and night, in sun or rain, eating bread and water once a day, until their families pay a ransom," according to Xicoténatl. Or warehouses full of human beings. In view of the evidence, the government created a specialised search team, with an investigation department and rescue force, but it has made no difference. It is estimated that in Mexico, 13 people disappear per day. One every two hours.

*   *   *

In Mexico, Mother's Day is celebrated on May 10. But for the last six years, this has been the day when thousands of mothers of the disappeared travel from all over the country to march together through the streets of the capital, demanding justice.

The mothers have travelled across Mexico in caravans where they demonstrate their sadness and rage. They have carried out hunger strikes and have stormed events with the president, legislators, state ministers and attorney generals.

Despite the work of the world's most important human rights organisations, including international bodies such as the U.N. and the Organisation of American States (O.A.S.), to demonstrate that there is a serious human rights crisis in Mexico, the authorities have not seriously recognised the problem; on the contrary, they try to hide it.

Even though the violence broke out in 2006, the government is yet to create a reliable missing persons database covering the whole country. Each federal body has its own laws regarding the registration of and procedure for dealing with unidentified corpses (some cremate them). Each cemetery does what it sees fit with the remains. There is not a single protocol or expert process for registering the characteristics of those bodies. And the disappearances continue.

Some of them occur within the labyrinths of bureaucracy, when the details of the corpses are not correctly recorded, thus impeding their identification.

I have never got used to the disappearances, even as they happen ever more blatantly, ever more massively.

The most spectacular has been that of the forty-three students from the Raúl Isidro Burgos Rural Teachers College in Ayotzinapa, Guerrero. They were attacked by municipal, federal and state police officers and in the presence of the military. The police and civilian-dressed armed men killed six people, wounded scores and disappeared forty-three students. In front of television cameras. En masse. Forty-three. Poor. Students.

The news shook the whole country. People went out into the street to demand that they be returned alive, and that justice be done, all chanting: "It was the State."

In the search for the students, countless mass graves have been uncovered. Witness statements led the police to places where, during the excavations, other bodies were found, not those belonging to the students. Some of them were complete corpses, still gagged with their hands tied. Others were no longer bodies, they were fragments of charred bone because their executioners had tried to turn them into charcoal. They were unrecognisable.

According to the P.G.R., that was what happened to the students, and false evidence was used to construct an untruthful version of events and close the case.

In the search for the students and others who had disappeared in the area, journalists also accompanied the relatives who travelled to places where people said the students were. The first such place was the hill at Pueblo Viejo, where 28 bodies were found.

The attacks against the Ayotzinapa students revealed other dramas.

That same month, scores of people in the area with a family member who had been disappeared gathered in a church in Iguala – in time they found that there were more than 250 such families. Overcoming their fear, they spoke for the first time of their shared pain and agreed to follow the example of the parents of the forty-three students: to look for and open hidden graves with their own hands in order to find their disappeared loved ones. The authorities had never helped them. Thus the organisation called Los Otros Desaparecidos (The Other Disappeared) was born. From November 2014 up to the present, they head out daily to comb the hillsides looking for their relatives. On their first day they found eight bodies.

They use machetes, shovels, picks, iron rods, their hands and fingernails, anything that can be used to dig. During their first expeditions, they wore dark glasses and hats or caps for fear of being identified by the armed groups that make their camps in those hillsides. Soon they lost their fear and began to wear black T-shirts, with the slogan "Son, until I can bury you I will keep looking for you" as a uniform.

From then on, the cries of "I found a grave" have not stopped.

Every time they find a skeleton, or the remains of a person, tears flow, throats become choked, a prayer is said, and everyone wonders which family is searching for this body.

The last time I saw this group of trackers, a year and a half after it was formed, they had become famous for having been the first to go out looking for bodies on their own initiative without waiting for the authorities to do it, and they were leading workshops on how to find graves and dig up bodies for fathers and mothers representing other families suffering their same plight, who have organised in other parts of the country, such as Chihuahua, Sonora, Sinaloa, Veracruz, Michoacán, Distrito Federal, Guerrero, Morelos and Coahuila.

They all trained with real forensic experts on a two-day theory course in Mexico City, which was followed by several days of fieldwork in Amatlán de los Reyes, Veracruz, where – no longer looking at the theory, but in real conditions now – the group of tracking families from Iguala taught them how to use tools such as spades, crowbars and pickaxes, how to identify the areas where soil has been disturbed, how many centimetres they should dig so as not to break bones, what death smells like, what to do when you find skeletons, how to preserve evidence. In sum: how to do the job that the government is not doing to find bodies.

Their method is this: Every time they see disturbed soil they drive metal bars made by blacksmiths into the ground, and hit them with a mallet, which the expert anthropologists deride. When they pull the bar out they sniff the end like bloodhounds trained to detect the stench of death. Then they bury it again, and so on, centimetre by centimetre

During the fifteen-day field course they found bloodied clothing, a number of bones and fifteen graves. This was known as the First National Brigade in Search of the Disappeared.

A month later, this same group, and another victim's organisation, travelled to Tetelcingo, Morelos, some two hours from Mexico City. There the Morelos state government was forced to exhume two mass graves where state officials had secretly buried 117 bodies. This would be the clearest example of how the government itself digs its own mass graves and disappears the disappeared.

Often, from the femicides in Ciudad Juárez to the present, human rights organisations have realised that the people they are searching for were thrown into mass graves even though they had been identified by authorities.

It makes me think that this may never change, because the cycle of impunity is never-ending: government officials still disappear people, whether directly, when they capture, and often kill and bury, the disappeared, or indirectly, when they do not look for them, do not help or protect the families looking for them, do not identify found human remains, or disappear the disappeared from the statistics.

Although I have been writing about these things for fifteen years, I always have a lump in my throat when I see families digging holes in the earth in the hope of finding their disappeared loved ones, bringing them back to the family, burying them close to home. When I see first-time mothers who still cannot assimilate what has happened to their children, and cry at any insinuation that they might be dead. When I hear these mothers say that they are not seeking justice, only the truth, so as not to cause any trouble with criminal groups; that they do not expect anything anymore from the authorities; that now they are not only looking for their relatives but also for all the dead, for any body, in the hope that just as they might find the bones which another family is waiting for at home, others might dig up the bones they are desperate to find.

Or when another of those parents is killed in retaliation for searching.

This image of fathers and mothers scratching at the earth with open hearts, with their own bare hands, with anger, frustration and sadness bubbling to the surface as they search for graves, encapsulates what this country has become. The country of mass graves.

Translated by Lucy Greaves

FRAGMENTS FROM A REPORTER'S JOURNAL

Lydia Cacho

I – The public side . . .

First of all I should tell you that in December 2006 I was tortured for twenty hours and then imprisoned. It happened because of my journalistic investigations into child pornography and the ties that Mexican governors, senators, police chiefs and businessmen had to the trafficking of women, girls and boys from across the continent. Though we now know that the orders were to murder me and throw my body into the sea, thanks to the solidarity of others and to precautions I had taken some months before, I am alive to tell the tale. I know the voices, names and faces of those who wanted to end my life in order to silence my voice. I am one of few who have survived the open season on journalists and defenders of human rights in Latin America. You should know that since 2000, more than ninety journalists have been murdered in my country, in addition to many reporter friends who have disappeared; we are still searching the country for their bodies.

You should know that the dirty war against ethical journalism is not new. The story began in 1934, when there was only a single paper factory in Mexico: the San Rafael monopoly, which supplied the newspapers and magazines of the entire country with the paper they needed. But that year, the workers rebelled against their pitiful salaries and lack of benefits, leading the country's print media into a crisis of forced silence. The newspaper and magazine bosses asked the federal government to help by granting them as soon as possible permission to import paper, and to exempt them from the onerous taxes on doing so as importation was not an easy task back then. The federal government, headed by General Lázaro Cárdenas, chose instead to found a state monopoly, and in 1935 it established the company Productora e Importadora de Papel S.A. (P.I.P.S.A.), which would supply subsidised paper to all the media in the country at prices and credits that would allow the press to subsist. President Cárdenas claimed that with this measure, all the states and provinces would have access to paper, fostering ideological diversity in printed media. The proprietors of the printing presses, who were already associated, supported the government and became shareholders controlled by the President of the Republic.

Little by little, corrupt power relationships were built between newspaper owners and politicians. Journalism only formally became a profession in 1949, when the Carlos Septién García School of Journalism – the first of its kind – was founded. Later, the Autonomous National University of Mexico (U.N.A.M.) opened its own school aimed at professionalising the media, though it would take at least two decades to consolidate the field.

*   *   *

According to the law, after thirty years the government would have the option of either dismantling or renewing P.I.P.S.A., so in 1965 the secret negotiations with the owners and directors of the most powerful media outlets began. Little by little an agreement grew out of the close-knit association between media and government that would not come to light until many years later.

The advent of the student movements in 1968 changed everything for Mexican journalism. There were thousands of accusations of forced disappearances, of massacres by special military units created expressly for the purposes of social cleansing and arresting hundreds who would become political prisoners. In response, Luis Echeverría Álvarez, strategist of the Dirty War and right-hand man of the then president Gustavo Díaz Ordaz, ordered his front man Mario Moya Palencia to deny paper to any media outlet that refused to publish "the historical truth". In other words, to deny the forced disappearances, just as Televisa news obediently did. The government, through P.I.P.S.A., had already decided on very many occasions to refuse paper to the provincial periodicals that gave voice to political opposition. An example of this was the repeated punishment of the *Diario de Yucatán*, which covered the conservative National Action Party (P.A.N.). The journalist Jacinto Rodríguez Munguía's research[1] into the National Archives clearly shows how the federal government monitored and controlled the media, and suggested tactics and strategies to governors on how to pressure and blackmail newspaper owners so as to consolidate the P.R.I.'s dictatorial command over public information.

Moya, who had been Secretary of the Interior (in charge of the federal espionage system), implemented a strategy that consisted of announcing that P.I.P.S.A. would soon be dismantled, which meant small and independent media outlets would be abandoned to their fate, without import permits or any access to paper. The more powerful media maintained their traditional, close relationship with the president in office and were not in danger of being shut down; however, they had accumulated multi-million peso debts to the government, which maintained a subsidy that enabled it to coerce and control the press. In the end, the media renegotiated to keep P.I.P.S.A. in existence. Meanwhile, journalism had been professionalised, and the leftist and libertarian movements in Europe, the U.S.S.R., and Central and South America exerted greater influence on the political culture of Mexican youth.

In 1970 I was seven years old, and the strange forced disappearances were a topic of discussion at my house, as were the self-censure of broadcast media and the student massacres. I learned that censorship has many masks. Meanwhile, the country's university journalism programmes were promoting the dignity of the profession and the notion of freedom of information. Journalists, feminist writers, and remarkable artists from all over the world inspired us: Oriana Fallaci, Simone de Beauvoir, Elena Poniatowska, Rina Lazo, Mika Seeger, Gloria Steinem, Roberta Avendaño, Tina Modotti and Marcela Lagarde; they all demanded a free journalism.

In the historical records of the Centre for Research and National Security (C.I.S.E.N.), Mexico's security services, there are thousands of pages describing the methods of political extortion used by Díaz Ordaz's government and his successor, Luis Echeverría Álvarez, against media owners. Álvarez governed from 1970 to 1976, but before that he was the politician who carried out the crimes against humanity committed against students and political dissidents under orders from Gustavo Díaz Ordaz (1964–70).

Seven six-year terms of the Institutional Revolutionary Party (P.R.I.) strengthened the corrupt power relationships between journalists and government. Newspapers and magazines consumed 12 million tons of paper per year, while publishers and textbook manufacturers needed only 1,500 tons. Political reforms in 1976–77 finally allowed the country to hold multi-party elections, and some media outlets began to break their ties with politicians and seek a freedom they had previously only imagined.

P.I.P.S.A.'s monopoly finally ended in 1998, and with that the media also regained a certain degree of freedom. It was then that the cloak of darkness was pulled back and we found out just who was really on the side of political power, and from that moment on arose the first wave of independent, freelance journalists. By that time, feminists had consolidated their critique of the misogyny inherent in the media, and of the lack of women in senior positions and as reporters in fields that had always been considered pre-eminently male territory.

Towards the end of the 1990s, a standard discourse had been established – though it bore little relationship to reality – regarding the pressure that political power exerted on media owners. Later on it was learned that most of the businessmen of journalism had only played at being victims, when in reality they were an integral part of the web of corrupting power.

In 2000, when the conservative P.A.N. party and its president, Vicente Fox, rose to power for a seemingly democratising term, it looked as if the media would be freed from government's so-called iron-fist control. During that time a new wave of young journalists, many of them women, made names for themselves for their steadfast ethics in investigating organised crime in the context of the falsely termed "war on drugs". But in actuality, too many of the thirty-two new state governors imitated to perfection the example set by their predecessors: extortion, corruption and alliances with the owners of media outlets; the public radio and T.V. stations became publicity centres for the new party in power. The owners of most media outlets had spent decades accustomed to earning more money by manipulating certain politicians than by doing good reporting. The elite journalists in the highest spheres main-tained this bad habit of collusion. But a new breed of free journalists had been born; the feminisation of editorial depart-ments was the foundation of a new freedom of expression and of information. Jesús Blancornelas was a much loved journalism teacher and the founder of the Semanario Zeta in Tijuana; he was the first to warn of Mexico's narco-politics, and he survived an attack from hired gunmen sent by a governor to kill him. He told me before he died that we – the female reporters with an awareness of human rights issues, the ones investigating links between power and organised crime, as well as the social cost of that degradation – we should never forget that we were journalism's salvation. Before dying he left his magazine in the hands of a brave woman: Adela Navarro, who in the midst of war has always known how to carry out courageous and ethical journalism.

The most recent reports from organisations that defend freedom of the press and information – including the Committee to Protect Journalists, Reporters without Borders and Article 19 – reveal that in 2015, 70 per cent of the deadly attacks and threats against the lives of journalists in Mexico come from the country's governors, police and military; the rest come from organised crime.

Freelance reporters and the new wave of free electronic media broke the alliances of our predecessors, and we revived the counter-power mission of journalism. We know very well that for sixty years we have been told a lie; now we know that the state's victimisation of the large journalistic empires is a pantomime that allows the latter to shore up their impunity. A closer look reveals that the majority of media owners, no matter how progressive they seem, have abandoned reporters to their fates. They exist only to defend their own interests: their ties to power, not to Truth . The few who defend us in the provinces have been bombarded, grenades have exploded in their editing rooms, and their directors have been kidnapped or shot. The truth is that the humanitarian crisis in Mexico and its resulting confusion comes from the fact that the collusion between press and power has left vulnerable those of us who have believed, since the dirty war of the 1960s, that the truth would set us free. The attacks on journalists are constant, from corrupt public servants and cartel hitmen alike, while the owners of large media outlets have left a void in place of human rights; like cruel generals, they have left their soldiers to their fates on this battlefield that is Mexico. All in exchange for paid publicity; journalism, too, has been gravely wounded by the neoliberal model of capitalism.

II – *The private side . . .*

Years have passed since that December 16, 2005, when an armed commando under orders from the governor of Puebla kidnapped and tortured me, with orders to kill me for having published the book *Los demonios del Edén: el poder detrás de la pornografía infantil* (The Demons of Eden: the power behind child pornography),[2] years during which I survived the contrived lawsuits brought by a gang of politicians with links to organised crime. During which I survived three murder attempts and two attacks, and seventeen death threats that I documented and proved before the authorities. I have left Mexico on five occasions in fear for my life, and five times I have returned home with my dignity intact. I have been fired from one of the most powerful newspapers in the country at the request of the federal government. I have published twelve books; I have been a journalist for twenty-five years, and every time I sit down to write, as now, a transparent fear settles over my eyes and makes me ask myself: Should I tell the truth? My hands keep going, my mind says yes, so does my heart. I confess to you . . .

It is dawn, dawn breaks and I look at the palms of my hands. I meditate while the leaves of the trees clinging to their branches praise life beneath the soft breath of the jungle's morning wind.

Only then do I think of those things I have not told you. The letters that, woven into words, remained hidden in the darkest night while you were sleeping, secure in the belief that publicly exposing injustice was enough to take down the enemies of truth, the masters of humanity's darkest nights.

Here I am alone, as one is alone when the body once more refuses to respond to the demands of a harrowing, seemingly endless litigation. It is too late to go back. Our enemies do not sign contracts that have expiration dates. And even if I could go back I would not, I would do it all again, I would return to the courtroom to defend my rights and the rights of others as if they were my own, because in a way they are. I have always been aware of the subtle, dynamic interconnection that allows us to endure on this planet together.

My ears refuse to hear the negative pronouncement again, the everyday no-you-can't. Nor will they heed the loving voice that recommends, like someone prescribing Aspirin for a headache, that I leave the country for a while, that I put my life on hold, leave with just the clothes on my back and go far away from the peace of my jungle house, from the sea that nourishes me, from the happy company of my noble dogs who need no excuses to love and protect me. That I leave behind my favourite pen I use to draw sunrises while I look out at the ocean, and this refuge that still retains the scent of my dead mother's embraces – my dead mother, whose absence reminds me of the pain of orphanhood. Some insist I should abandon the security of my warm bedroom, the sweet smell of the coffee I make every morning in a corner of my kitchen, from where I look out at my favourite palm tree while the infusion treats me to its sharp and cloying smell of awakening. They say it nonchalantly, that I should leave the playful sound of the fountain in my garden where lively carp swim while I meditate in silence, the smell of the orange tree growing there whose sweet flowers gives off light every time I pass it. They ask me to leave, like a nomad. As only a criminal fearful of the law would leave.

I will not leave for ever. Just long enough for them to know that I will not give up, not even with a contract out on my life.

I never told you how indignant I am at being a person pursued by injustice. I stand alongside many thousands of others also hunted by the injustice that in Mexico has become a means of emotional colonisation, a system that paralyses some of its victims and fills others with rage. Sometimes, most of the time, it drives them to flee and never return.

Never have I pronounced these words aloud: every time I flee death, a little of my happiness spills into foreign territory, never to return to me; shreds of my life husked away into the void.

I have not told you that for ten years ... no, wait, sixteen. I have to go back to my diaries to remember when my words first acquired the power to summon danger. When my intuition and knowledge, my intelligence and investigative skills, my ability to defend and educate, all became lethal darts.

More than two decades have passed since the beginning of this journey during which I had to learn, in silence and with only my convictions as allies, to detect in my saliva the bitter taste of real fear, to look over my shoulder every time I turn a corner, to smell danger like someone sniffing red roses on an April afternoon. I learned alone, because no-one told us that being journalists and activists is not looked upon kindly in a country given to hypocrisy, to double standards and the hateful professional scapegoating of martyrs.

I never told you how I debated in silence, searching for the exact words to tell you – any of you who wanted to listen – that the heroism they all talk about is a perverse ruse, a pool of muck I never let myself sink into. I wondered if it was worth it to go into the cave and drive out the bats, the ones that on starless nights look like sparrows, and only close up are clearly dark *chiroptera*. I questioned whether I should name the desperation that drives me involuntarily to keep following the patriarchal script, in which the only women who do good for good's sake are selfless saints (preferably nuns). How to go against the monumental discursive farce that permeates everything? The media, those who grant prizes, the human rights experts who believe we must be exceptional to lead, as if leadership were a unique gift only for a chosen few . . . Exceptionalism is a trap that relegates us to ostracism; it serves only as an excuse for those who are not willing to be part of the collective change.

We choose our jobs, certainly; convictions, though, and principles and values, grow unnoticed in the human spirit until one afternoon, in maturity, we discover that they cannot move very far from our consciousness because they have melded to it with the strength that allies metals to make bronze. The conviction that rejects dogma is weightless and strong as the flame of a candle lighting a dark room; the ethic that accompanies it will not fit in the clenched fist of intolerance. Both of them silently inhabit every word, every mysterious action of one who lives by telling the stories of other men and women who felt voiceless before.

So busy was I with telling those people's stories that I never told you what it is like to live the anxiety of moving from city to city, from country to country, dragging your feet and creating speeches in thanks for the prizes that are really provisional shields, recognitions of something that by all rights should simply be validated by its social usefulness. The truth, so hard to come by in this sorrowful Mexican autumn, seems to demand stars and laurels, statues and applause, because very few people believe in its vital, inherent, concrete, value. The prizes have become a kind of bizarre protection. Some bring us to weave wider networks, to expand our horizons; others stuff us into little marble boxes like diminutive trophies, hidden oddities that come – like ships full of the swaying bodies of mournful refugees – from unsalvageable countries, ruthless places incomprehensible to the outsider's naked eye, or to the one-eyed gaze of the people who, by looking outside of their country, do not see inside their own hell.

Nor did I tell you that this fame thing is really a charade, that I am not interested in satisfying the needs of a public that clamours for spectacle so it can flee from the real and essential responsibility calling them to act right here, right now, alongside us, with urgency, discipline and compassion, with strategy and conviction.

It was then that an idea took hold of me . . . reputation, I told myself, is what matters in a world as absurd as ours, because it is born of credibility. And that belief was confirmed when I saw the crass and prostituted reporters coming with their pens and their spears to attack our credibility, to dig around in the little privacy I had left, using the trifles they found to knead deliberate lies. Because they understood too: there is irrefutable vulgar heroism in the violent people who win the battles of corruption, torture and death; but these same people are poisoned as if with venom by the heroism of those of who understand that journalism, the true counter-power, has human rights at its core. This heroism wounds them like a poison dagger, makes them taste the fear in their saliva. The patriarchs never expect a woman to be valiant and right.

We all are afraid. They fear losing the power they have won through oppression, economic violence and lies. We fear losing lives – our own and our loved ones' – for daring to rebel, to riddle our profession with coherence, for being honest in a country seduced by the illusion of magical realism that hides the tragedy of planned inequality, of systemic racism, of dehumanising capitalism and structural sexism.

I never told you that every night in the hospital, all those nights when my body wanted to give up, I cried until I fell exhausted into a passing dream. My sobs became a river and the river became tears, my feet would not walk and I felt like a pariah whose life was reaching its end out of pure fatigue.

One day I thought there was nothing left to say, that no-one could bear up against so much pain in her soul, so much indignation pumping through her veins. I hugged myself in the hospital room with the fear of a lost little girl in a desert of uncertainty; I thought I would die from a torture that returned every night to remind me what I had lived through, the nightmare that yanks out your eyes so you can no longer see hope. One afternoon the doctor came in and explained to me that the physical exhaustion was the result of post-traumatic stress from the torture, from the taxing pressure, from working so arduously collecting horror stories, from listening to hundreds of exploited boys and abused girls tell their tales so I could make them known to the world.[3] My mind understood the meaning of that explanation, but my spirit – which is also in my mind – repeated no, no, no more suffering, no more pain, no more fear, not for me or anyone (and then I knew why so many victims submit to their captors). As the doctor left the room and I closed my eyes, pretending to be asleep so no-one would know that the enemy was winning the battle within me, that his subjugation over the course of years, the threats, the persecution, the state spying, the paying off of judges and witnesses, the salaries of the police torturers, the death of that little Salvadoran girl victim, the pain of those hundreds of abused girls who told me their stories, and the sadness of my loved ones who protect me and suffer for me – it was all stifling my breath like an immense mountain of coal. I closed my eyes to ensure that no-one could yank them out by their roots, and as long as I kept them closed, the landscapes of my happy childhood could be reborn: images of my mother who had inspired me, of my grandparents who survived the Second World War and were reborn in Mexico. I was also reborn, little by little without knowing. I felt like a refugee in my own country who, before reaching solid ground, had been sure I would drown.

Nor did I tell you that on a certain night in May, still sick from exhaustion and with the shadow of a fear the colour of bile that visited me every night after the long judicial testimonies, I thought that death was my friend and nothing was worth anything anymore. They kill you that way . . . first your body collapses, and then your spirit concludes that maybe there is no future for you, because you want no more dark nights, or idiotic questions about your pain and your fear. Because now you cannot understand why the hell others cannot understand this task of reinventing traditional journalism to be one of peace with a human rights perspective. Why cannot they understand that this is the way to understand wars and their information feeding dynamics? The way to reveal the secret of that morbid, addictive contempt for life that we created by showing images of corpses piled up like rocks in the desert, or of bodies hanging from city bridges, decapitated heads on the front pages of newspapers, a pornographic display of a country that is rotting unawares, where we are socially indoctrinated to believe we have lost the battle against impunity and violence. Because the fact is that we live as if we are the ones who have been decapitated, as if it is our collective spirit the narco-traffickers have hung from the bridges, and those grey, piled-up bodies are our dreams, now become a shapeless mass of indifference. It is our civic strength that is buried in thousands of clandestine graves, where those who died in the battles of narco-power lie side by side with the student victims of forced disappearance.

The fetid stench of blood and the media's standard discourse have blinded us to the concrete fact that we are facing the same strategy of state terrorism strategy that Colombia lived through before us, one that made millions of people suffer from the stigma of being seen as an execrable and unsalvageable nation. Millions were driven from their homes, thousands of sons kidnapped and enslaved as hitmen, thousands of daughters turned into enslaved dolls for the mafia or soldiers for the guerrillas. And we, stupid as we are, refuse to understand the story of those who were our cellmates in this global prison of narco-government, who shared the infamy that has seeped like an underground river from south to north. Not to mention the flow from north to south of domineering, wanton violence, the sale of arms, and the U.S. war strategies to debilitate democracies. We look at the horror and its consequences, but never at its origins and the concrete ways to stop it and face internal conflict.

Again and again I have recognised the naked truth before my eyes. Twenty years ago, when a gang lawyer put a gun to my forehead and demanded journalistic silence; ten years ago, when I was released from prison after being unjustly sentenced; two months ago, when I faced my torturer in a court for six hours, while he smiled, sure of his near impunity. Each time I had the indescribable, solid and implacable certainty that something must be done, something significant and on a mass scale, finally to free ourselves from structural violence and abuse. To release ourselves once and for all from the absurd conviction that this country does not belong to us, that it is the nation of others, the water of others, the mines of others, education for others, the freedom and privilege of others, our female bodies appropriated by others. We the dispossessed must end this madness.

A dizzying clarity occasionally overtakes me, and my desire to say everything, to hear and tell it all, is revived. Like a little girl holding in her hands a baby bird just fallen from its nest, I go through life showing something that we think is possible: freedom in the making, some tiny wings, a diminutive sparrow that some day will rise up through pale skies after the storm and the thunder.

I believed that it was misery talking to me, but later I found, thanks to the poets and writers who were with me during so many solitary nights, that it was otherness that wounded me to my soul. So many times I have been *the others*, so many times I walked in their shoes, that without knowing it I stopped being myself, the solitary reporter. I became us, and I feared for us. It was not death I desired, but the excising of that multitude that inhabits me after twenty-five years of being a journalist confronting a system that abhors justice and rewards institutionalised abuse.

I discovered one afternoon, imbibing the blue sky with my eyes, that after being so near the mothers of the disappeared, I began unknowingly to disappear. I feared for their sons and our daughters, and from showing so much strength to those in power I involuntarily made many of the dispossessed believe that I held a vital, hope-bringing power in my hands. They turned me into a symbol because I dared to challenge the cruel abusers tirelessly and head-on, without negotiating with the powerful. The symbol inhabited me slowly, but I gave it little room to grow in my heart while I was distracted in the daily battle of life and death. I feared my power, which was not conventional power. I feared the power of knowing the truth and naming it as I would a bird just fallen from its nest. I rejected it like one refusing her own story out of pure exhaustion; I wanted to be a normal woman, in a ramshackle

country with cruel or weak people in power, and brilliant intellectuals preaching from atop a golden mountain. I feared having the
answer because I knew that there would be no calm, no rest or
respite or forgetting ... only truths that are out there waiting for
us to write, to tell them, chronicle and report them. Truths like
leaf-cutter ants that never stop moving in hordes, invading cities
and homes. Living truths inhabited me with their foreboding and
I knew how to name them with first and last names, how to trans-
late them so that others could understand them and use them in the
service of social justice as glass beads, as tools, as whips.

In silence I feared I could never again be that simple woman
who writes poetry in secret, who dives into the depths of underwater caves, who laughs heartily at English comedians; I felt
nostalgia for the I that I had been before becoming us, that simple
woman who cooked sweet crepes and lamb in red wine, or who
spun tortillas on the hotplate and made rice with beans and green
chillies. That I from before no longer exists, she was discarded
along the way without my knowing.

I made myself a solemn promise: I would never turn into a
cynical journalist like those cavalier colleagues of mine, war cor-
respondents who swell with manliness from seeing so much death,
who little by little have been bled dry of hope until they drink the
honey of cynicism. Cynics are dogs thirsting for blood, for a fight.
I have wanted nothing to do with them. I distance myself from
their seductive words and their tedious and mocking lessons, their
parties with toasts and blood-stained drugs, their loud and bewitch-
ing fame and absurd celebrity status.

And one afternoon like any other, after responding to a thousand questions about my research, I picked up my pen and a white
page, pristine like the tail of a cloud protecting me from a brilliant
light . . . and just like that I discovered I am incapable of bowing

subserviently as so many others have done, and I decided it is time to close the notebook, empty the fountain pen, say goodbye to that way of looking at the world. I ventured in search of new registers, new voices, and other ways of living, without fear of retaliation or fear of my own power. I breathed like one emerging from the sea after a long and solitary dive. It was then and only then that I could write these confessions, the secrets of a reporter who in her diaries tells of the little life led by the one who narrates immense, multiple lives: the lives of those who matter.

That is why I never told you how for years I have kept myself safe from harm in the arms of poetry; how with other voices I sailed – as on a life raft – through imaginary worlds. You have no idea how many novels led me to live in other realities less dangerous than mine, than ours. How many written voices breathed new life into the paths my own words took. Walter Benjamin was not wrong when he claimed that "there is a sphere of human understanding that is inaccessible to violence: the true and singular sphere of understanding, which is language. But language and its comprehension do not always extend along the horizon that unites us; at times, some people speak words and others shout barbarisms that clash like swords in a dreadful babel." That is why in the privacy of my studio, in the jungle tower I inhabit in solitude, language comes to rest gently on my naked body, on my bared soul, where there is no room for violence; I have blocked its way by following my instinct. I want only to hear wise words that show me the way, not the ones that drag me towards a pre-determined destiny of the famous.

You do not know, because it is a private ritual, how much life is renewed in me every time I lose myself in the sea, when I swim down through its depths where the human voice has no place, there where the light reinvents itself and the earth thrums without human intervention. You do not know, nor would you have reason to understand, why I need those successive isolations, and so much silence, or why sailing free of land, without gadgets or pretensions, fills me with peace.

Nor does anyone know how fervently I carry out my morning rituals, when I merely receive in silence – and sometimes in overwhelmed gratitude – the arrival of a new day, a day when I can look down at my hands and know I still exist for the words that name me. No-one knows how I breathe and meditate to take in the vital air that allows me to keep writing every day, how I listen to music while I prepare my breakfast, and how I climb the stairs doing a little *paso doble* to a tune I just heard. I reach my studio at the top and give myself over to the task of writing, of planning my work with a mug of coffee in hand and a pile of stories in my notebooks, a host of living faces in my camera and a rainbow of voices on my recorder.

Nor do you know, though maybe you can intuit, how important love is for me. How I delight in succulent kisses, in sweet, furious embraces, how I enjoy with all my humanity the frollicking of two warm, damp, soft, delirious bodies. Every encounter traces a new line on my landscape, every ecstatic tremor resuscitates my strength. The dance of intimacy colours my life with happiness. Losing passion, for me, is non-negotiable.

Like one seeing a new sunrise, I enjoy the daily messages from my sisters and my brothers, the continual I-love-you-daughter from my worried father, and the anecdotes, memes, emoticons and kisses from the girls and boys who make up the vital force of my big family.

I never told you that my happiness and pleasure are not fortuitous, because I care for them and cultivate their flowers like jasmine. I nourish them with vital nutrients; take my melancholy

out for a stroll under the marine sun so it can slough off all the bad.
I tell my lungs, with my hand at my chest, that they must breathe
every morning; until that breath reaches my belly, nothing is true.
My body knows this, and it walks to the rhythm of my breathing. My arms reach out, my legs dance as though searching for the
happiness lost during nights of anguish. I dance to revive the rite of
vital emotion, I play my drum to tell the earth that we are still here
to defend her, and to defend our right to the unhurried joy that has
nothing to do with power and everything to do with compassion,
the simple and uncomplicated human encounter – the kind that
does not savage, does not abuse, does not kill: the kind that loves.

I never told you that every day, all the days of my life, I struggle
with the death that lurks in various forms, and I emerge victorious
because this life deserves me and I deserve it too. Because in my
heart I live with every one of my fifteen journalist colleagues and
women's rights defenders who have been murdered at the hands of
powerful narco-politicians, and with every one of my twelve friends
who have disappeared. I have not told you that every time I answer
the phone at night I am afraid there is another lost life behind the
call, or another threatened comrade, or another companion fleeing
the country to save her life. I never told you that there is nothing
in this world like survivor's guilt, that at every funeral, in every
communiqué and during every tireless search, those of us who have
survived the others wonder: Why am I still here? And we will never
find a valid answer. We are both those who are gone and ourselves.
When the blank page will not accept one more story, their spirits
are behind me, their hands on my hand, their words in my voice.
Because no-one kills the truth by killing journalists.

Perhaps I never told you any of this because I knew that no-one,
absolutely no-one, should live being tortured or stalked, fleeing
death for twenty years simply for having decided to assume her

civic responsibility and answer the call to make this a better world.

I write without stopping because the others live in my words with me, and when I am gone you will know that I told you how the days and nights are lived alone in a country that, for now, kills its journalists and its activists to keep an outrageous, unjust, and arbitrary power system alive. A system unquestionably exposed and weakened by the work of those who have died along the way, and by those of us who have decided to live in spite of the torture and the seductive voice of self-censorship that promises a calm and placid life within the celebrity elite of conformists.

Here we are again, looking out the window toward a possible future that needs honest words, trustworthy power, and the revolution of dangerous ideas. You and I are meeting on a fateful afternoon in Latin America; what others see as a "spring", to us signals a ruthless autumn to come. We must prepare for it by recognising our pain and achievements and our individual power to exercise and foster the human rights that belong to us. Indignation and justice will save us, but rage and blinding hate never will. That is why many, like me, have chosen the former and closed the door to the latter.

Indignation is the ink with which I write the names of those hundred thousand dead Mexicans, the sixty thousand disappeared, the twenty thousand boys and girls kidnapped by drug cartels; I am indignation, and I am the others. Now, after a half-century of life, I walk more slowly, but my steps have traced a route that knew no limits; as long as I live I will walk in my name and the names of the women who are gone and whose legs can walk no more, but whose ideas must never die. We are the utopia our grandmothers dreamed of.

Translated by Megan McDowell

III

MAKING A STAND

THE DREAM OF JESÚS FRAGOSO

Emiliano Ruiz Parra

I – Agrarian history

In his descendants' memories of him, Don Jesús Fragoso Aceves, or
El Chango (Country Boy) as he was known, is dressed as a farmer,
in cowboy hat, homespun trousers, and sandals, a rough bag slung
over his shoulder. This was how he was dressed, like a poor Indian,
when he went to the Supreme Court building, one of the major
centres of power in Mexico City, and walked into the offices of
the justices, who would rise from their benches to greet him with
respect, even reverence.

Many years earlier, even before people began adding the honor-
ific "Don" to his name, Jesús Fragoso took part in the first agrarian
assemblies in his village of Guadalupe Victoria. The year was 1955
and the people were alarmed. A minority faction of villagers were
trying to sell off two large fields named Potrero del Rey and La
Laguna, which the people in their rural town had been using for
some ninety years. Good pastureland in the dry season, the fields
turned to wetlands during the rainy months. Thousands of birds
flew south from Canada in the winter to enjoy the warm lake water,
while the villagers hunted for ruddy ducks, coots, mudhens, wood
ducks and other migratory waterfowl.

The rumour mill was abuzz: they are going to sell the common
land. Then the story was confirmed. Lawyers showed up in their

suits and ties with an official document from the state of Mexico
(or Edomex as it is generally known, to distinguish it from nearby
Mexico City). The common lands of Guadalupe Victoria "have
been adjudicated to the state government", in the words of File
210-1-8605, signed by Jorge Jiménez Cantú, Secretary of State
for Edomex. The lawyers displayed the sales contract and, indeed,
there were the signatures of a few people from Guadalupe Victoria,
selling fields that had belonged to them all.

The villagers who had sold the land defended their position.
They were disgruntled with the way the village had parcelled out
its land and they laid claim to the lake and the meadows. They
were not alone. They boasted the support of the governor of
Edomex, a guy born in Atlacomulco named Salvador Sánchez
Colín. These fields, they said, are going to be for the governor.

Alarmed by the situation, most of the villagers in Guadalupe
Victoria began to organise. It was true, some fifty villagers wanted
to sell the land. But more than 250 were opposed to the sale.
These common lands, they said, were left to us by our grandparents, they belong to us all, and we should all be free to continue
using them in common. But they were poor folk. They had no
land documents and no money for lawyers. On 5 October 1957
they elected Jesús Fragoso Aceves (who had turned thirty on
25 June that year) to represent them in the defence of their land.
His first task was to reconstruct the property records, because
nobody had the documents. A labyrinthine job awaited him, requir-
ing years of research and paperwork in government agencies.

*   *   *

It took Jesús (El Chango) Fragoso five years to gather the papers
detailing the history of the fields of Guadalupe Victoria, his village,

today a neighbourhood in the north of Ecatepec, a former rural town that has become a populous working-class suburb of Mexico City. The year 1865 had been one of the most tumultuous in Mexican history. French troops had invaded the country and installed Archduke Maximilian of Habsburg, who crowned himself Emperor of Mexico. President Benito Juárez, a Zapotec Indian, had packed the legitimate government of the country into a horse-drawn carriage and fled north, pursued by the invading troops and pro-imperialist Mexican forces.

Perhaps the national events brought it about. Ángel García Quintana had recently bought the hacienda of Santa María Guadalupe de Portales (situated where Guadalupe Victoria is today), but he had fallen behind on his payments to the former owners of the estate. He was not a rich man. The purchase money came from his wife, Josefa Tijera, who had died without a will. Finding himself in a tight spot, with the added pressure of the invaders' roaring cannons, García Quintana came up with a plan to save his estate: he would sell the least productive part of the hacienda – the wetlands of Lake Xaltocan, a rocky stretch of land, and the pasturelands. A good thousand hectares. And who would be his most interested buyers? The field hands who worked on the hacienda itself.

The villagers of Guadalupe Victoria (or Pueblo Nuevo as it was called back then) hailed mainly from the state of Jalisco in the west of the country. The previous owners of the hacienda of Santa María de Guadalupe de Portales (a family named Ansorena) had imported their labour force from Jalisco. On every trip they had carted back ten or fifteen men, and over the years the field hands had brought their families to join them. The hacienda owner rented small plots of land to the families, where they put up shacks with thin pine-slat walls and roofs tiled with century-plant leaves, the traditional housing of the poor Indians of the region. At first they all saw each other as kin, and many shared the surname Fragoso.

In nineteenth-century Mexico it was exceptionally rare for field hands on an agricultural estate to be given an opportunity to own the land they tilled. So they jumped at the chance. Each family turned over their savings: the poorest put down 10 pesos each; the richest, 500. Between them all, the sixty families, after seven years of scrimping and sacrificing, put together nearly 20,000 pesos in gold (plus another 2,000 pesos for the deed to the land). They paid off the last penny in 1872 and became the legal owners of five ranches: De Valdez, El Rosal, La Troje, El Obraje and Ranchería de Pueblo Nuevo.

By then Benito Juárez had recovered the presidency and had Maximilian executed by a firing squad. Juárez was born a Zapotec Indian, and as a poor country boy he tended sheep for a while in his village of Guelatao, Oaxaca. Possessed of an exceptional character and intelligence, as an adult he became the undisputed leader of Mexican liberals. Mexico, in the view of his followers, needed to modernise, and their notion of modernisation left no room for indigenous culture or traditions. The Constitution of 1857, written under Juárez' influence, banned the collective ownership of land that indigenous peoples had practised since pre-Hispanic times. Juárez and the liberals were the great promoters of capitalism in Mexico, and the prime showcase for the new capitalist relations was precisely the Mexican countryside, even if it meant trampling on the century-old traditions of the country.

So the sixty rural families of Guadalupe Victoria bought their land under the Juárez laws depriving communities of the right to own land collectively. Now, sixty people were too many owners for one estate, but civil law made allowances for them to buy the land jointly (just as a married couple may own property jointly). They remained in this legal category for decades. With the passing of the generations, the original sixty joint owners multiplied among children and grandchildren. Eventually they agreed to work their land under two sets of rules: first they parcelled out more than 600 hectares as private property, dividing the land in proportion as to how much money each family had contributed in 1865. Then they left in common ownership the Lake Xaltocan wetlands and the meadows so that everyone could fish, hunt waterfowl, and graze their livestock.

As highly as the story of this purchase speaks for the organising abilities of the people of Guadalupe Victoria, we should not idealise the community; exploitative relationships were reproduced inside it. One villager, Ángel Fragoso Gallo, amassed a tidy sum through loansharking and used it to buy up fields, becoming thereby a substantial landowner. He hired the former owners of his land as field hands and set up his own *tienda de raya*, a company store that used a system of short-term loans in exchange for purchases of basic provisions, turning his workers into lifelong debtors. The time came when Ángel Fragoso was the only boss offering work to the farmhands in the village.

In 1910 a revolution had begun in Mexico, leading by 1917 to the most progressive constitution in the world up to that time. One of the heroes of the revolution was Emiliano Zapata, the head of the Liberating Army of the South, whose slogan was "The land belongs to those who work it". In that spirit, the new constitution rolled back the Juárez land laws and promoted the collective ownership of the countryside. The communities that owned and worked their land in common were called *ejidos* and their villagers were called *comuneros*.

*   *   *

By April 20, 1962, Jesús Fragoso Aceves (El Chango), could recount this history with documents in hand. The time had come for the revolution to do them justice. On that afternoon the village assembly of Guadalupe Victoria confirmed him as their representative, and in a letter addressed to President Adolfo López Mateos the villagers asked to be recognised as *comuneros* and to be given legal title to La Laguna and Potrero del Rey, the two properties that had been set apart from the parcelling out of the cropland.

In addition to their recognition as a community with rights to their land, the villagers of Guadalupe Victoria distributed their cropland. Just as their predecessors had done in 1925 and 1940 with Potrero del Rey and a portion of Rancho de Valdez, they used a lottery system. They allocated the fields only for the purposes of farming; legally, the whole parcel still belonged to the community as an entity. Lake Xaltocan was almost dried up by then, drained by the Great Drainage Canal that had been laboriously completed between 1865 and 1900. So they divided the former wetlands into 265 lots of 8,500 square metres a piece plus another 75 lots of 4,250 square metres each, and they distributed them to be farmed.

Gaining recognition as *comuneros* was a way of keeping out of the clutches of politicians who wanted to steal their land. Common lands belonged to the nation, to the Mexican state (which in turn allowed the communities use-rights over them), and were inalienable, not for sale. There was a purpose behind this law: to prevent the great capitalists from turning the clock back to the time of Porfirio Díaz, assembling large estates and treating their field hands like slaves.

If the fields of Guadalupe Victoria were declared private property, however, they would be subject to sale. And you can be sure the political bosses were eager to get their hands on such prime real estate. The minority faction of Guadalupe Victoria no longer boasted the support of Salvador Sánchez Colín, who had left the governorship in 1957, but rather that of the new governor of Edomex, Juan Fernández, who (according to the dissidents) was going to buy the land from them.

El Chango got the bureaucratic ball rolling. The engineers of the Agrarian Advisory Board (C.C.A.) – a group of specialists that issued technical reports – went to the village, convened assemblies, pored over documents, took measurements, and on July 3, 1964, published their report, affirming that the residents of Guadalupe Victoria in the north of Ecatepec had the legal capacity to be recognised as *comuneros*.

Their common lands, according to the C.C.A., covered 392 hectares (twice the size of the principality of Monaco and nine times that of Vatican City), divided into La Laguna (310 hectares) and Potrero del Rey (82 hectares). The C.C.A. declared that there were no internal conflicts and asserted that "there are no parcels of private property that should be excluded from the area to which they are to be given title". In other words, they annulled all the land sales to the political bosses from Edomex.

It had taken him ten years, but El Chango had won the legal battle. Or so it seemed. But then things began to fall apart. On September 24, 1964, forty-seven dissidents sent a letter to the president of Mexico demanding the suspension of the villagers' recognition as *comuneros*. They wanted to divide the land according to the terms of the original purchase in 1865 by making the 392 hectares private property and thus subject to sale.

Strangely, the C.C.A. began to rule against their own studies and reports: on March 5, 1965, they called for a halt to the process of recognising the common lands. They suspended their earlier decision.

As long as Juan Fernández remained in governorship (1963–69), El Chango found himself gradually losing one battle after another. The dissidents obtained lawyers, wrote letters, and initiated legal proceedings. On the national level, the situation had turned bloody: on October 2, 1968, elite Mexican army soldiers massacred a group of peaceful student protesters in the Plaza de Tlatelolco in the centre of Mexico City. The massacre was a warning to the whole country: whoever refuses to submit to the will of the state will be met with bullets and repression.

On June 9, 1970, the blow fell against Guadalupe Victoria. President Gustavo Díaz Ordaz, the man who had ordered the Tlatelolco massacre, signed the decree denying the villagers of Guadalupe Victoria the right to become *comuneros*. His argument was absurd: the sixty original purchasers in 1865 had bought the land under the constitution of 1867, which deprived communities of the right to collective ownership of land; therefore, a century later and under a different set of laws, they had no right to be *comuneros*.

An odd explanation for a regime that claimed to be heir to the Mexican revolution. Díaz Ordaz' decision was so ridiculous that it contradicted a legal opinion issued by his own administration. On March 4, 1970, the president's legal advisory board had upheld the villagers' right to be recognised as *comuneros* by the simple logic that, though they had bought the land under the Juárez laws, they had functioned between 1917 and 1965 as a *de facto* community and should be recognised as such.

It must be said that Díaz Ordaz may have merely been acting as the instrument for this blow against the villagers. The 392 hectares of Guadalupe Victoria had attracted the attention of the most powerful man in the country, President Luis Echeverría Álvarez (1970–76). Though Echeverría would not be sworn into office until December 1, 1970, in keeping with the curious customs of the P.R.I. regime he had actually taken over the reins of the country from the moment he was unveiled as the official party's presidential candidate. Officials made sure the villagers of Guadalupe Victoria knew that it was a bunch of Luis Echeverría's close relatives who wanted the land for a private business deal, setting up a dairy operation to supply milk products to the Valley of Mexico.

Ever since the Tlatelolco massacre of October 2, 1968, hundreds of young people had turned to radicalised forms of struggle, joining guerrilla groups and revolutionary organisations aimed at overthrowing the state. Echeverría responded with the Dirty War, a wave of political repression that swept across the nation. Some 1,300 young people were disappeared by agents of the state (we never heard from them again); many more were murdered, tortured or illegally imprisoned.

Guadalupe Victoria was living through its own dirty war. Roberto Aceves Herrera, the village historian, recounted the repression that his community experienced from 1968 to 1983. Hundreds of police would take over the streets in the early hours of the morning, arresting dozens of men and women, harassing them and marching them through the streets in their underwear before throwing them into jail. They beat pregnant women with the butts of their rifles and used tear gas to break up political meetings.

But Jesús Fragoso did not give up. On June 15, 1973, he filed an appeal against the president's decree. No-one was surprised when the Second Judge of the Federal District rejected his appeal. Undaunted, El Chango jumped straight back into the fight, taking the case to the highest court in the land, the National Supreme Court of Justice, seeking to overturn the presidential decision.

The government responded even more viciously: on November 5, 1973, 500 police occupied the village. Officers arrested villagers tilling their fields and tossed tear gas at women who came out to protest. Meanwhile, more thugs were putting up concrete posts and fencing off La Laguna and Potrero del Rey with barbed wire. For years afterwards, Guadalupe Victoria was caught in an absurd situation: hundreds of armed police, manning security booths and out on patrol, guarded a fence enclosing an area that contained nothing but fields sown with maize and beetroots as well as some oats and barley, and a few wetland pools where herons and swallows nested.

The fence went up in Guadalupe Victoria precisely at harvest time, and the crops rotted in the fields. The government was trying to wear the villagers down through hunger and terror. Don Jesús Fragoso spent long periods hiding in caves in the hills because the police were searching for him house to house. They grabbed his mother, Antonia Aceves Díaz, and "beat her like beasts", recalls Cecilio Aceves Herrera, a cousin of Don Jesús and a village chronicler.

His brother, Roberto Aceves Herrera, another village chronicler, wrote: "The village said, 'Those who are on the outside should rescue those who are on the inside [of the jail],' and that is what they did, until only a few remained [free]; the ones most wanted by the judicial police were the communal representative Jesús Fragoso and his brothers Refugio and Israel Fragoso. Several times all three were in jail together." Police officers had notified the villagers that the land had already been sold: the P.R.I. politician had obtained a loan of 660 million pesos from the development bank to buy the land and set up their dairy operation.

While he was on the run, Don Jesús became a sculptor. He made stone sculptures of Tlaloc and Ehecatl, the gods worshipped by the emperor Moctezuma. Serpents, frogs, beetles. Jesús and his cousins Roberto and Cecilio Aceves Herrera claimed the Aztec past as their own and devoted themselves to the task of documenting pre-Hispanic settlements in Guadalupe Victoria. Having no money now to hire a lawyer, El Chango read law books and taught himself to be a lawyer. He specialised in criminal law – to defend himself against being jailed – and also became an expert in agrarian law.

It was during these years that he arrived at the Supreme Court dressed in sandals and cowboy hat, and the judges greeted him with respect, even reverence. He was a frequent presence. For years the judges saw him work tirelessly, formulating writs, presenting arguments, bringing up judicial theories, dusting off speeches by revolutionary legislators, and holding forth on constitutional law.

At last, after a long struggle, Don Jesús Fragoso, a poor and persecuted farmer, won one of the most important victories in the history of rural Mexico: on March 13, 1980, the Supreme Court ruled in his favour, overturning the presidential decree from 1970. Those 392 hectares belonged to no-one but the village of Guadalupe Victoria and they were safe, the highest court in the land declared, from an arbitrary decision by the president.

Highest court? Only on paper. Throughout the P.R.I. regime (1929–2000), Mexico was under the six-year monarchy, as Daniel Cosío Villegas termed it, of the president of the republic. So the police continued to dole out kickings and beatings as if the Supreme Court had done nothing. It was not until the night of September 15, 1980 that hundreds of men and women, outraged and fed up with the abuse, left their houses and with their bare hands tore down the barbed wire enclosing their fields, an ominous net representing the pillage by politicians set on robbing them blind. They took advantage of the fact that it was a holiday night (Mexico celebrates its independence on September 15) and the police were absent or drunk. Rip down the wire! Rip it down!

Their struggle had only just begun. They pulled down the barbed wire, but the police did not withdraw until 1983, when the country was going through an economic crisis brought on by the national debt and falling oil prices, and President Miguel de la Madrid (1982–88) was looking to quell social conflicts. From then on, instead of turning to the police for repression, the government used bureaucracy. The government now posed the question: what is the scope of the Supreme Court's decision? It was an absurd question, a malevolent question, but the government clung to it in order to keep it from being put into effect.

And so began a new battle for Jesús Fragoso, this one in a quagmire of courts and paperwork. The Supreme Court decision was sent back to the Superior Agrarian Court, which forwarded it to the District Agrarian Court, which asked to see the report from the C.C.A., which discovered new mistakes and sent it back to the District Court. Here I am saving the reader from all the trips to the Ministry of Agrarian Reform and the civil courts and the recycled technical and judicial reports that were demanded here or there to gain time and delay the Supreme Court decision from being carried out.

I have summed it up in one paragraph but all this meant sixteen long years that further poisoned relationships between neighbours, including relatives. The country changed once more: in 1992, President Carlos Salinas de Gortari (1988–94), Mexico's answer to Ronald Reagan in his addiction to neoliberalism, amended the 1917 constitution. For the first time in 75 years, common lands could be sold into private hands (even when they were recognised as *comuneros*, the villagers of Guadalupe Victoria could sell their land so long as they agreed on doing so at a village assembly). Salinas opened the doors to the return of large agricultural estates. Under the new agrarian laws, the 23rd District Agrarian Court took on the Guadalupe Victoria case on November 26, 1993. More Kafkaesque episodes: the case file travels in and out of government offices, accumulating more and more documents until it swells to 26 volumes in length.

At last, on April 10, 1997, the anniversary of the assassination of Emiliano Zapata, Judge Fernando Rojo of the 23rd District Agrarian Court delivered justice. He ruled that the Supreme Court had been correct: Guadalupe Victoria was a de facto community and should be given legal recognition; their 392 hectares were properly classified as inalienable. In other words, any deeds of sale concerning land within its borders were null and void. Only the residents of Guadalupe Victoria could make use of the wetlands and meadows in La Laguna and Potrero del Rey.

But not yet, because in Mexico no decision is binding until it is published in the official government register. Four months went by before, on August 8, 1997, the judge's sentence was published in the *Diario Oficial de la Federación*.

Now there could be no doubt. The people of Guadalupe Victoria could enjoy their 392 hectares without fear of having them stolen by governors or presidents. Don Jesús Fragoso Aceves, seventy years of age, was the legal representative and historic leader of a triumphant community that possessed an exceptionally valuable expanse of land. After forty years of lost battles, Don Jesús Fragoso Aceves had won the war.

II – Urban history

On January 6, 1996, Leticia Solorio spent the night in Golondrinas for the first time. She had hammered four wooden poles into the ground and, in place of walls, had wrapped cloth from large sugar sacks around them. The next morning Leticia and her two young daughters woke up, soaking wet and exhausted after a sleepless night. After the night's rain, the neighbourhood of Golondrinas greeted them in all its splendour: their house was a tiny island, a clearing amidst a sea of maize and alfalfa fields, surrounded by puddles where salamanders swam and snails emerged from the mud. Over there she saw a mole and a rabbit scurrying, and herons sliced the air like winged arrows.

But how had it all begun for Leticia and her neighbors in this parcel named Golondrinas, inside the common lands of Guadalupe Victoria? It had begun one year earlier, in 1995. The worst economic crisis in modern Mexican history had pushed hundreds of thousands of people from their homes, forcing them to seek shelter on the outskirts of cities, in what then was still cropland. That crisis was the final breaking point, but not the only one. Ten years before, on September 19, 1985, a 7.9-magnitude earthquake had destroyed hundreds of buildings in the centre of Mexico City, killing 5,000 people by the government's reckoning; N.G.O.s estimated a death toll of 40,000. Thousands of victims sought refuge in the outer suburbs of the nation's capital.

Though, to be more precise, we would have to look back several more years, to the decade of the 1970s. The Mexican government was promoting an industrial corridor in the village of San Pedro Xalostoc, Ecatepec, Edomex. Farming communities suddenly saw their fields overrun by factories; their *ejidos* (communally owned lands) were turned into working-class neighbourhoods, and their old mule trails became avenues crowded with buses and pickups crammed with factory workers. Throughout the 1970s and into the 1980s, San Pedro Xalostoc was transformed into the epicentre of strikes during an era in Mexican history known as "the workers' insurgency".

It is less than fifteen kilometres from San Pedro Xalostoc to Guadalupe Victoria. In the 1970s, the villagers of Guadalupe Victoria were dealing with the enclosure of their fields and the beatings by the police. The government had decided that their village and their fields belonged under the jurisdiction of the municipality of Ecatepec in Edomex. Repression was undermining their

morale. They were not alone in their misfortune. The Mexican
countryside as a whole was falling into bankruptcy, sending
thousands of field hands silently into exile in the United States.
The villagers of Guadalupe Victoria, deprived of their fields, sought
other means of making a living. Some became artisans. Some took
jobs in the industrial zone. Others worked in construction. Many
women became domestic servants in middle-class homes in Mexico
City. They would live in their employers' homes five days a week,
returning to the village for Saturday and Sunday.

A curious character made his appearance in Ecatepec during
those years; for economy's sake, we will call him "the estate agent".
He wears pointy boots and a cowboy hat. He shows up among the
villagers and offers them hard cash for their fields. A cool 100,000
pesos. He buys up a hectare here and a hectare there. He divides
each of these hectares into fifty or seventy lots of 120 square metres
each. He offers these bits of land for sale at a price of 25,000 pesos.
They are wasteland. Rocky fields. No water, electricity, sewers,
pavements or roads. It does not matter. All he has to do is advertise
in a sports paper: "Parcels for sale." Or pin a flyer to a tree: "No
home? Living with relatives or renting? Come see us." Within a
couple of days, one or two hundred people in urgent need of shelter
will call: those forced from the city by the 1985 earthquake or the
1995 economic crisis.

But these sales are fraudulent. Or "irregular", at least. Because
his customers are buying fragments of land that were distributed
to the *ejido* community by the agrarian reform following the revolution. By law, these fields belong to the nation. Their owner is the
Mexican state, which grants use-rights over them to the village
farmers, and they are inalienable. The law forbids or complicates
their sale. But these things are taking place on the ground: the
villager signs a deed of sale with the estate agent. The agent signs a

similar deed with Leticia Solorio (or any other new resident), who agrees to pay him 700 pesos a month for the next five years. In less than 24 hours, Leticia shows up with her four wooden poles to build a shelter and make her dream of owning her own house come true. But every one of these deeds and sales is worthless in the eyes of the law. These fields still belong to the Mexican state.

By 1990 Jesús Fragoso, El Chango, is still fighting the good fight, but the villagers of Guadalupe Victoria have grown tired of waiting. They decide to divvy up the 392 hectares, even though they are still the subject of a lawsuit against the nation. Their children and grandchildren have multiplied and so are inheriting small plots of 1,000 square metres, and finally of 600 square metres. Some of them plant maize. Others wait for the fraudulent estate agent to show up so they can sell out to him. Still others learn to be estate agents themselves and sell their plots to new residents.

And everyone knows that carving up the property of the Mexican state and selling it as house lots is against the law in Edomex. The new resident (the "settler", people call him) lives in terror: any day the police may appear, throw him into the street, and destroy his cardboard shack. But he has no reason to worry; the country has made a transition from an authoritarian regime to a (more or less) democratic one. The P.R.I. is no longer the sole ruling party. Now it has to compete with opposition parties that join the electoral campaign for public office. Not even two decades have passed, but how distant 1976 seems, when José López Portillo was the only candidate running for president and he won with just a shade under 100 per cent of the vote.

We are in the decade of the 1990s and there are ballot boxes to fill. The P.R.I. sees that the estate agent can be very useful, and they come to an agreement with him: impunity in exchange for votes. This urban cowboy feels powerful now. He has got the government behind him! He grows bolder and kicks up the fraud, selling the same lot two or three times over. Or he pays the villager 10 or 20 per cent and then runs off. In a few years, the estate agent has become a problem for the ruling P.R.I. So he reaches a final agreement: he takes his winnings and disappears.

The estate agents have unwittingly discovered a gold mine: the land transfer. The villager sells a field for 100,000 pesos and the estate agent makes a million. But there is something even better: its political profitability. The settlers are hostage to the P.R.I. government. Want water? Support the P.R.I. candidate. Want electricity? Turn out at P.R.I. rallies. Want pavements? Vote for the P.R.I. Want clear title to your land? Join the P.R.I. Refuse to bend your knee? Watch out, because we're going to throw you out on the street and smash up your cardboard hut.

The urban periphery is no longer simply a place: it becomes a relationship of exploitation, a modern pact of serfdom in which the government (the P.R.I.) offers protection and public services in exchange for political fealty. This process is written down nowhere. But it is quickly learned. Settlers are poor and have no choice but to put up with it. If the settler is a man, he leaves home before daybreak and commutes two or three hours to his job. If she is a woman, she stays home. She goes for water, sometimes walking kilometres to bring home a couple of buckets. She sells food in the local markets. She knits sweaters. And she is the one, almost always, who participates in the political activities mandated by the P.R.I.

Jesús Fragoso, El Chango, notices that times have changed. The land he has spent years fighting for will never be maize fields again but rather housing tracts for the poor. His neighbours from Guadalupe Victoria have also been swindled: estate agents got deeds of sale from the villagers and disappeared without paying.

The era of estate agents soon ended. El Chango now faces a new character, the "housing advocacy association". Being an estate agent entailed legal risks. The new method is safer: hide behind a phantom organisation. If a legal problem arises, change the president, the board of directors, and nobody's the wiser. P.R.I. politicians fostered these associations and hid behind them.

In 1993 Jesús Fragoso had his first run-in with one of these phantom organisations. At 3.00 in the morning on November 2 (Day of the Dead in Mexico), the new neighbourhood of La Joya was invaded by 1,500 police, some of them on horseback, who attacked the settlers and destroyed their houses. According to the government, this tract of land belonged to the Popular Pro-Housing Union of Settlers, a P.R.I. front group. In reality, it was part of the 392 hectares that the village of Guadalupe Victoria was trying to recover through the courts.

Don Jesús Fragoso was outraged, and that morning he came out to lead a protest of some hundred neighbours. His boldness cost him dear. The police arrested him and five others. They threw him in jail for land-grabbing (grabbing his own land!), racketeering and assault. The repression against the residents and El Chango was so violent that the U.N. Committee for Human Rights asked the Mexican Foreign Ministry for information about the evictions.

A few months later people began settling in the dried-out basin of Lake Xaltocan. They called this area La Laguna. Don Jesús realised that the process was inexorable and he raised a new demand: the construction of a university, a public institution for vocational studies that would be open to the grandchildren of the former farmers and the new settlers alike. He was self-educated. His relatives had not been taught to read or write. Their struggle for the land made them autodidacts. Don Jesús had read more law books than most lawyers. His cousin Roberto Aceves Herrera had taught himself to be a historian and had written the history of his village from the Pleistocene Age to the present. But they were exceptional cases. The young people, he thought, deserved a better future. Taking classes to become qualified certified professionals. No more being dirt-poor field hands, factory workers, or domestic servants.

In those years when Don Jesús proposed his dream of a public university, Mexico was going through one of its greatest upheavals. On January 1, 1994, the indigenous people of Chiapas rose up in rebellion and a few months later the P.R.I. candidate for president, Luis Donaldo Colosio, was assassinated in Tijuana, across the border from the United States. Hundreds of new neighbourhoods fostered by the P.R.I. were named in Colosio's memory. So it was that La Laguna was renamed Colonia Luis Donaldo Colosio, or Colosio for short. This decision left no doubts about which party was in charge there.

And yet down in the underground another actor was beginning to emerge: the left. In the 1970s and early 1980s a workers' insurgency had arisen across the country, including in the industrial corridor of San Pedro Xalostoc, Ecatepec. Dozens of strikes were suppressed by police truncheons. This process had left a few labour leaders scattered here and there. It had also given rise to a new generation of rebels who moved to the outskirts of the big cities, where they organised social struggles for water, electricity, and pavements and streets. One of them appears in this story: Faustino de la Cruz.

Faustino was an indigenous Nahuatl speaker who had migrated to Ecatepec to seek work in a factory. He had not yet turned thirty when he began challenging the P.R.I. for political control. On his free evenings, Faustino studied to become a school teacher. And he already had one political coup to his credit. In the *ejidos* of

San Cristóbal, another village in Ecatepec, he had established a neighbourhood primary school.

Don Jesús Fragoso learned of Faustino's efforts. He offered him one hectare in the new Colosio neighborhood to build three schools: kindergarten, primary, and high school. The young school teacher got to work. He organised the neighbours and convinced them that it could be done. They would build a school, even if they only had cardboard to build it with, bring in teachers, and in time the Ministry of Public Education would have to recognise it, validate the classes, and pay the teachers' salaries. The school was an urgent necessity in Colosio: the nearest school was three kilometres away on foot (there were no buses).

While Faustino organised the school, events were developing at breakneck speed. On April 10, 1997, the 23rd District Agrarian Court ruled that Jesús Fragoso and the villagers of Guadalupe Victoria were in the right, both legally and historically. They had won, after forty years of defeat after defeat: they were *comuneros*! The 392 hectares belonged to them alone! And on August 8 the decree was published. Yes, even though thousands of people were living there now, even if Leticia Solorio and thousands more like her had built shacks of wood and cardboard to sleep in.

Beginning on that day, August 8, Don Jesús Fragoso became a key figure in northern Ecatepec. El Chango was fine with letting his land be turned into housing tracts. But he repudiated the P.R.I. The P.R.I. had been harassing him for forty years. They had attempted to steal his land. They had beaten his mother. They had thrown him in jail time and time again, along with his brothers and neighbors. The estate agents of the P.R.I. had defrauded his brothers, his cousins, and his neighbors in Guadalupe Victoria. So El Chango wanted nothing to do with them. Anybody who wanted to reside on a plot within their 392 hectares would have to be approved by the Committee on Common Lands of Guadalupe Victoria. Now the villagers were in control, no longer the P.R.I. politicians.

Faustino de la Cruz, the young leftist leader, said goodbye to the residents of Colosio on the afternoon of Saturday, August 23, and went home for the night. The nine cardboard classrooms were finished and ready to open for classes on the first day of school, August 25. But around 3.00 in the morning some 500 police drove into the neighborhood. They fired into the air to scare off any protests. Using mechanical diggers they destroyed the classrooms and carted off the benches and blackboards. The P.R.I. mayor of Ecatepec, Jorge Torres, justified the destruction: the classrooms were built, he said, on land belonging to the Union of Civil and Private Associations for Popular Housing in Edomex. Another phantom masthead.

The following day, at 11.00 in the morning, the residents of Colosio marched to the mayor's office in Ecatepec. Don Jesús Fragoso was there. He told them, so that everyone could hear, that the Committee on Common Lands of Guadalupe Victoria was giving them one hectare of land, and that nobody should stand in their way, because they were under his protection.

A few days later another political rally was held. Don Jesús Fragoso, in the name of the Committee on Common Lands, gave the title to the land for a public high school to the National College of Professional Technical Education (C.O.N.A.L.E.P.), a public educational institution. He invited Faustino de la Cruz to be present. Also there, uninvited, was Rodolfo Valdés, the municipal administrator of Ecatepec. The same man who had ordered the destruction of the schools in Colosio. As soon as he saw him, Jesús Fragoso had him thrown out.

"And tell Jorge Torres [the mayor of Ecatepec] that Faustino has my full backing. If he's attacked, threatened, or intimidated again, the mayor can expect to see me with 3,000 people, because the people are in charge here, not him, a puppet imposed on us by corruption. That's what Jesús Aceves has to say to him, and if the mayor doesn't like it, we'll meet him in the open."

A few days later Jesús Fragoso Aceves was murdered.

On September 6 he held a party at his house. One by one his guests departed, until only one remained, who shot him in the head. His cousin, the village chronicler Roberto Aceves Herrera, aged thirty-three, carried on Don Jesús's struggle. He, too, was murdered. He was kidnapped on April 4, 2001. His lifeless body was found on April 11. They had mangled his left hand.

Don Jesús's murder was strategic. Today, nineteen years after his murder, the community has no legal representative. Its residents accuse the agrarian courts of obstructing their assemblies in a way that prevents them from resolving their issues. The villagers of Guadalupe Victoria have a right to compensation for the housing projects that have sprung up on their land. But to get it, they will need legal representation.

The settlers on the 392 hectares meanwhile remain in legal limbo. They are living on common lands belonging to the village of Guadalupe Victoria. Their housing is "irregular". Lacking title to their own homes, they are hostage to the modern pact of serfdom: P.R.I. politicians argue that they have no obligation to supply the settlers with water, electricity, or sewers, because they are squatting on common lands. But if they were to support the P.R.I. ...

The land history of Guadalupe Victoria is no mere anecdote. Its branches reach the upper echelons of Mexico's political system. The most stable political faction in the country arose in Edomex in the 1940s: the Atlacomulco Group. This group pulled off a political coup in the 2012 election; it conquered the presidency with the P.R.I. candidate, Enrique Peña Nieto, who had been the governor of Edomex from 2005 to 2011. His election to the presidency would have been impossible without his former control over Edomex, which had been based in part on the exploitation of the modern pact of serfdom with impoverished neighbourhoods on the outskirts of Mexico City. They have administered the "irregularity" of the housing situation. Ecatepec now has more than 1.5 million residents. And the title to 50 per cent of its area is "irregular". On this pretext, the politicians squeeze the residents for monthly sums of cash, or demand political support from them in exchange for water or paved streets.

The dream of Jesús Fragoso, to establish a public university on the common lands of Guadalupe Victoria, remains a dream.

Translated by David Frye

WAR MADE ME A FEMINIST

Marcela Turati

I

IT IS HARD TO PINPOINT the precise moment when I became a feminist, but I do know the transformation began around the time when I first reported on a war, a war that has been raging for more than a decade in my home country. I shall venture to sketch out two reference points: Ciudad Juárez and 2010.

At that time I had been a freelancer for around a dozen years, and had volunteered to cover what came to be known as "the war on drugs", from the city considered the epicentre of violence in Mexico. It would have been on a par with Baghdad in any contest for the title of the most lethal city on the planet, even though I was unaware of such facts to begin with. Back then, all I knew was that Ciudad Juárez was familiar to me, as a frontier post I had previously reported on, located only three hours away from Chihuahua City where I grew up.

There was no one moment of epiphany to which I owe my conversion. My memory holds a kaleidoscope of significant instants. I remember following in death's footsteps across the flat and deserted city, its centre in ruins, already absurdly scattered and dispersed by bad town planning, where sweatshops sit side by side with boarded-up housing estates, car breakers' yards and vacant lots, where dust storms pile up dunes, trees and pavements are lacking, and weather tends to the extreme.

By this time, Ciudad Juárez had already turned into a national scrapyard of the dead, and newspapers published the scores for murders on a daily basis. Known as the "executionometer" they kept count of the number of corpses as if they were goals in a football match.

In articles I published in *Proceso* magazine, I noted things such as the following:

> The violence in this city has given rise to all sort of sordid stories, all of them true. There is the tale of a man from Colonia Champoton who, weary with coming across corpses dumped outside his office every morning, hung up a sign reading *No corpses or rubbish to be left here.* In November one of the bodies dumped on the plot was his daughter. He himself did not see it for by then he too had been killed. Or the tale of a woman from Juárez Valley who saw a dog passing by, pushing something along with his snout. She thought he was playing with a ball: a largeish round mass, but it was sticky and flesh-coloured and turned out to be a man's head. Or again that of some high school kids who discovered a corpse wearing a pig's head, dangling from the school railings. Or bridges, where at dawn headless men materialise. Or policemen who run away because they feel so frightened. Or the little girl sacrificed when a fleeing man grabbed and used her to shield himself from the bullets.

I travelled all round the city meeting funeral directors known as vultures, or kept night watches with tabloid crime reporters who showed me places where massacres had taken place. I interviewed cops, businessmen, priests, academics and politicians at their work places; only occasionally would they ever take me to sites where the events had unfolded.

It was in neighbourhoods devastated by tragedy that I began to notice danger zones that had become "hot spots", and came across a sisterly group of women who seemed to be working independently, but whom I later found to be collaborating with others, scores of them, struggling without making a show of it, on the front lines of our domestic war. I followed them on a couple of occasions, until I could no longer take my eyes off them.

At their side I encountered one of the secret worlds that women devise when obliged to confront a war. I saw more clearly than ever before what an ethics of caring for others truly means, a female way of facing a social emergency. (At that time, I had no idea that my fate would be to share theirs.)

I discovered women who tried to exorcise the paralysing horror one could breathe in the air, who offered *reiki* and flower therapies. There were street artists who used stencils to spray-paint poems or gave acrobatic classes and staged hip-hop concerts in the parks where executions had taken place and neighbourhoods where no-one ventured onto the streets. They spontaneously turned themselves into bereavement counsellors in the struggle against grief, forming support groups in the *barrios* most deeply affected by the tragedy. And there were activists who dealt with the havoc wrought by the levels of violence, including child malnutrition. Women lawyers who listened to victims and took up their cases, even those that would involve challenging the police and the military.

The overwhelming majority of those seeking to repair the devastation were women.

2

In November 2010, in the city of Chihuahua, I was invited to a meeting of victims of the indiscriminate violence then spreading across the country. There I met mothers, wives, sisters, family members of the disappeared along the northern borders, who had formed their own local groups to seek out their missing loved ones. As if they were the sole inhabitants on a planet of pain. A week later, in *Proceso*, I described their plight like this:

> Ever since their loved one failed to return home, they have become nomads. Prompted by the laws of the heart, they run the length of the country combing state attorneys' offices, highways, hospitals, prisons, morgues, cemeteries, wastelands and common graves in their searches.

I watched them taking notes like schoolgirls, listening to workshops on how to operate georadars that can detect human remains underground; how a D.N.A. analysis works; the rights they have to convene judicial investigations into their loved ones' disappearances; how the Inter-American Court of Human Rights functions; or how to contact researchers at the United Nations.

One old woman in the audience raised a painful question: "If they give me a sack of bones and tell me it is my son, how do I know if it is or not?" The teachers who run these workshops are also women. There is the daughter of a guerrilla murdered in the 1960s who studied forensic techniques, a lawyer and theologian who has founded a human rights organisation, and a former worker from one of the sweatshops who, having fought as a mother regarding her child's disappearance for many years, trained herself as an investigator and worked until she recovered her daughter's remains. They had obtained their knowledge through witnessing the drama of young women being disappeared in Juárez City and the whole State of Chihuahua in recent years. In Ciudad Juárez, femicide had imposed, horribly, a kind of technical training.

I observed them exchanging information, uncovering common mechanisms to apply to individual disappearances (for example, that several were disappeared on the same section of the motorway, or on the same day and in the same place). They put forward the idea of posting a blog in order to recover their absent ones' life stories. They drew and wrote their feelings (broken hearts, family trees, empty houses with slogans such as *My God, I pray to you for strength and help*; *I continue the struggle for love of my son; Our family is so-sad but ever in struggle against the monster; A thankless journey, with no end in sight*). They bade each other farewell with tears, and whispered the same phrase into each other's ears, over and over: *Don't you give up. Don't you give up. Don't you give up.*

This was the first time I cried.

3

I met up with these mothers, wives and sisters of the disappeared a year later, in 2011, together with the writer Javier Sicilia who, ever since the murder of his son, led two nationwide "victims' caravans", appearing as painful exhibits of the human suffering caused by the drugs wars.

The women travelled alongside the poet, but they were not the protagonists. They were the backbone of the whole movement, like the women who took part in the Mexican Revolution, but who never became famous, and of whom scant written record has been kept.

Sicilia, the poet, took up the threads of his life again. But they carried on, demanding justice. I follow them, seeing their hunger strikes outside the Attorney General's office; in the processions of nomadic mothers who for eleven long years have walked the train tracks searching for their disappeared sons and daughters; on public occasions, they demand that the government should meet them, the relatives; they hang commemorative plaques listing the names of their loved ones for whom they search. On an almost daily basis, they put emotional messages regarding their absent loved ones up on Facebook.

Disappearances reached such epidemic proportions – over 26,000 people have disappeared since 2006, according to the latest official figures – that every May 10, Mother's Day, they hold a march in Mexico City where the faithful pray, demand, insist those they wish to celebrate be returned to them. After attending the first Mother's Day march in 2012, I wrote the following in *Proceso*:

> Look at all of them together. There they are, the madwomen, screechers, who don't know how to behave in public. You'll have spotted them marching up and down the highways, camping out in public squares, blocking streets. From the moment they rise, they start talking to someone who isn't there. They're the ones who upset the good folks at church when they raise their pleas and prayers at the end of Mass. Their main pastime seems to be keeping watch at the doors of government offices. On occasion they gain access to some presidential event where they call out to ask for the president's assistance. Others even manage to obtain airtime on television, repeating the same timeworn slogans. They can be identified by their apparent uniforms: a T-shirt or a placard bearing the photo of a young lad, or a young girl, and the same expression in their eyes, the same shape of the mouth or arc of the eyebrow.

Without knowing quite how it happened, I became a collector of female voices. My notebooks, like a music box, are full of women's voices, victims suffering beneath the weight of violence, or rebelling against the state, or they are redeemers in a tragedy. Every one of them a protagonist.

Few men accompany them on their journey. They go out alone on almost every occasion.

When I happen to meet a husband or son belonging to one of the women, I always ask: "What's going on? Where are the rest of the men?"

To which I never get a definitive explanation, though they try.

Señora Julia Alonso's husband – they being the parents of Julio, disappeared in Nuevo León in 2009 when he went to a reservoir to enjoy himself with friends – told me that while his wife kept on searching, he would continue working in order to maintain the search economically. Because it is expensive. Because it goes on for years.

Others have outlined similar responses.

Alberto Rodríguez Cervantes, a psychologist from the north of the country, who has assisted some of the men at his family therapy workshops held for the searchers, told me that the macho culture preventing men from revealing weakness means that it is much harder work for them to express their feelings over the loss of a son, and that it is almost impossible for them to ask for help.

Those in the same situation admit how hard it is to maintain a mask of inscrutability.

"One of them related how he had to lock himself in the toilet to cry for his son, because the culture of machismo counts on him to be the strong man of the family. Yet his whole life has fallen apart: he lost his job, fell ill, is under psychiatric treatment, and takes incredible quantities of sleeping pills in order to get any rest," the psychiatrist from the Centre for Women's Rights in Chihuahua explained.

Sociologist Martha Sánchez of the Central American Migrants' Movement once told me that the drug traffickers have a sort of superstition concerning the maternal image, explaining why it is the mothers who gather in dangerous places to seek their sons. No-one dares to touch them. The way is left open for them.

I heard this on numerous occasions: males are the targets of the "hunting raids" (of every ten killings or "disappearances", nine are of men). They know they can disappear, or be executed. This is why, when it comes to searching, they try to make themselves invisible; it is the women who insist on making themselves public.

Carlos Beristáin, a Basque doctor and psychiatrist, explained in an interview he gave me, that at times of violence or during a process of militarisation, such as that being lived on a daily basis in Mexico, family roles reach crisis point, as the men find themselves most exposed to death and conscription, and they take the weight of the impact on the lives of their families, communities, and on themselves.

There is no single answer to this. It could be a mixture of all of these reasons. It could also be related to something women feel in their wombs.

A little while ago, a Central American *mamá* who travelled to the capital with some thirty other mothers in a nomadic caravan, who were also searching for their children, responded to a photographer who attempted to console her: "You can never know what I feel because you'll never be a *mamá*. You have to go through pregnancy and giving birth in order to understand."

In the course of the interviews I made with them, I noted how different the language of these mothers was.

They always talk about broken hearts, empty bellies, anguish in the soul, intuitions and hunches, paths watered with tears, lives torn to shreds, mother love, babies they once rocked in their cradles. And they cry . . . at the least provocation, they cry.

The men, in contrast, mention the sadness, how their lives were torn apart by the separation, often recounting the facts, the place where it all happened, all the clues they have been able to gather, all the dates, and the names of the suspects. They rarely cry.

In a press release before Father's Day, the women from AMORES said the following of their husbands. "They suffer after the disappearance of their sons and daughters, even though they don't show it. They cry with us. They have complex emotions and feel desolation, just like us, even though they don't make it public. We, the women of AMORES, bear witness to this; we know their worries. But culturally the men were not raised to express their emotions, and thus they repress their feelings and live isolated in their pain, which sometimes leads to illnesses.

(The disappearance of the forty-three students from Ayotzinapa Teachers College in September 2014 broke this pattern. Here both fathers and mothers can be seen searching for their sons and demanding justice.)

4

What I saw was that from that moment on, following this itinerant war and recounting it in the words of the victims, from people who had survived it, viewing it from the standpoint of a fight-back, of sowing life on razed earth – was that I had changed. This new me had, among other new identities, one defined as feminist. Not because I might want to fight with the men to win superiority or fame. Because I saw with a new intensity – something I'd never even glimpsed before – the role of women who go forth to shelter other people. In March 2011, I described the role of women like this:

> The weight of violence in the drug war is borne by women. It is they who gather up the corpses belonging to a family member murdered in a hail of bullets, then denounced/ presented to the world as a common criminal. It is they who travel the length and breadth of the country – knocking at doors, putting up posters, conducting their own research – to uncover the whereabouts of the husband, son or brother, any or all of them disappeared. They are the ones to who organise in order to come out and demand clear explanations regarding the mass killing of their sons. It is they who remain on the home front – at homes now without a man, but with an abundance of children to feed. It is they who accompany other women in their quest for justice or those who treat the wounds of both male and female survivors of this war.
>
> They are our contemporary Antigones, those who live by the laws of blood, even when it means rebelling against the state.

Suddenly I found I was one of them.

In 2006, together with some colleagues, I founded an organisation (called *Periodistas de a Pie* – "Grassroots Journalists") intended to dedicate itself to train journalists covering stories about the poor. But when the Mexican war began, the violence, which we encountered as journalists and were completely unprepared for, changed my life and plans.

The direction within the organisation also changed in an attempt to deal with the state of emergency.

Once again, I found myself surrounded by women with whom I shared a double workday: both writing our own copy, and teaching and advising reporters on the risks of being killed.

The workshops we organised were about how to survive writing a story, how to understand drug-trafficking, how to interview the child survivor of a massacre, how to encrypt information which could put us at risk and how to cleanse our souls, in order to be able to continue covering such news without losing our sense of joy in living.

Before we knew it, we were a hub and contact point, ready to respond in case of emergency. The journalists with whom I worked to establish this network, reacted at whatever hour of day or night, not excluding the final tense instants before the paper was put to bed, when we received calls for help from colleagues in some distant region of the country, desperately pleading for aid because they knew they were about to be killed, and were in need of refuge. Or pleas for psychological support for journalists loath to go out to work in the wake of some traumatic event, like a fire or some other attack on their editorial office.

From being ordinary reporters, all of a sudden we were now campaigning for human rights, and we began to be called – not without sarcasm – "defenders" or "activists".

In 2010 we held our first march demanding justice for murdered and "disappeared" journalists. With a tape recorder and notebook in one hand and the photographs of the late remembered in the other.

Ever since the devastation began, we, as female journalists, proposed we use our network to look after other colleagues. Soon, in other parts of the country – starting with Ciudad Juárez – other reporters inspired by our movement, founded their own collectives. Although it was mainly men who were being killed and "disappeared" in Mexico, as women we could not continue as if nothing were happening, without providing protection for everyone through training courses, assessments, demonstrations to demand justice, campaigns to highlight the situation of the Mexican press.

The leaders of all these groups are journalists who cover human rights, aged between twenty and thirty years old. They belong to a generation sickened by the corrupt relationship between press and power, and take upon themselves the responsibility to look after others and to avoid being silenced.

Traditional journalism organisations are different. They are typically made of men comfortable with speaking in public and networking. We, in contrast, cried the first time we picked up a microphone. Often the cameras and media attention took a lot out of us. And we do so much silent work: spending time in meetings, taking collections for the families, searching out psychologists and lawyers.

The circle closed when women human rights defenders sought us out to persuade us to join a network of women defending rights, not exclusively for feminists, although it arose within the movement, learning to take care of each other. It was an invitation to link hands with women friends in jumping the waves. At times the waves turned into tsunamis and wreaked destruction.

It cost me to acknowledge being a feminist. But I know I am no longer the same. That ever since 2010, I look on things with a fresh eye. Ever since I saw what could no longer be denied: the presence of the "reconstructors" who rebuild from the ashes up, in a

MEXICO – RETURN TO THE ABYSS

Sergio González Rodríguez

IN 1996, I FOUND myself in the border zone abyss of Ciudad Juárez and El Paso, Texas for the first time. I never imagined that what was taking place in that region was a sign of things to come, or which were already happening and which we were ignoring, across the whole country.

I am referring to institutional deterioration, corruption, and the inefficiency and negligence of the authorities; to the overwhelming power of organised crime, the synergy between economic and political power and large-scale drugs trafficking; to women and minors, and even little girls' defencelessness against the predatory, macho behaviour that prevails in Mexico; and to the ever increasing number of crimes that go unpunished.

Thus a criminal pattern unites what might be called the systemic causes, that is, the insatiable greed of ultra-liberal capitalism and the multinational industry of assembly plants, and human settlements with precious little infrastructure and low standards of living. The most wretched neighbourhood in the middle of the desert, subject to extreme heat in summer and strong winds and sub-zero temperatures in the winter. All in exchange for the worst salaries on the planet.[1]

In the 1990s, Ciudad Juárez experienced an extremely rapid growth in population due to the need for a workforce able to undertake painstaking, technically demanding work, which women were able to do. Their prominence on this border led to the male population rejecting them.

The migrant population of young women and adolescents from poor families were simply looking for work and a way to improve their lives, and came from other parts of the state of Chihuahua or neighbouring states, such as Zacatecas, Coahuila, Durango and still others further south.

From the early 1990s, murders of extreme cruelty and with signs of multiple sexual abuse began to be reported, in which almost all the victims were women, minors and little girls who had been abducted prior to the murders and whose bodies appeared both on the outskirts of Ciudad Juárez and in central areas of the city.

Criminologists and other experts identified in this a recurring pattern, which in time would come to be identified as serial in nature, and carried out by at least two criminal groups operating out of safe houses in complete impunity. Nevertheless, despite being denounced by civil agencies, academic investigators and journalists, both the authorities in Chihuahua as well as the federal authorities shied away from any kind of in-depth investigation into the available information or the evidence of complicity between members of the large-scale drug trafficking groups based in Ciudad Juárez and figures with economic and political power in Mexico.

Eventually, under pressure from the federal government, the disappearance, abduction, torture and murder of dozens of women on the border was attributed at the time to "intra-familial violence", a problem that is in itself very serious in the country as a whole. Now, a more distressing version of events tends to predominate: that there never were any serial killings of women, that the femicides never existed, that it was all a "myth" or an "urban legend"

· invented by out-of-towners. Unfortunately, the reality contradicts the official lies.

The ever erratic and contradictory manipulation of data on the murders of women has been a recurring response by those in the Mexican government, who insist on denying the facts documented not only by independent investigators, but also by international bodies. The Inter-American Commission on Human Rights (I.A.C.H.R.) has already condemned the Mexican state for, among other things, its official figures on violence against women in Ciudad Juárez.[2]

In the last few years, murders and disappearances of women and girls in Ciudad Juárez have increased. To date, the situation for women on this border has grown worse since the last decade of the twentieth century, as seen in a report from the research centre El Colegio de la Frontera Norte (C.O.L.E.F.) entitled "Spatial and temporal behaviour of three paradigmatic cases of violence in Ciudad Juárez, Chihuahua, México: femicide, homicide and involuntary disappearances of girls and women (1993–2013)". This is from the report: "Justice remains veiled. Furthermore, with the escalation of missing girls and women since 2008, and the discovery of female skeletons in the years 2011, 2012 and 2013, we can say that the commitment to the eradication of femicide remains unfulfilled."[3]

When I visited San Cristóbal Ecatepec, the disturbing memory of Ciudad Juárez sprang to life.[4] Ecatepec ("windy hill" in Náhuatl) dates from the pre-Hispanic era and has a population of around 1,700,000, with women making up a small but significant majority.

Under the jurisdiction of Mexico State and bordering the northeastern part of the Mexican capital, Ecatepec records the highest level of femicides (murder accompanied by a pattern of misogynistic behaviour and extreme violence)[5] in the entire country, as well as high rates of homicide. It also has a huge number of rapes, sex crimes and forced disappearances of women and girls.[6]

Ecatepec spread out from the colonial architecture of its centre until a layout had been created based simply on growth, without any kind of planning whatsoever. As people emigrated from their exhausted rural communities, they sought to settle in the centre of the country in search of work, in the face of the industrial modernisation of the second half of the twentieth century. The result has been a suburban environment where modern buildings, poverty, marginalisation and inequality all intersect, and whose appearance is that of a post-apocalyptic slum permanently under construction, that never quite fulfilled its promise of domestic improvement, having started with poor quality building since blighted by neglect, wear and tear and chaos.

At some crossroads in Ecatepec, as a foil to the chaos of traffic congestion and the polluted air (despite the wind that is a feature of the region), there are monuments and civic sculptures whose rigid stone and copper presence is only interrupted at one spot along the trajectory by a gigantic, multicoloured effigy of Our Lady of Guadalupe, visited by half a million pilgrims every December 12, the day of the "mother of all Mexicans".

In these disconnected streets, nothing remains of the idyllic landscape that, a century and a half ago, a lithograph of Ecatepec might have captured: the clear air, the distant, placid lake, the silhouette of a colonial hacienda, the fields full of crops and the maguey plants scattered under the white clouds and the evening sun.

Nowadays, industrial accidents and car crashes, organised crime, gangs and police aggression have imposed a dreadful stigma on Ecatepec that seriously damages all productive activities (trade, industry, transport, etc.) and the daily lives of the local people, who must put up with a severe shortage of public services such as water.[7]

Residents tend to be suspicious of strangers, afraid they might be kidnappers or criminal spies in pursuit of their victims. In 2015 alone, there were 63 lynchings in Mexico, with the majority occurring in the capital and in the states of Mexico and Puebla.[8]

The discovery in 1995 of the remains of a mammoth on communal land in Ecatepec[9] highlighted the sort of contrasts that exist in this suburban enclave, still tied to agricultural activities and with a large number of irregular human settlements, as well as the difficulty it has had in reconciling its ancestral history with modern life, based on organised guidelines.

In the list of Mexican cities and their quality of life, Ecatepec comes second to last.[10] In 2013, for instance, a gas tanker exploded in the city, killing 19 people and injuring more than 30.[11] In Ecatepec, as in all of Mexico now, *No vale nada la vida* (Life is worth nothing), as the *ranchera* song, with mariachi accompaniment, by José Alfredo Jiménez goes.

Nonetheless, in the face of doom, many people and civil groups fight every day to better their lives by reporting corrupt authorities and institutional failings.

In Mexico, only 1 per cent of each and every crime committed per year is punished by law. Every day, 51 people are murdered, every four hours a woman is raped and every day, 13 people are forcibly disappeared.[12] Reality always ends up overtaking fiction.

In their 1928 *Threepenny Opera*, Bertolt Brecht and Kurt Weill constructed a parable about a London ravaged by a boom in criminal activity and corruption, which ends by inverting the conventional order to impose a sense of cynicism and political amorality. This is Mexico today.

Mexico's ruling classes, whose wealth is concentrated in 36 families, appear far removed from this social catastrophe, which has its origin in the signing of the North American Free Trade

Agreement (N.A.F.T.A.) with the United States and Canada in 1994: there are currently more poor people than ever in Mexico, although exports and foreign investment have increased in unprecedented ways. In the last two decades, more than ten million Mexicans have had to emigrate to the U.S. in search of work,[13] whilst organised crime and common offences became widespread in a rapidly modernising society.

The old homogeneity and years of authoritarian presidential rule and one-party rule saw an increase in the expectation (never fulfilled) of a transition to a healthy democracy. What appeared instead was a fragmented, polarised society, given to breakdowns in social norms under an a-legal state, which functions via its dysfunctions, that is, outside and against the law in a perverse fluctuation, while pretending to respect national laws and conventional international law. Its political character combines a mix of bureaucratic and juridical formality and an apparently reformist pragmatism, which manages the effects – but refuses to combat the deep-seated causes – of the country's problems.

Thus not only has there been an increase in the age-old problems of poverty, inequality and marginalisation, but also in corruption, lack of transparency, inefficiency and a lack of respect for human rights from institutions themselves. Mexico is the most corrupt and insecure country in the world, according to the Organisation for Economic Co-operation and Development (O.E.C.D.), despite the fact it is now defined as the tenth largest global economy.[14]

Seen from the outside, this paradox is not only astonishing but also tragic and troubling; when experienced from within, it implies daily resistance to the new forms of oppression and exploitation that lie in store for other countries in the world that keep acceptable standards of living out of reach of the majority of their

populations. There is here an apparatus of government and subjectivity that consists of the idea and the practice of the normalisation
of abuse, injustice, violence and de-humanisation in both public
and private life.

In other words, reality as unreality, where anything liminal,
shadowy, uncertain or unspeakable is expanded and deepened. A
horizon with no prospects in sight for most people, summed up
by the title and contents of a 1999 novel by the now deceased
writer Daniel Sada: *Porque parece mentira la verdad nunca se sabe*
(Because it looks like a lie, the truth is never known).[15] The Mexican
penumbra.

In the summer of 2014, there was a demonstration in Ecatepec
to protest against the rule of crime. The demonstrators wore
white, and their grievances can be summed up by this message
on one of their placards: "The police don't patrol, they extort and
repress".[16] In 2009, when the current president of Mexico, Enrique
Peña Nieto was governor of Mexico State (2005–11), there had
already been demonstrations in Ecatepec to mourn the femicides
taking place there.

Since then, the government's inclination has been to downplay
the problem. For instance, the federal statistics agency indicated
that in 2012 there were 388 murders of women, while the authorities of Mexico State recorded only 281. In 2011, slightly more
than half of women aged 15 were subjected to some kind of
violence; almost half of all women suffered some kind of intimidation, sexual abuse or physical aggression in a public space. Between
2012 and 2013, around five thousand women were raped.[17]

In 2012, the categorisation of the crime of femicide came into
force in Mexico State, including the correct protocol to follow
when investigating the crime. Nonetheless, such measures are far
from resolving the problem of violence against women. In fact,

due to the technical and administrative demands of the regulatory framework, investigations into femicides became more complicated. Of the 281 women who the local state government say were killed in 2012, only 62 were investigated as femicides.

The following year, there were 30 files on femicide, which according to the National Citizen Femicide Observatory, a civil agency, means that "the real figure of women murdered in the state is unknown".[18] Between 2011 and 2012, there were 1,258 reports of women and girls being forcibly disappeared in Mexico State.

In 2014, when the Grand Canal on the outskirts of Ecatepec was drained at a place known as "Devil's Curve", 21 bodies were found, of which 16 were young women or girls and five were men.[19] A civil agency stated that, in actual fact, the number of bodies found was 46. The authorities' actions were limited to minimising the discovery,[20] typical behaviour among politicians and government officials and which is due to the inertia derived from the a-legality (being outside and against the law) of Mexican institutions, and which has become proof of the deepseated negligence displayed when they find themselves obliged to tackle cases of misogynistic violence.

Among the remains found in the Grand Canal was the skull of 14-year-old Diana Angélica Castañeda Fuentes, who disappeared months earlier as she was on her way to a friend's house in the centre of Ecatepec. On September 13, 2013, the girl was seen for the last time as she crossed the bridge to the district of Tecamac. Her family reported her disappearance to the authorities and asked around themselves, sticking up posters in the neighbourhood. The police, meanwhile, said they had investigated without success. It would be D.N.A. analysis that revealed the victim's identity.[21]

Also identified, amongst further remains found later on in the same canal, was Mariana Elizabeth Yáñez Reyes, eighteen years old. She disappeared on September 17, 2014, after leaving home at 9.00 p.m. to go to a nearby internet café to print off some documents for a scholarship application. A neighbour reported hearing screams in the street at the time. Nothing more was heard of her, nor did the authorities explain why or how the victim was murdered. Her family had to settle for the official version of events, which said she had been positively identified, which they subsequently found dubious: "I don't believe them," declared the victim's mother.[22]

In 2015, forced by pressure from civil agencies, Mexico State authorities declared a "gender alert due to femicides", a legal mechanism which triggers the allocation of additional resources to deal with the problem.[23]

With its symbolic connotations of a river of death and waste, the Grand Canal makes for a disturbing metaphor of Mexico's modernisation.

Mexico City was founded on a small island in the marshy region of a high plateau, which sits at 7,350 feet above sea level. Since colonial times, and throughout the nineteenth and twentieth centuries, the capital suffered from several serious floods. In order to prevent this, a large amount of construction work was carried out.[24]

In 1604, for instance, a dyke was built in Ecatepec, and two centuries later there was a proposal to build waste pipes out towards the River Tula, which flows into the River Moctezuma and then the River Pánuco, until finally ending up at the Gulf of Mexico. In the nineteenth century, tunnels and canals were built to decrease the flow of water, which is very heavy on the plateau during the rainy season.

From the second half of the twentieth century onwards, the Grand Canal was complemented by a deep drainage system after diverting the rivers that crossed the rapidly expanding capital and suburban areas. If the damage was contained in the capital, the suburbs and neighbouring areas resented being saddled with the problems originating with these engineering works, of which the ominous flow of "black water" – raw sewage – was the symbol.

In 1977, the writer Armando Ramírez published his novel *Pu*, later re-published with the title *Violación en Polanco* (A Rape in Polanco),[25] in which he narrates the story of a criminal orgy on board a bus, which ends in the sacrificial murder of a woman who the delinquents kidnap in a rich neighbourhood and then throw into the Grand Canal on the outskirts of the capital of Mexico State, as if she were an Aztec sacrifice.

Ramírez' literary premonition seems chilling now when we observe that, in the State of Mexico alone, misogynistic violence is currently at the following levels: "Records spanning the period between 1990 and 2011 reveal Mexico State's tendency to be the place where most women are killed in the country; in these twenty-one years, it was number one on eleven occasions for mortality rates due to attacks on women."[26]

It is worth remembering that Mexico State is the most densely populated in the country, and went from having 10 million residents in 1990 to nearly 16 million in 2010. The historical and current difference between the municipality of Ecatepec and that of Ciudad Juárez is huge: in 1990, the border city had half a million inhabitants; now it has 1,300,000. As such, it is a fallacy to compare cases of misogynistic violence in both places with the aim of illustrating how the authorities have acted in response to their respective problems.

If the question of femicide in Ciudad Juárez reached inter-national levels of impact, commanding a huge amount of coverage in the press, on the radio and on TV channels in several countries, giving rise to documentaries and even Hollywood and Mexican films, as well as other abusive uses such as a line of cosmetics based on the "style" of the city and its surroundings, it is due to the tenacity of human rights organisations, feminists, female academics, journalists and researchers who brought the subject to the public's attention and that, over time, we have seen worsen thanks to impunity: the macho abuse of victims, the boom in crime, the lack of respect for human rights and the corruption of the Mexican government.

Against such tenacity, state and federal authorities, as well as powerful groups on the border, unleashed an intensive crusade to discredit the accusations and questions being asked. Instead of collaborating so as to establish the facts, they financed costly campaigns to "clean up" the image of Ciudad Juárez, which a substantial number of local media outlets, businessmen and various spokesmen aligned themselves with.

The focus of this campaign was to deny the existence of the femicides and attribute them to causes unconnected to economic and political spheres and responsibility. Such a propaganda-based approach, which focused on damage limitation, became common practice in similar cases on the part of the country's ruling classes.

The cartography of violence against women in Mexico is overwhelming: the female murder rate is above the continental average; resorting to the so-called "gender alert" tends to fail; in most of the country, the crime of femicide has no legal definition; proving such crimes is very difficult, due to the legal, bureaucratic and administrative requirements that must be satisfied; and, what is worst of all, every day six more women are murdered.[27]

The country's challenge, as José Ramón Cossío, a magistrate at the Supreme Court, once told me, consists of making the constitutional norms effective: that is, ensuring that they are obeyed. However, in both the prevailing subculture of authoritarianism in México and among citizens in general, the law and figures of authority are distrusted, and what is favoured instead are personal initiatives, pragmatism, taking the law into one's own hands, and an ideology that privileges the superiority of individual liberty over collective responsibility. An attitude influenced by oligarchy.[28]

Theory of negative evolution: from a conventional point of view, one might think that the social behaviours described here are derived from some sort of historical "backwardness", and that all that has to be done is improve the education system, propose legislative reforms and comply with international laws so that, in some undefined future, things will get better. Such a perspective, as mechanistic as it is delusional, overlooks that fact that the deficiencies, irregularities, paralysis and lack of development are also forms of social control that serve political and geopolitical interests based on the survival of the fittest.

The deterioration of Mexico's institutions is a direct result of both the North American Free Trade Agreement (N.A.F.T.A.) and the Security and Prosperity Partnership of North America (S.P.P.), which Mexico endorsed along with the U.S. and Canada in 2005, by way of an executive mandate signed by the then president of the Republic, Vicente Fox Quesada, and the fact that this ought to have been approved by the Senate, as stated in the Mexican Constitution, but was not.[29]

From then on, and under the imperative of subjugating Mexico's sovereignty to the principle of the United States' "national security", whose reach encompasses the entire planet ever since 9/11 and the geopolitics that subsequently emerged, Mexico unleashed a war against drug trafficking in its territory subject to the military directives of North American Command and the United States' new military and diplomatic doctrine, which declared that terrorism is equivalent to drugs trafficking.

Before such a change, drugs traffickers in Mexico kept a low profile as they carried out the violence that benefited their criminal activities. In obedience to the new criminal policy backed by the United States, criminal groups were incited to attack each other in order to "exterminate themselves". This "balkanised" the country.

It was out of this convergence of factors that Mexico's profound crisis at the start of the twenty-first century arose, the explosion of violence and insecurity propelled by the war machine of the United States, which has the largest arms industry in the world and, contradictorily, the largest market for drug consumption world-wide. At the same time, it sells weapons indiscriminately to drugs traffickers and other criminal groups, and to the Mexican armed forces and police forces.

Mexico provides the dead men and women. Thousands and thousands of them.

Between 2014 and 2015 alone, Mexico bought arms and military equipment from the U.S. for a sum of $3.5 billion. Mexico has become a violent country that produces yet more violence, and one in which each person has a personal, familial or affective story of the daily horror that reappears in their dreams and night-mares. In my case, it has a title: Extreme Violence as Spectacle – I Within.[30]

As I investigated the murders of women in Ciudad Juárez I was threatened, kidnapped, beaten and tortured, and ended up in hospital. I survived and, later on, I was kidnapped again, threat-ened, and subjected to psychological torture. In both cases, the torturers were trying to intimidate me so that I would call off my investigation.[31]

Despite all this, I consider myself fortunate: I managed to survive. Something that, unfortunately, proved impossible for many of my journalist colleagues. Between 2000 and 2015, 103 journalists were killed and 25 were disappeared.[32] According to international organisations, Mexico is one of the most dangerous countries in the world in which to carry out investigative journalism, not only because of the criminals lying in wait, but also because their corrupting power has turned the police and government officials into their allies.

If a journalist comes close to revealing these illicit links, he or she will be in danger, as will his or her family. And there is no institution that protects journalists. Their only defence is to publish and to take a prominent role in public life, with all the risks implicit in this resolve.

In 2015, for example, the photojournalist Rubén Espinosa Becerril, aged 32, was killed on the night of July 31 in an apartment in Mexico City. Murdered along with him were the women Nadia Vera Pérez, Yesenia Quiroz Alfaro, Olivia Alejandra Negrete Avilés and Mile Virginia Martín. Three of them showed signs of rape and torture.

Espinosa Becerril had left his native state of Veracruz because he was being persecuted by the state government for doing his job of providing information. He knew he was being threatened and persecuted. His friend Nadia Vera Pérez, a social activist in Veracruz, had previously stated that the governor, Javier Duarte, would be responsible for any action against her or her colleague's physical integrity that might take place.

When the scene of the crime was discovered, the government of Mexico City dismissed the idea of a serious investigation into any possible responsibility of the governor of Veracruz or his subordinates and instead, took great pains to attribute the four murders to the victims having been mixed up in drugs trafficking. This resulted in the criminalisation of the female victims, with no clear evidence, by employing inconsistent, contradictory documentation littered with unfounded assertions. The accused, who were coerced by torture into declaring themselves guilty, relied on the help of other individuals who were still at liberty even though their existence was known to the authorities.

To this date, the government of Mexico City maintains this stance. But what if Rubén Espinosa Becerril's killing is the perfect crime? What if the government of the state of Veracruz, weary of the criticisms and accusations ordered the annihilation of its critics by using hired killers? The government of Mexico City refused right from the start to investigate this possibility.[33]

Espinosa Becerril was a photojournalist but also an artist.[34] He specialised in images of social demonstrations which sought justice or respect, and his success in this area has two principal features: the first is the face of a person in the middle of a crowd, or rather, facing the uncertainty that surrounds them; the second consists of discovering the revealing contrasts of Mexico's political framework and its corrupt politicians and officials. As well as their informative nature, both aspects reveal a certain oblique position that invites reflection.

The dialogue with its subjects implied by Espinosa Becerril's pictures alludes to a principle of identity in conflict, one that he understands how to transmit to the viewer, one in which the gaze becomes the obsessive centre that gives meaning not only to the image, but to the person and citizen facing up to a hostile or threatening reality.

Espinosa Becerril's camera is revealed as a humanising gaze from where multiple relationships are expressed before others. Sometimes, when the photographer is the subject of his own image, he covers his eyes with dark glasses, as if trying to erase himself or vanish inside the image itself.

One of his colour photographs shows an indigenous or mestizo person with a scarf completely covering their face, evoking a world that is simultaneously real and imaginary: flowery, starry, full of multiple folds. Dispossession transformed into wealth.

Another black-and-white image shows a phenomenally large advert at an urban crossroads, which shows a man (we only see half of his face), his eyes out of shot, holding a camera phone out in front of him. A kind of self-portrait by transference in a landscape of traffic lights, street lamps, road signs, wires and an ominous, cloudy sky.

The motif of people walking or circulating on marches or demonstrations is a frequent one in Espinosa Becerril's photographic output, although time and time again it lays bare the contrasts at play in collective political participation: the icon of the Mexican Revolution (Emiliano Zapata) in front of a little girl, her expression sad and set; a lighted candle illuminating the face of a young woman; the placard standing out in the middle of the crowd: "We demand justice! We reject violence!"; the armed police officer who tries to obscure his face with his hand; or the official, portentous portrait of the governor.

The fragility of a modest person in simply existing was one of the photographer's preoccupations, an artist who, as his images show, saw his role as standing side by side with those who lack everything and yet still possess an undeniable dignity.

Among the photos in his catalogue, there is one that moves me in particular: a colleague had to take a photo of Espinosa Becerril as he points his camera straight ahead. Behind him, another colleague follows after him. Or is he the one who is capturing a colleague who, at the same time, is personifying him? In this shot, Rubén Espinosa is simultaneously there and not there in the middle of this mountainous spot flooded with smoke or mist, a few trees in the background. Danger stalks him, and he persists. Always with us: he lives in us by his absence. Nimble, unflinching, faithful, forever lying in wait. An endless lucidity that holds us in its embrace.

The generous response of the creative imagination to brutality.

In the state of Veracruz, as in many parts of the Mexican Republic, the rule of law has been replaced by the rule of crime.[35] The figure of the police hit man or the hit man policeman has come to be emblematic of institutional corruption. Day after day, in the midst of such drama, people live in a border zone between fear and desperation. A world turned upside down with regards to the basic rules of coexistence.

How should we confront such adversity? The demand for re-establishing the rule of law spans a wide variety of registers, which in terms of culture reveals something critical: it is only via high-art, aesthetic perspectives that we can hope to transcend conventional condemnation, almost always stifled by the saturation of distressing headlines and images and figures that compete against each other in the global media market. What is urgently required is a balance between emotion and reflection.

This is the case with the photographs of Koral Carballo, born in 1987 in Poza Rica, Veracruz, who has assembled her own personal vision for capturing the daily tragedy of living in a region where negativity and destruction proliferate under political formalism and a-legality. The photographer's approach breaks the mould of photojournalism, in which she is trained, and conveys a metaphor of the daily apocalypse that coexists with an understanding of the atrocious in all its philosophical breadth.

Koral Carballo's photographs express how she, as a person and as an artist, has reflected on the violence she has experienced and witnessed in others, its comprehensive impact on public and private spheres. The images simultaneously shed light on "the nightmares one has as a consequence of witnessing violent scenes" and allude to "the need to speak about violence, in a place like Veracruz where this is prohibited".[36]

What does Koral Carballo speak about? About the blood in
rivers or pools, whose colour is incorporated into nature and
reflected in vegetable or mineral textures; about animal or human
bodies ravaged by the aggression of their surroundings; about the
lunar sign, which reads as a dark omen; about flesh in repose of
which it is impossible to say whether it is alive or dead; about the
clearing in the forest that exudes an ominous atmosphere, where
the earth takes on connotations of soft ash; about the profile of a
half-finished slum rising up from the smoke of a bush fire; about
the mythical force of a young girl's face and her hair blowing hope-
fully in the wind. Or else she speaks about caged stones, which, in
her vision, evoke the idea of the subjugation of the natural world.

Koral Carballo reinvents the malevolence of historical context
and transforms it into a compassionate substance where the
torment of violence becomes a strength that is not only a figurative
but also a verbalised trope of the meditation, chanting, shouting
and words that break the silence, which the savages, a product of
the collusion between politics and crime, would like to impose
upon people. Words that hint at other things; images that are
eloquent in their immediacy.

Unlike the usual tendency among artists and writers who seek
a fiery rhetoric to reflect cruelty, injustice and aggression (which
ends up nullifying the content they are trying to highlight, since
anything added to the forcefulness of reality ends up looking super-
fluous), Carballo opts for precision, the painstaking focus of which
comes from the effective clarity and synchrony with regards to the
object or subject portrayed, whether situations, scenes or people.

Koral Carballo forms part of the great photographic renaissance
in Mexico (which can also be seen in other fields of cultural
production, such as literature, art, film, etc.), characterised by the
way its images, as seen by the viewer, shape what is inscribed in

each photograph as well as the way in which the viewer is affected by the aesthetic/artistic gaze. This gaze, in turn, returns us to reality: the images infect, enrich and supply us with new perceptions and concepts. Such a visual strategy excludes a merely literal approach.[37]

In this emerging photography, the simple ingredient of the testimony or accusation is transcended to open the image up to elaborations that bestow a sort of honour on the object/subject portrayed (the events even acquire a personal identity), relational aspects, perceptive frameworks, reflections on oneself and bewilderment: the vanishing points of the imagination, which are aimed at the viewers and which the photographer has examined and explored first. As such, the testimonial or accusatory aspect gains the additional value of being freed from the immediacy of the causal in order to offer an expansive element of interpretation and conjecture, which resists the threatening reality.

The function of the image becomes complex, stripped of the simple stimulus–response dynamic, which tends to be the norm in the ultra-modern audiovisual sphere. The results here are intelligent images.

Koral Carballo represents an undeniable creative will and all the admirable critical significance this implies. She is an example to follow in the midst of brutality.

Terrestrial hells are temporary, and Ciudad Juárez, San Cristóbal Ecatepec, Mexico City or Veracruz are fated to disappear, provided that the truth and the depths of the adversity facing them are acknowledged, and if from their ruins we can construct a present and a future greater than the penumbra of today.

Translated by Rosalind Harvey

STREET CHILDREN

Juan Villoro

The child and the tree

My parents separated in 1969. My sister Carmen and I moved with
our mother to an apartment in Colonia del Valle, an area in which
the traditional kind of houses had begun to give way to middle-
class buildings.

My father rented a nearby apartment. My sister and I would
visit him at the weekends. A man of philosophy, he lacked all
domestic skills. The place was cold and dark; the windows gave
onto a car park and none of the furniture seemed destined to be
around for long. We would eat off paper plates, as if we were on a
camping trip. The lack of creature comforts captivated us: it was
far from normal, and that made it apt for adventures.

We would have a heater on when we slept. I liked the gentle,
rhythmic sound emitted by its infrared tubes. As I listened, I imagined myself on a train to Veracruz. On one occasion my father set
up the heater too close to the bed and the blankets caught fire.
We extinguished the flames with a fabulous deployment of pillows.
My blanket was left with a hole in it, but my father acted as though
nothing had happened. The following weekend I was pulling a
charred blanket up to my chin.

Life with my mother was more orderly but she was rarely at
home. She worked as a psychologist at the Child's Psychiatric

Hospital and would return little inclined to analyse her children's squabbles.

When I turned thirteen, Colonia del Valle became a place of discoveries. I sometimes thought about staying out in the street, never going home. I imagined myself – with a corrosive, frankly masochistic morbidity – becoming a tramp, living in the hollow of a dead tree in the Forest of Chapultepec. My disappearance would mean my parents joining forces to find me; the marriage would not be rescued by love, but by the distressing sight of me as a hobo who had forgotten how to wash and how to speak Spanish.

My passion for the city merged with early melodramatic leanings. I wished I could give it all up, impoverish myself in the metropolis; I would be a pauper, taking on the glazed expression of a castaway, my skin besmeared with lowly grime; I would metamorphose into one of the dispossessed, thereby forcing an attitude of regret on my parents for ever having broken up.

It was very unusual to get divorced in those days, and I did not dare discuss the subject with my friends. Though nowhere near as tragic as destitution, war, poverty or illness, in social terms a separation still equated to failure.

The courteousness with which my parents treated one other was little different to the cool amiability of their cohabitation, but things could always get worse. How long would my father go on living surrounded by paper plates? He would soon be looking for another woman, another fate, other children.

Curiously, the feeling of abandonment made me yearn for a life more solitary still; solitude so frightened me that I sought to overcome it by imagining I was the one abandoning everyone else. At thirteen the only way for me to do that was to become an untouchable. I would leave my clothes and my toys behind, I would forget the language. This last detail is striking to me now; being a beggar does not necessarily entail stopping speaking, so it was me who added this extra calamity, picturing the *telenovela* moment when my parents would find me and, seeing I had lost the ability to converse with them, realise it was too late.

I dreamed of this escape from reality until one day I met a boy who had actually lived in a tree.

Jorge Portilla, a philosopher friend of my father's, also lived in Colonia del Valle. His children came across a boy in a treetop one afternoon and the author of *La fenomenología del relajo* (The Phenomenology of Relaxation) decided to adopt him. Years on, Jorge, the eldest, would compare the boy with Kaspar Hauser. All of a sudden there he simply was, this person with no background whatsoever.

The former street urchin did not grow a great deal and went on to find work as a jockey at the Hipódromo de las Américas, later moving to the U.S.A. where he won various derbies. Each Christmas he would send the family that raised him a photo of his wife and children. As far as I know he never went back to Mexico. The path laid out for him involved going away, becoming a champion rider, racing towards the finish line eyes narrowed against the onrushing wind.

Knowing that a child had lived in the street confirmed for me that this could be my destiny. I savoured the possibility, as though sampling a harmless dose of poison. Deep down I knew myself incapable of putting it into practice, and for that same reason enjoyed it; it was *an idea*. For the son of a philosopher, that was as good as going around with a gun.

Since that time, when I come across a child in the street I feel a mixture of guilt, nostalgia and shame, all at the same time. Mine were the tragic fantasies of a basically well-off child; I could afford them. I never came face to face with any real danger.

When I see a child who is alone in the world I remember what it was I did not dare to be, and I understand – feeling that I do so too late – that my tedious and humdrum existence kept me from the shame of it.

The temple of lost causes

Mexico City's Church of San Hipólito is situated a stone's throw from Alameda Park, at the corner of Avenida Hidalgo and the Paseo de la Reforma. At 2 a.m. the night air is punctured by the melancholic strains of an accordion; to one side of the church, leaning against some shop shutters, a busker tries to win change from the people coming out of the bars.

Nearby a lorry waits for dawn to set off with its consignment of goods. There is a slogan on the front bumper: "Love goes with me everywhere." In the dark beneath the chassis lie several indistinct shapes – sleeping children making the most of the warmth from the engine.

The number of people who go out at night in Colonia Guerrero makes for a lot of after-hours activity. Agustín Lara, the legendary musician-poet, sang in the cabarets and lived in a number of different places in this barrio. It is a place for dancing and for vaudeville shows, with the Salón México, the Blanquita Teatro and the bar where "Paquita of the Barrio" stakes a claim to women's liberation, disarming the male public with her stock line: "You listening to me, you good-for-nothing?"

So-called "gentrification" has not been visited on this part of the city – the "modernisation" that entails raids to physically remove unwanted inhabitants. There are all sorts of *cantina* bars and one-night hotels, the clients of which are the preferred targets for the street children: begging money from them, selling stolen flowers, or, on a small scale, selling drugs to them.

And it so happens that they have gathered in a place of great historical resonance. August 13, 1521, saw the fall of Tenochtitlan, and as it was Saint Hippolytus's day, he became the city's patron saint.

Hippolytus was a bishop, and a figure of some controversy. In 217 he was labelled the "anti Pope" when he spoke up for excommunicates. In a near miracle, he managed to reconcile with Rome and on August 13, 236, his remains were returned to the city along with those of some other exiles.

Not many people know about Hippolytus, this saint of inclusiveness. A bit part actor in a religion with more than its fair share of leading roles. Chance had it that he would go on to become a patron saint in Mexico, but he did not even become a big name here. "His" church received a Judas the Apostle altar in 1982 – the patron saint of lost causes. Since then it has usually been referred to by this name, which makes a kind of sense in a country that has lost its way.

The last recorded Marian apparition took place across from the Church of Saint Hippolytus or Saint Judas, in 1997, when the Virgin Mary appeared in Hidalgo Metro Station. During the wettest part of the year, a street seller noticed that the moisture had left the outline of Mexico's patron saint on an alley wall, just where the wall met the ground in a natural niche.

Hidalgo, where Metro lines 2 and 3 meet, is one of the city's busiest stops. The miracle immediately made people want to visit the place, and the name of the station only added to the sense of wonder (Miguel Hidalgo sparked Mexico's struggle for independence from Spain when he raised a flag bearing an image of Mary in 1810).

Street children have sought refuge at this intersection, unaware of the church's link with lost causes, or that Mary appeared beneath the pavements where they lay their heads. Fate, that great lover of symbols, has deposited them at this crossroads of mixed hopes.

The capital of Mexico became a hub for street children in the twentieth century. Many arrived from the provinces (particularly Mexico's southern states) and Central America, others from the outlying barrios, towns and districts that make up the most heavily populated macropolis on the whole of the American continent.

I met up with José Ángel Fernández to discuss the subject. Mexico City's Public Notary no. 217 is one of the hardest-working champions of street children. Taught in his youth by the Marist Brotherhood, and a graduate of the Law Faculty at the National Autonomous University of Mexico, he remembers the precise moment in which his social vocation became clear to him: September 19, 1985, at 7.19 in the morning. The devastating earthquake that day confronted him with the need to do something for the place where he lived. He took part in the rescue operations and saw that there was a bigger, more protracted task to be done, helping the most vulnerable: the young.

The March sun flooded the small terrace attached to his offices. As he smoked, Fernández recalled the establishment of Pro Niños (Championing Children) twenty-three years earlier, an institution that in 2016 has 1,600 regular donors: "There are over 17,000 street children; 5,000 actually on the streets and another 12,000 in a 'street condition', meaning they might be able to get a roof over their heads for the night, but not on a permanent basis. Then another 200,000 who'll do three or four day stints on the street. Only 10 per cent are girls: it's almost impossible for them to survive, they immediately get drawn into prostitution. Then there's the second generation, children of the homeless. They don't know any other way of life, it's a shock to them to see a clean knife or a shower. We've got a thousand children off the streets in our twenty-three years, which is a lot, but not enough."

Every now and then a clerk would come out to the table where we were talking, and the notary would dash off a signature; on went the transactions under his name, while he described an alternate Mexico City, a place where a clean knife can be unsettling to a child who has only ever eaten with his or her hands: "The earthquake created new spaces for street children. For years they were the main inhabitants in the centre. They lived in what today is the Solidaridad Park, next to the Alameda Park. While the centre was being rebuilt, they left, scattered throughout the city. Previously they'd live together in large groups, now they go around in threes and fours. A lot have been sent back from the U.S.A. without adults to accompany them – that's a violation of international accords. You'll come across a nine-year-old holding a three-year-old's hand; not siblings, sometimes even originally from different countries, but they've joined forces somewhere along the way. Mexico City is the least bad place to wind up, elsewhere all manner of things might befall them, trafficking networks, people who'll kill them for their organs." Fernández points to my pen: "We've got kids, former gang members in Central America, they could kill you with one of those."

Objects take on different meanings in a context of fear and violence. As I carried on taking notes I thought of knives and forks, how they might feel threatening to a child who's never set foot in a kitchen before. Or how my work implement of choice could also transform into something else entirely. What depths would one have to plumb for a pen to become a murder weapon?

Families: the fingers on a hand

There are no street children who do not have family problems. Violence, instability and addiction are ubiquitous features of their pasts. In the Pro Niños home, I spoke to a young man named

Alejandro – tall, good looking, and with a melancholy look in his eye. I spent a little while with a group of boys who were living there and some others who were on a visit. He came over almost immediately to tell me his story.

He first spent time on the streets at the age of seven. Born in Colonia de los Doctores, he had been familiar with the central parts of the city from a young age. His mother had three children from previous relationships. He had not seen her at this point for four years, and it had been a good deal longer since he had last heard from his father. He recalled his father beating his mother when she was pregnant with Alejandro's sister; the girl was born deaf mute. One of his half-brothers was arrested as a minor after taking part in an armed robbery.

Alejandro has managed to rise above this chaos, and believes good can still come out of it. He turned twenty-one on February 22, 2016. He had an office job and was thinking about studying management. He had given up trying to see eye to eye with his mother ("She just won't stop and think about things"), but wanted to make sure his sister didn't suffer: "I worry she might cut herself, self-harm. She can't talk to anyone, she's shut up in her head."

Alejandro paused and glanced at the other Pro Niños children, who were playing basketball in the yard alongside where we sat talking. Then, taking my hand, he looked me in the eye: "Every sibling is a finger," he said, grasping my index finger, "and this one's me." His sister's name is Karina, a girl who cannot speak and who has received no support whatsoever. The dream of the boy who survived the streets was to rescue her. Her fate pained him, as though she were a part of his own body. Karina was in his hands – she was the ring finger.

Alejandro's heartrending desire to make something of a devastated family contrasts with the self-satisfaction you tend to hear in the voices of people whose main achievement in life is to have inherited a large sum of money.

Mexico is a pyramidal country in which certain surnames dominate almost all branches of the economy. In the summer of 2015 I flew in a jet operated by the Mexican Aeromar company, its "executive" line. The inflight magazine heaped praise on the country's main consortiums, and highlighted the fact they are mainly family businesses. The economy was seen as a natural offshoot of tradition and decency; encomiums were dedicated to businesses run by relatives, and not to those operated by professionals from outside the tribe. Without meaning to, the article emphasised something about Mexico: here, family is a luxury.

The jobs worked by poor people almost always entail shifts of eight hours or longer, and on average subject them to a four-hour commute – two hours each way. According to a study by the Organisation for Economic Cooperation and Development (O.E.C.D.), of the thirty-four countries surveyed, Mexicans worked the longest hours (an average of 2,228).[1]

Nurseries are inadequate and state schools will not take children for whole days. This being so, who is supposed to look after them? For some the family amounts to the transmission of power, a way of accessing business interests established by their ancestors (success in business depends on inheritance); for others, it is the vertigo inside which one must operate while trying to avoid homelessness and jail.

Another boy I met at the Pro Niños home in Colonia Buenavista, near Tlatelolco, was Leonardo. We played a brief game of football and he put a number of goals past me: "A pleasure playing with you," he said, with no little irony. He was the first to come over and start talking to me.

He wore a "Dallas" beanie on his head. He intially struck me as timid, but gradually did become talkative, and was quite deliberate over his choice of words.

One of his eyelids drooped – the result of an accident. He would scratch his forearm as he spoke and look down at the floor. Sometimes he would smile at nothing, stop for a moment, before going on with his tale: "I never met my father. My mother raised me on her own, and she had kids by other men. I used to abuse the youngest boy; I didn't know I was doing it. Mama drank a lot because she would come home really tired from her job as a security guard. She'd work 24-hour shifts, then have 24 hours off. Her knees would hurt from being on her feet so much. I was a good student – I was even appointed one of the school banner bearers! But Mama didn't have the money for the uniform so I got kicked out. Then I went to vocational college but again we didn't have enough money for the books. I once went and photocopied some books, and got in trouble. Mama had to look after all her kids and Grandma too, money was always short."

When his mother would fall asleep drunk, Leonardo would help himself to the dregs. He started going to parties, tried drugs (first marijuana, then solvents), and left school without his mother noticing – nor did she notice when he began spending two or three days away from the house at a time. Her exacting job involved watching over company buildings, but prevented her from watching over her own child.

Leonardo was born in Ecatepec, to the north of Mexico City, the area with the highest population density and the highest crime levels in the country. But he did not see it as a violent place. Maybe it was just familiarity, the strange acclimatisation that meant he also did not know when he was abusing his little half-brother. Over time he had learned to relate to people worse off than himself. Some children come to the day centre in a "street condition", like

Leonardo – that is, not living full time on the streets, sometimes going home, getting a change of clothes and a decent meal. Then there are those who have never had a roof over their heads and come to Pro Niños with some very serious issues. Getting better is no easy thing if you are surrounded by those who have had it worse. Leonardo found it hard at first to cope with spending time amongst kids who were in such a state – they made him feel like he was breaking down. Little by little he discovered an ability to identify with them, realising he was in a position to help. The thought of indifference came to worry him: "I'd like to be a psychologist, sometimes I spend so much time listening to people's problems they start crying."

When he was seventeen Leonardo had a job as a waiter in Colonia Roma. He almost got fired when an Argentinian customer asked for a Coca-Cola and a coffee and he brought them both at the same time. "He didn't say he wanted the cold one first and then the hot one."

Any luxury that exists in Mexico is contingent on poverty. A security guard who cannot supervise her child patrols a property for 24 hours without a break, and a youngster with no money for his school uniform must satisfy the demands of hot and cold in a restaurant.

Leonardo was studying to become an electrician, and thinking of completing the course online. He made huge efforts not to become distracted by all the online temptations. "I know, within me, it's bad if I watch videos." He had met German volunteers at Pro Niños, awakening an interest in that country: "I want it all, but I have to take things step by step: sometimes I catch the Germans saying things wrong in Spanish and it makes me think I could learn German." He smiled. "At least enough to speak it as badly as they do."

He made a pistol with his fingers and, with a wink, fired an imaginary shot.

Palliatives, not solutions

"80 per cent of Mexicans don't take part in public activities because they think they're just political activities," said José Ángel Fernández as we made the long trip from his offices in the south of the city to the Pro Niños centre of operations in Tlatelolco: "The church disseminated a culture of charity, and that prevented civil society from organising, and then the government has been so pro-welfare that it doesn't actually get people out volunteering. We do this from a feeling of simple charity: we're not after converts. It's very important to help in an unprejudiced way. Personally I hate actually getting my hands dirty, but there are other things I can do."

The street children phenomenon can only be understood if we see how attractive the streets are for people who opt for this way of life. It may end up as tragedy but it begins as an idyll of laziness and fun.

Mexico City is the perfect scenario for this. In a city that has been unable to define the exact size of its own population, nothing could be easier than maintaining one's anonymity. Children can get lost without being looked for, and the climate is kind enough to live outdoors. But the decisive factor is the treatment they receive from fellow citizens.

Tense and mistrustful situations abound in the city, and the community very rarely organises itself without the government prompting it do so. It could be said that we live in an empire of indifference. And yet, intermittently and spontaneously, millions here do give support to others. Not because of any programme but on the basis of feelings and impulses.

Who worries the most about other people? In 2010 I interviewed

Daniel Goñi Díaz, director of Red Cross Mexico, and he told me that, year on year, they find it to be the less well off who give most money.

It is quite common, when a beggar comes up to a taxi, for the driver to hand over a coin and for the passenger, usually someone with a higher salary, to give nothing. In the city whose stock exchange depends on the price of U.S. dollars, an economy based on centavo coins operates. It is no coincidence that the Mexican word for the perennially homeless person, the equivalent of the *clochard* who accepts penury as an existential condition, is *teporocho*; this literally translates as "tea for eight", alluding to an economy based on centavo coins (in the days when the term was coined an orange or cinnamon tea spiked with alcohol cost eight centavos).

Handouts have gradually become quite considerable. There are few organised initiatives, but no lack of people who feel impelled to donate clothes, food, the odd centavo. One of the effects is that children are able to survive on the streets. It is not a solution, it is a palliative; rather than offering ways out of mendicancy, it enables a slightly nicer version of it to continue.

Anthony Burgess, in his novel *Earthly Powers*, pointed out how good the English are at guarding against emotions, except for when it comes to their pets. Whereas in Mexico it is the norm for animals to be maltreated. Here we tend to cordon off a place emotionally that is reserved for children. Few countries tolerate more resignedly the noise, outbursts and the sheer rudeness of young ones. We see a hotel or a restaurant that does not admit children as a fascist enclave.

Street children receive more clothing and toys than they need. This is the fundamental reason why Mexico City is such a hotbed for minors without homes and families. Awful things have driven them to the street, but the hopes it awakens are equally strong – of a life without scholastic impositions or hygienic obligations, like the one so many children yearn for after reading Jules Verne's *Two Years' Holiday.*

"The street is one big party," says Fernández. "It's useless telling children to get off the streets: they have to become convinced of it themselves. This was why we set up the Day Centre, which is a transition shelter where they can come and be for a little while, eat, clean themselves up, without any obligation to stay. They have to leave their drugs at the door and they get them back on the way out."

The 1985 earthquake gave fresh impetus to street life. Large numbers of buildings were left empty in the area of seismic activity, which included central parts of the city. The ruins became the children's own ghost town. In the documentary "Night and Fog" (1955), Alain Resnais looks at the German towns that underwent bombardment during World War II. The only signs of life in this panorama are the children playing in the wreckage – like some eerie amusement park. What was once a neighbourhood has become a labyrinth, where they run and play with disquieting innocence.

And so it was after the earthquake: those who lived in the sewers returned to the surface and began occupying neighbourhoods and palaces from the time of the Viceroyalty (*c.* 1500–1800).

A couple of decades passed in which children lived in the shadow of the "old town". As new properties were built and old ones restored, they were forced to cede territory, but this is still where their numbers are most concentrated.

Do people really care about the city's children? Interest in them quickly morphs from affection to abuse. Very few survive the double prong of being on the street and the trafficking networks. Drug gangs, which go from strength to strength, have turned their sights on the young and homeless: "Twenty years ago, 60 per cent of the kids could take it or leave it," says Fernández. "Nowadays 95 per cent of them need to go through some kind of detox to even begin to recover. They're using different stuff too. Before it would be paint thinner, turps, glue, all of which is very damaging to the body, but not so addictive. Gangs exposed them to other drugs (marijuana, crack), and they turned out to be model addicts."

Around San Hipólito, at all hours of the night, whistling can be heard. It is a communication system far more efficient than social media.

To everything its historical moment, even whistling. The art of communicating in this way has gradually been disappearing from the city, and perhaps it will only live on as the legacy of the outcasts who use it for emergency rendezvous.

Outside the church of lost causes, the children still whistle for good luck.

To sleep underground

"90 per cent of street children have a parallel identity; on the street, their identity is substituted by other people knowing them. When they finally reveal their names it's because they've decided to make a change in their lives." After a quarter of a century fighting the problem, José Ángel Fernández has an aphorism to sum up destiny: "The worst affront to an individual is to grow up." I think of Peter Pan's phrase: "I won't grow up." As children, street dwellers can be tolerated and given help. All that awaits in adulthood is jail or general decline.

It so happens that across from Pro Niños' centre of operations in Colonia Buenavista, at No. 277, Calle Zaragoza, stands a Police Academy. Either side of the street represents an aspect of the country: the lawless children and those who supposedly uphold the law.

Laura Alvarado Castellanos, Director General of Pro Niños, speaks with great aplomb on the risks posed to the city poor by juvenile delinquency, shortcomings in the home and a lack of aspiration. She says, revealingly: "The most intelligent ones go out on the streets." You need initiative, willpower and adaptability if you are to survive there. But this is all changing: "Thirty years ago, the street was a place where solidarity could be formed, with the newspaper vendor, at the corner shop, with taxi drivers. But nowadays you have the gangs and they see street kids as the perfect drug mules. Also, no-one's going to come looking for them, so they've already in effect disappeared, and when they get involved in crime they learn to become even more invisible. Many of them don't look like beggars, they have a place to wash, they can sleep in a hotel, they camouflage themselves so that they can carry on selling drugs in the street. Another change we've seen is that they've become more consumerist. You might think they've got nothing, but it isn't so; they get paid to transport the drugs around, and they use too; they buy mobile phones, clothes, and they follow all the online and *telenovela* stereotypes they see. We've found it harder and harder over the last five years to find ways of connecting with them. They used to be more isolated, but nowadays the people who hooked them into crime keep an eye on us, they warn us to back off. One of our volunteers was kidnapped."

A psychologist with a degree from the Universidad Iberoamericana, Laura Alvarado Castellanos introduces me to some peculiar phenomena of street life. Like the large numbers of children abused in adolescence who then self-identify as gay because, that way, it feels less degrading to have been raped. It is a complex form of taking responsibility for the crimes done to them.

Before introducing me to the children at the Pro Niños centre, she informs me that many of them will tell their stories to get money. They know people are interested, and fashion their narratives according to their circumstances. This gives me pause; I wonder about my own part in this chain.

Laura volunteered for a number of years at a youth offenders organisation called the Consejo Tutelar de Menores (Youth Advisory Board). She was assigned to incarcerated youngsters who had no family, so no-one would be visiting them. There she learned that violence in the family is part of the problem, but the most serious things are social exclusion and a lack of alternatives. This is why the articulate and sharper ones seek out a more challenging and entertaining fate – the street, where they can embody dashing tales.

Once more I am reminded of my hopes of getting lost forever in the Forest of Chapultepec. I felt this same temptation, and now I share something else with them, the swapping of stories for money . . .

I ask Laura where street children congregate. As well as the old town, there are bastions like the Taxquena Metro station, which is surrounded by large car parks where they can assemble.

Not every homeless child sleeps exposed to the elements. At all hours of the day there are youngsters asleep in Metro carriages, with no fixed destination. They board and then rest in the false night of the underground, lulled by the rocking motion. These are children who work at night and find temporary shelter in the trains that move about beneath the city. They might wake and find themselves south, north, east or west – if night has fallen, they ride the train one more time with their eyes open.

On March 31, 2016, I interviewed a young man named Christian at another of the Pro Niños centres in Mexico City, the halfway house "Casa de Transición a la Vida Independiente" in Colonia Santa María la Ribera, where youngsters are allowed to stay for up to two years, until they are able to stand on their own two feet. Christian spent several years sleeping in the Metro by day and selling his body at night. It is hard to imagine anyone having been through more horrific things. And yet, at seventeen years of age, he spoke of the damage done to him with a sense of humour. He would smile, make a joke, touch the curly lock of hair that fell down the left side of his face, and glance around mischievously before returning to some dramatic moment from his life. His wounds had not entirely healed and he was still considered more vulnerable than most, but he showed a toughness far greater than many of the others in the shelter.

Christian mentioned strength a good deal, but not in the physical sense. His fortitude was based on humour. If something took his interest, he would cast a sidelong smile, the look of an intelligent troublemaker.

Like Leonardo, Christian was born in Ecatepec. And he had a similar family story to other street children. "I saw my father once but I don't remember what he looks like." His father disappeared and his mother had a child by another man, though it died soon after the birth. Then came a third child by a third man, this one given up for adoption. Drugs made it impossible for his mother to care for her children. Christian was raised by an older lady, and she was good to him, though he was constantly up to mischief: "I'm a joker, I like pranks. I was really bad when I was small; I loved breaking stuff and escaping out the window, loved it. Now I say stuff that might come across as offensive, but I'm only joking."

His adoptive mother put up with the broken crockery because he did unusually well at school. In his first trimester he got sixes, in the second sevens, and in the third tens – as though his grades depended on the nearness of holidays. The problems began later: He failed third grade, the same in fourth grade, and left school altogether in fifth grade.

His adoptive mother died when he was ten, and he was sent to live with his grandmother, who went back to her village soon after that. Christian moved in with an aunt. She was the fourth and the worst person to take charge of him. She was the one who took him out of school, and she forced him to sell sweets in the Metro. He saw nothing of his meagre profits, and would get a smack at the smallest protestation. The aunt had five children, all of whom she treated well. She took all her anger out on the stepchild: "If it rained it was my fault, I'd get a beating for that as well."

After a time she started sending him out to sell pirate C.D.s. He bought the blank discs in the barrio of Tepita, she would burn the music onto them and he would sell them in the Metro.

Until that time he had not had any friends. "I was always a loner," he said bluntly. "I can be a talker, but only with certain people." And then one day a girl burst in on his solitude. Her name was Norlendi, she was two years older than him and also lived in Ecatepec. "We used to play clapping games," said Christian, putting his hands up as if touching someone else's palms. "And we told each other our secrets. It was the first time I had the feeling of being understood by someone."

When he went to Norlendi's house, he was surprised to see a family that functioned without resorting to violence. "To me it was normal, people getting a beating. All my uncles hit their wives. It hadn't occurred to me that life could be different." He began spending more and more time at his friend's house until one day his aunt came to get him, boxing his ears as she dragged him through the door. Norlendi's brothers tried to stop her, even threatening to call the police – a phrase that in Mexico lacks any real force and only made the aunt laugh.

She forbade him to go back to Norlendi's house, saying they

were drug dealers. "That was a lie, she just said it because they had a better house than us."

Perhaps what hurt was the different treatment enjoyed by his cousins. They could leave school without getting in trouble, and they did not have to work. As Laura Alvarado Castellanos said, unfair treatment can be worse than physical violence.

One day Christian sold a pirate C.D. to a man for 300 pesos. It suddenly struck him as absurd to go back to his aunt's house. Important dates were fixed in his memory: "It was December 14, 2012," he says. That day, at thirteen years old, was the day he began living on the streets.

"I was cold but I didn't feel alone. My first night was hectic, I met someone on drugs, then another person who tried to assault me (luckily I'd already hidden my money in a shoe), then someone I knew drove by and took me back to his house, but when we got to the front door I turned and ran off into Ciudad Azteca. I didn't sleep at all that night, and when morning came the first thing I did was buy the Shakira C.D., "The Tune Robbers". It cost 99 pesos. Then a coffee and some bread. I got on the Metro and slept as the train went round and round."

A couple of weeks before deciding to leave home he had met Erick, a man ten years his senior. They had hit it off at the time, and now, not knowing which way to turn, Christian decided to call him. He tried all day, seeing his coins swallowed by public telephones ("One of them took a whole five-peso coin") until finally Erick picked up. Erick said he would help, they agreed to meet at his house and from there he took Christian to a hotel. "I'd asked for help and I wound up with a boyfriend. But I did fall in love with him over time. No-one has ever loved me like Erick did. Things went really well until my birthday, January 18. He asked me to help him download some documents from the internet, but the computer was really slow, and when he came back nothing had downloaded yet. He accused me of being in chatrooms with other men, he had a fit of jealousy and hit me. I felt guilty, I thought he was in the right. From then on he'd beat me every couple of weeks and I would feel like it was my fault, like I was getting things wrong. He lost his job and claimed it was because we were spending so much time together. Again, I felt like he was right. After that the beatings were the least of my worries. He stopped letting me go out, and he wouldn't let me go online either; I was trapped. My aunt had beat me in the past but at least I was able to go out; now I was getting beaten and I couldn't go anywhere. I carried on thinking he was justified in what he was doing, until he started bringing younger boys to bed. I told him he shouldn't do that, he threatened me, made me join in. He never used condoms. He'd beat me, and that would turn him on and he'd want to fuck. To me it felt more like rape than anything, but if I didn't let him, he'd just find other boys to do it with. I'd think: 'They can leave, but I've got it good because I'm the one he keeps on.' I'd console myself by saying that. He'd take them to the cinema or the ice-cream parlour, but I lived in the house."

I asked if there were not some good moments to justify living there. "There were," he said, "but not many. It went on for a year and a half, and then, as with my aunt, God came to me one day, and after one more beating I ran away." He went to Norlendi's house, stayed for three months, then returned to Erick. He found it impossible to leave his abuser, someone whose affection he hoped to win back. He finally decided to break the cycle, only to stumble into another: a friend connected him with a prostitution ring.

"Sex was the only thing I felt I was good for," he said. He started working one of the strips in the city centre, the bastion of corporate offices and hotels on Paseo de la Reforma, between the statues of Diana the Huntress and the Angel of Independence. Mexico City is an inverse Eden, a place where a minor can buy solvents to get high, and get a room with an adult, selling his body alongside transvestites on the city's main thoroughfare.

Christian would be up all night, sleeping the days away on the Metro. "In my case the clientele didn't vary much. I remember there'd be a few fair-haired guys working, and they did manage to reel in good-looking customers, but I just got the old guys, the drunks, the addicts, disgusting. There was one nice man, all he wanted to do was talk, and he gave me 2,000 pesos. I'm still in touch with one customer, this guy who just wanted to do stuff with my feet; he friended me on Facebook the other day. But some of them made me sick. One liked using a dildo on me. Use it on yourself, I thought. He became obsessed and was constantly sending text messages."

Some customers asked him to get high with them. Though he tried to resist, he had to use amyl nitrate and sometimes crack, never enjoying it. "I tried cocaine out of curiosity," he said, "but it made my hands shake and I dropped it everywhere. I never stole from anyone, I couldn't do it, there were lots of times when I had the chance but I think, deep down, I'm too much of a good person. I made friends in the night, another boy called Christian, and one called Jair. We'd play clapping games, and sometimes we'd get hired as a pair, or all three. Then the two of them went off together and I felt really alone again. It was a bad time. I went back to Erick, my only love, and the beating started over. I started slipping away, giving up, I thought about suicide. I began sleeping by a Banamex cash machine on Reforma, I was skin and bones at this point, I hardly ate, drank water from the taps in the Sanborns restrooms. That's how I was when I met a guy from Honduras who told me about Pro Niños. At first I thought it was some kind of jail, they'd lock you in, abuse you. When I finally decided to come and check it out, the shelter the only thing on my mind was eating and getting some sleep. Mind you, when I got here I still had my Shakira C.D.s, I always kept them with me."

With the support of Pro Niños, he started to see his past for what it was and learned to talk about his experiences with a fluency I saw for myself. He had missed a year of elementary school (ages 5–11), and within five days had managed to pass the exams. Then, in a space of six months, with only the use of study guides, he caught up on the secondary stage of education (12–15). He had an alert mind, but complained that he found it hard to concentrate: "I find it impossible to read a whole book, *Rubius* [a comic] is about all I've read, I've got that in my room." He was in "prepara-toria" when we spoke (ages 15–18), taking classes in English, swimming, drama and guitar. I asked him where he saw himself in five years' time. "On camera, or in front of lots of people, talking about important stuff."

And did he still see Norlendi? "She's pleased I'm doing better, but she isn't wild about the person I've become. I'm more outgoing now but less of a joker. I like to laugh about the things that hurt me. My sense of humour is very cutting. I had syphilis and when I was cured of it, it was like getting over an obstacle, now I can laugh about it."

I asked him about his dreams, and he said he couldn't remember them. Then he thought for a few moments, blew his hair out of his face and said: "When I was on the streets, selling myself, I imagined singing at a concert hall; I had a feeling that everyone in the audience loved me. And recently I have started to dream. I see the Christian my aunt used to hit, but he's me as I am now, and he fights back, he doesn't let her."

He had been watching foreign films with subtitles in English as a way of learning the language, and said he would like to travel to Spain and England. Also that he wanted to have a small dog one day, perhaps a chihuahua.

I asked if he had ever thought about having a tattoo. "I have, but I wouldn't want to not be able to donate blood – if I got hepatitis or something . . ." And what tattoo would he get? "The Shakira logo! No, that would be silly, something else." He stopped for a moment. I did not need to ask any follow-up questions; he sat thinking, very absorbed, about what marks he would like to make on his skin: "I'd get a wolf," he eventually declared. "Wolves are aggressive, they're survivors."

How would he describe his character? He said he was like music: "My personality's like a sponge. When I listen to Shakira I'm sweet (when I met Erick everything was love and everything was also Shakira), with Gloria Trevi I'm bold, cheeky, with Miley Cyrus I get in people's faces. I'd like to join the three together, but each has its place: I can't be Miley Cyrus at a funeral!"

Does Erick still come looking for him? "He just has been, actually, and I'm doing therapy to stop myself from falling for him again. I know he's bad for me." On occasion, having told his story so many times, Christian lapses into the third person – not with the vanity of a football star, but as though all these things had happened to some other person: "Christian's quiet, keeps himself to himself, finds it hard to make friends." This is how he talked of the past; the first person was reserved for the present; and there was another facet to the quiet Christian: "I like to be listened to, particularly by large groups of people. What I'd like to do is teach sexual health."

With the interview over, I walked through the Colonia Santa María la Ribera down to San Cosme station. I took the train towards Hidalgo station, the place where a miracle occurred, opposite the church of lost causes.

Before I got there I saw a child sleeping deeply. He slept as only a person can who knows that this is his only home in the treacherous Mexican night.

The orphan who saved a president

The self-willed hell I wished for in my youth (getting lost forever in the Forest of Chapultepec) was another child's paradise.

Guillermo Prieto, a writer and liberal politician, was born in 1818 in Molino del Rey, near Chapultepec, when the country was engaged in its struggle for independence. In *Memorias de mis tiempos* (Memoir of My Times) he recounts a childhood spent in the countryside; in those days Molino del Rey had yet to become part of Mexico City. Prieto would go to the lake, crossing through the forest with its thousand-year-old Montezuma cypresses as he went.

He wanted for nothing as a child; he grew up well loved and with all kinds of sensory stimulation, much of it related to food, something he always enjoyed. Upon the death of his grandfather, there was sufficient money for the family to move to a central part of the city. The Arcadia of that time changed, though, with the sudden death of his father at the age of thirty-three. The consequences were dramatic: "My mother never recovered," Prieto writes in his memoirs. "Strangers took over the family assets, which were considerable." At thirteen, he went to live with a family of dressmakers and became accustomed to wearing worn-out shoes.

He would visit his mother periodically. He found her immersed in a mental fog; a woman of thirty, gentle and serene in appearance, no longer able to relate to anyone around her. She would not always know who he was, but she liked the bonbons he brought. Prieto would come away bathed in tears, though never entirely losing hope for her recovery.

He did not have money for books but discovered literature in a public park. Poets would compete with one another in Alameda Park by hanging their sonnets up in little wooden frames. Prieto learned rhetoric by reading these over and over: "Alameda Park was my great poetic gymnasium," he writes.

One night he overheard the dressmakers talking of their struggle to make ends meet; they had stopped eating so that they could continue to feed him. A little later, a cholera epidemic swept through the city, and his brother nearly died.

At fifteen, Prieto felt he had to do something to bring his troubles to an end. Enraged by the life he had been dealt, he went to see the Minister of Justice, Andrés Quintana Roo. In 1833 Mexico was still an experiment of a country, yet to define itself. In this, a scenario in which hopes outweighed reality, a child could go and knock on the door of a government minister. Quintana Roo wept when he heard this young man's tale – a young man almost exactly the same age as the nation. He found him a job that meant he could pay for the care of his mother, help his benefactors and continue to study.

Four years later, Prieto read a poem in front of the president, Anastasio Bustamante. The statesman was so impressed that he asked for the young man to come and see him in his office. A brief meeting was enough to join the pair's destinies. Bustamante had a bed set up for the young poet in the governmental palace and put him in charge of editing the *Diario Oficial*, which recounted the government's day-to-day workings.

In his biography of Prieto, Malcolm McLean says: "And so the poor young orphan achieved, by dint of his own efforts, a position as a trusted employee, a respectable place in the presidential household." The surprising thing is not for a young man to have talent, but for him to have received such support.

Prieto went on to become one of the foremost writers and liberal politicians of the nineteenth century; the Palacio Nacional lodger became the republic's staunchest defender. Later President Benito Juárez appointed him Treasury Minister, and he in turn went on to save Juárez's life: in Guadalajara, Prieto at his side, Juárez was ambushed by some enemies. As bullets flew, the writer who learned to read in a public park is said to have come out with the line: "A brave man is never an assassin." At these words, the killers put down their arms.

Prieto was an exceptional witness to the vicissitudes of life in the Mexican capital, the independence struggle and the North American invasion of 1847, experiencing famines, epidemics and endless changes of government in his time. His fate was as hard to predict as that of Mexico in the nineteenth century. Between the ages of thirteen and nineteen there was every chance he would share the trajectory of street children today, but he received the backing of a country just as unsteady as him, one that had barely begun to consolidate itself. The Minister of Justice opened his door to him, and the President offered him a bed in his home.

Prieto placed his confidence in a fledgling nation. Vicente Quirarte was right to describe his career in the following way: "The fatherland was his profession."

There was a time when a child could call at justice's door and be admitted.

Things are different in 2016. Tonight around San Hipólito, next to the Alameda Park where Guillermo Prieto learned the art of poetry, children will make their beds beneath a truck or down in the sewer.

Translated by Thomas Bunstead

APPENDIX 1

REGISTER OF 94 JOURNALISTS, BROADCASTERS AND PHOTOGRAPHERS MURDERED IN MEXICO SINCE 2000

Between January 2000 and May 2016, Article 19 has documented the murder of 94 journalists in Mexico in possible relation to their journalistic work.

Since the beginning of Enrique Peña Nieto's six-year presidential term, which began in 2012, the death count of journalists stands at 21. Oaxaca and Veracruz are the deadliest states during the current administration, with 5 murders in Oaxaca and 6 in Veracruz.

The office of the present Governor of Veracruz, Javier Duarte of the Institutional Revolutionary Party (P.R.I.) began in December 2010, and has been the deadliest on record for journalists: in addition to the case of Rubén Espinosa, who was murdered in Mexico City in 2015 where he was living in exile having fled Veracruz, 16 journalists have been murdered in the state during Duarte's time in office.

Of the 94 murdered journalists, 87 are men and 7 are women. The most recent case is that of Manuel Torres (Veracruz).

(Updated in May 2016)

Translated by Sophie Hughes

Date of death	Name of journalist /photographer or broadcaster	Media outlet if known
2000		
1 February	Luís Roberto Cruz Martínez	Multicosas
9 April	Pablo Pineda Gaucín	La Opinión
19 July	Hugo Sánchez Eustaquio	La Verdad
2001		
19 February	José Luís Ortega Mata	Semanario de Ojinaga
9 March	José Barbosa Bejarano	Alarma
24 March	Saúl Martínez Gutiérrez	El Imparcial
2002		
17 January	Félix Fernández García	Nueva Opción
16 October	José Miranda Virgen	Imagen
2003		
13 December	Rafael Villafuerte Aguilar	La Razón
2004		
19 March	Roberto Mora García	El Mañana
22 June	Francisco Ortiz Franco	Zeta
31 August	Francisco Arratia	Freelance
28 November	Gregorio Rodríguez	El Debate
2005		
8 April	Raúl Gibb Guerrero	La Opinión
16 April	Dolores García Escamilla	Stéreo 91
17 September	José Reyes Brambila	Milenio Jalisco
2006		
6 January	José Valdés	Not specified
9 March	Jaime Olvera Bravo	Freelanción
10 March	Ramiro Téllez Contreras	EXA FM
9 August	Enrique Perea Quintanilla	Dos Caras
27 October	Bradley Roland Will	Indymedia

Date of death	Name of journalist /photographer or broadcaster	Media outlet if known
10 November	Misael Tamayo Hernández	El Despertar de la Costa
15 November	José Manuel Nava	Excélsior
21 November	Roberto Marcos García	Testimonio
30 November	Adolfo Sánchez Guzmán	Orizaba en vivo
8 December	Raúl Marcial Pérez	El Gráfico
2007		
6 April	Amado Ramírez Dillanes	Televisa
23 April	Saúl Noé Martínez	Interdiario
8 December	Gerardo García Pimentel	La Opinión de Michoacán
2008		
5 February	Francisco Ortiz Monroy	Diario de México
8 February	Alfonso Cruz Pacheco	El Real
8 February	Bonifacio Cruz Santiago	El Real
7 April	Teresa Bautista Merino	Radio Copala
7 April	Felicitas Martínez Sánchez	Radio Copala
23 June	Candelario Pérez Pérez	Sucesos
23 September	Alejandro Fonseca Estrada	EXA FM
9 October	David García Monroy	El Diario de Chihuahua
10 October	Miguel Villagómez Valle	La Noticia de Michoacán
13 November	Armando Rodríguez Carreón	El Diario
2009		
13 February	Jean Paul Ibarra Ramírez	El Correo
22 February	Luís Méndez Hernández	Radiorama
3 May	Carlos Ortega Melo Samper	Tiempo de Durango
25 May	Eliseo Barrón Hernández	Milenio
28 July	Juan Daniel Martínez Gil	Radiorama
23 September	Norberto Miranda Madrid	Radio Visión

Date of death	Name of journalist /photographer or broadcaster	Media outlet if known
2 November	Bladimir Antuna Vázquez	Tiempo de Durango
23 December	Alberto Velázquez López	Expresiones Tulum
31 December	José Luis Romero	Línea Directa

2010

8 January	Valentín Valdés Espinosa	Zócalo
29 January	Jorge Ochoa Martínez	El Sol de la Costa
3 March	Jorge Rábago Valdez	La Prensa
12 March	Evaristo Pacheco Solís	Visión Informativa
28 June	Francisco Rodríguez Ríos	El Sol de Acapulco
6 July	Hugo Olivera Cartas	La Voz de Michoacán
10 July	Guillermo Alcaraz Trejo	Omnia
10 July	Marco Martínez Tijerina	La Tremenda
16 September	Carlos Santiago Orozco	El Diario
5 November	Alberto Guajardo Romero	Expreso

2011

25 March	Luis Emanuel Ruíz Carrillo	La Prensa de Maclova
1 June	Noel López Olguín	Noticias de Acayucan
13 June	Pablo Aurelio Ruelas	El Regional
20 June	Misael López Solana	Notiver
20 June	Miguel Ángel López Velasco	Notiver
27 July	Yolanda Ordaz de la Cruz	Notiver
25 August	Humberto Millán Salazar	A Discusión
24 September	Elizabeth Macías Castro	Primera Hora

2012

28 April	Regina Martínez	Proceso
3 May	Guillermo Luna	Veracruz News
3 May	Esteban Rodríguez	Veracruz News
3 May	Gabriel Huge	Veracruz News
18 May	Marcos Ávila	El Regional de Sonora
14 June	Víctor Manuel Báez	Milenio
14 November	Adrián Silva Moreno	Freelance

Date of death	Name of journalist /photographer or broadcaster	Media outlet if known
2013		
3 March	Jaime González	Ojinaga Noticias
24 April	Daniel Martínez Bazaldúa	Vanguardia
24 June	Mario Ricardo Chávez	El Cuidadano
17 July	Alberto López Bello	El Imparcial
2014		
11 February	Gregorio Jiménez	Notisur
29 July	Nolberto Herrera	Canal 9
11 August	Octavio Rojas	El Buen Tono
11 October	Atilano Román	Locutor / Así Es Mi Tierra
22 October	Antonio Gamboa	Nueva Prensa
2015		
2 January	Moisés Sánchez	La Unión
14 April	Abel Bautista Raymundo	Transmitiendo Sentimientos
4 May	Armando Saldaña	EXA FM
26 June	Gerardo Nieto	Nuevo Siglo
30 June	Juan Mendoza Delgado	Escribiendo la Verdad
2 July	Filadelfo Sánchez	La Favorita 103.3 FM
31 July	Rubén Espinosa	Proceso / Cuartoscuro
2016		
21 January	Marcos Hernández Bautista	Noticias en la Costa
8 February	Anabel Flores	Sol de Orizaba
20 Feburary	Moisés Lutzow	Radio XEVX
25 April	Francisco Pacheco	El Sol de Acapulco
May 15	Manuel Torres González	Noticias MT

APPENDIX 2

ABOUT ARTICLE 19 MEXICO AND CENTRAL AMERICA

Article 19 Mexico and Central America is an independent, non-partisan organisation that promotes and defends the progressive advancement of freedom of expression and freedom of information for all people, reflecting the highest international human rights standards, and thus contributing to the strengthening of democracy.

In order to accomplish its mission, the primary functions of Article 19 Mexico and Central America are:

- demanding the right to disseminate information and opinions across all media;
- investigating threats and trends;
- documenting violations against freedom of expression;
- intervening in cases where individuals' or groups' rights have been violated; and
- helping to develop public policies in its specific field of action.

In this sense, Article 19 Mexico and Central America envisions a region where all people can: express themselves in a free, safe and equal environment; exercise their right to freedom of information; and, subsequently, facilitate society's participation in making informed decisions about themselves and their environment, effecting the realisation of other individual rights.

Article 19 was founded in London, England, in 1987. The organisation takes its name from Article 19 of the Universal Declaration of Human Rights:

Everyone has the right to freedom of opinion and expression; this right includes freedom to hold opinions without interference and to seek, receive, and impart information and ideas through any media and regardless of frontiers.

The Mexico and Central America office began operations in 2006.

Translated by Sophie Hughes

NOTES

Elena Poniatowska: Preface

1 "To disappear" was first noted in English as a transitive verb by US author Joan Didion in her book *Salvador* (London: The Hogarth Press, 1983, p.57). The 1980s was a period of military dictatorship, dirty wars, the prelude to "US interference" via the Contra war. In Spanish and across Central America the term was used to mean both forced abduction followed by absence, indefinite until evidence proves its mortal finality.

2 <http://www.jornada.unam.mx/2013/11/03/opinion/a03a1cul>

3 Carmen Aristegui is an admired Mexican journalist and TV presenter, who is known for her critical investigations of the Mexican government. She presents the news programme *Aristegui* on CNN in Spanish, and contributes to the opinion section of the periodical *Reforma*. She was fired from her regular role on Mexico's MVS Radio in March 2015 following allegations of a conflict of interest on the part of President Peña Neto and his wife.

4 "Interruptions from the West (3) (Mexico City: The 1968 Olympiad), trans. Eliot Weinberger, from Octavio Paz: *Collected Poems 1957–1987* (New York: New Directions, 2012)

Felipe Restrepo Pombo: Introduction – Narrating the Downfall

1 Translation of "New Manifesto of Infrarrealist Journalism" by Diego Enrique Osorno by Jennifer Adcock.

Juan Villoro: Collateral Damage – Living in Mexico

1 "Sunstone", *The Collected Poems of Octavio Paz 1957–87,* trans. Eliot Weinberger (New York: New Directions, 2012).

Anabel Hernández: The Hours of Extermination

1 For many years the students have been under attack from the government in many ways. The government does not want to have to maintain the school, and deals forcefully with the students' protests. There had been two earlier incidents: in 2007, when one protest was dispersed, 250 people were injured, two seriously. In December 2011, a similar event occurred, during which Jorge Alexis Herrera and Gabriel Echeverria were killed by the federal and local police. No official went to jail for these crimes.

2 The intelligence agencies of the Mexican government had been monitoring Ayotzinapa for many years because former students of the school, for

example Lucio Cabañas, had later joined the guerrilla movement in
Guerrero.

Diego Enrique Osorno: I'm the Guilty One

1 P.P.G. Industries: North American company, founded as Pittsburgh Plate
  Glass in 1883. P.P.G. Industries is "a global supplier of paints, coatings,
  optical products, specialty materials, glass and fiber glass".

Marcela Turati: The Graves Correspondent

1 F.E.M.O.S.S.P. was set up in 2001 by President Vicente Fox and closed
  in 2006 before Felipe Calderón came into office.
2 Factories in Mexico assembling e.g. electrical goods from parts made
  elsewhere (often the U.S.A.) and enjoying special tax breaks. A *maquila*
  is a "processing fee".

Sergio González Rodríguez: Anamorphosis of a Victim

1 This text is a chapter from the book *Campo de Guerra* (Barcelona:
  Anagrama, 2014) by Sergio González Rodríguez that was awarded the
  Anagrama Essay Prize in Barcelona in 2014.
2 José Zamora Grant, *Derecho victimal. La víctima en el Nuevo Sistema penal
  mexicano* (México, Instituto Nacional de Ciencias Penales, 2009), 215.
3 Alejandro Linares Zárate, *La Justicia. Su simbología y valores que concurren
  en su aplicación* (México: UAMEX, 2005), consulted February 4, 2013:
  <http://uaemex.mx/indentidad/docs/JUSTICIA.pdf>; on the pyramidal
  concept of positive Law, that affirms that any norm bases its validity on a
  higher norm: Hans Kelsen, *Pure Theory of Law*, translated by Max Knight
  (Los Angeles: University of California Press, 1967).
4 Franz Kafka, "Before the Law", Nahum N. Glatzer (ed.), Franz Kafka,
  The Complete Stories and Parables, 3–4, translated by Willa and Edwin
  Muir (New York: The Quality Paperback Book Club, 1971). Originally
  published in the independent Jewish weekly, *Selbstwehr*, 1915.
5 "Anamorphosis – a word that appears in the seventeenth century though
  related to previous compositions – proceeds via an inversion of elements and
  functions. Rather than a gradual reduction to their visible boundaries, it is
  a dilation, a projection of forms outside themselves, executed in such a way
  that they are configured towards a specific point of view: destruction via
  re-assembly, escape implying a return [...] An anamorphosis is a puzzle, a
  monster, a prodigy": Jurgis Baltrušaitis, *Les perspectives depravées*, Volume
  2: *Anamorphoses* (Paris: Flammarion, 1996), 7–8. First published, 1955.
6 My argument here follows Giorgio Agamben's line of thought, when he

states: "bare life, that is, the life of *homo sacer* (sacred man) *who may be killed yet not sacrificed* [...] An obscure figure of archaic Roman law in which human life is included in the juridical order solely in the form of its exclusion (that is, of its capacity to be killed)", Agamben, *Homo Sacer: Sovereign Power and Bare Life,* translated by Daniel Heller-Roazen, (Stanford: Stanford University Press, 1998), 12. "Its capacity to be killed" is a fact in Mexican society, where the index of unpunished crimes is absolute.

7   S.A., "Homicidas de edecán, al servicio de El Teo", *El Universal,* August 8, 2009. Also consulted February 4, 2013: <http://blogs.periodistadigital.com/ Hermosillo.php/2009/08/07/p245576->.

8   A case noted by S.G.R., the victim's name has been changed to protect his identity.

9   A case noted by S.G.R., the victim's name has been changed to protect his identity.

10 A case noted by S.G.R., the victim's name has been changed to protect his identity.

11 Human Rights Watch, *Neither Rights Nor Security: Killings, Torture and Disappearances in Mexico's War on Drugs* (New York: Human Rights Watch, 2011), 72.

12 Ibid., 68.

13 A case noted by S.G.R., the victim's name is changed to protect his identity.

14 A case noted by John Gibler, *To Die in Mexico: Dispatches from Inside the Drug War* (San Francisco: City Lights, 2011).

15 A case noted by S.A., "Patrulla fronteriza mata a un mexicano", El Universal/lavanguardia.com.mx, October 12, consulted February 4, 2013: <http://www.vanguardia.com.mx/patrullafronterizamataaunmexica- no-1392881.html->.

16 *U.S. Navy Survival, Evasion, Resistance and Escape Handbook* (U.S.A.: Department of Defence, 2011, Kindle Edition), location 36–41 and following.

17 Article 3, 1.d. of the Geneva Convention, 1949, in respect of the treatment of prisoners of war states: "the passing of sentences and the carrying out of executions without previous judgement pronounced by a regularly constituted court, affording all the judicial guarantees which are recognised as indispensable by civilised peoples", consulted February 4, 2003: <http://www.icrc.org/ihl/WebART/375-590006>.

18 A critical analysis of the origin and meaning of this phrase can be found in: Jimmy Sun, "*Inter arma silent leges*", U.S.A., CS 1993 Final Project May 14, 2007, s.f., consulted February 4, 2013: <http://www.eecs.harvard.edu/ cs199r/fp/Jimmy.pdf>.

19 Barry D. Watts, *Clausewitzian Friction and Future War* (Washington D.C.:
    McNair Paper 25, October 1996), 2 and following, consulted February 4,
    2013: <http/com.mx/books.google.vom.mx//books>.

20 Nicolas Skrotzky, *La Terre victime de guerres* (Paris: Les Dossiers de
    l'écologie, France, 2002).

21 Slavoj Žižek, *Looking Awry. An Introduction to Jacques Lacan through
    Popular Culture* (Massachusetts: MIT Press, 1992).

22 Jurgis Baltrušaitis, "'The Ambassadors' of Holbein'", in *Les perspectives
    depravées*, Tome 2. *Anamorphoses* (Paris: Flammarion, 1996), 125–160;
    Slavoj Žižek, "Looking Awry", *October* 50, Fall, 1989, 30–55.

23 For a study of war generations and, in particular, the fourth generation or
    4GW: Thomas Hammes, *The Sling and the Stone* (U.S.A.: Zenith Press,
    2006, kindle edition), 212–16.

24 Eyal Weizman, "Walking Through Walls", Transversal Texts,
    <http://www.eipcp.net/transversal/0507/weizman/en> Also: Sean J.A.
    Edwards, *Swarming on the Battlefield: Past, Present, And Future*
    (U.S.A.: Rand Corporation, Kindle edition).

25 On the effect of social networks on the war against drug dealing in Mexico:
    Andrés Monroy-Hernández, Emre Kiciman, Danah Boyd, Scott Counts,
    "Narcotweets: Social Media in Wartime", U.S.A., Microsoft Research, 2011,
    consulted February 4, 2013: <http://research.microsoft.com/pubs/160480/
    ICWSM12-093.pdf>.

26 Weizman, op. cit.

27 Rubén Martín, "Narco y violencia en Guadalajara", *El Economista*, March
    12, 2012, consulted February 4, 2013: <http://eleconomista.com.mx/
    columnas/columna-especial-politica/2012/03/12/narco-violencia-
    guadalajara>.

28 René Ramón and Israel Dávila, *La Jornada*, September 7, 2012,
    consulted February 4, 2013: <http://www.jornada.unam.mx/2012/09/07/
    estados/032n1est>.

29 S.A., "Desmantelan una red de comunicación de Los Zetas", *Excélsior*,
    August 24, 2012, consulted February 4, 2013: <http://excelsior.com.mx/
    index.mx/index.php?m=nota&id nota=855319&seccion=
    seccion-nacional&cat=1>.

30 Jean Clair, *Hubris, La fabrique du monstre dans l'art moderne*, Paris,
    Éditions Gallimard, 2012.

31 For a selection of official propaganda against drug trafficking:
    Alejandro Poiré Romero, *Porqué el narcotráfico se hizo más violento
    en los últimos años?*, México, Gobierno Federal, August 21, 2011:
    <http://presidencia.gob.mx/blog/blog -alejandro-poire/;

also, consulted February 4, 2013: http://www.youtube.com/
watch?v=rPFR0Yif4>.

32 The data describing these vehicles comes from: S.A., "Blindados del narco,
monstruos inoperantes", *La Razón*, June 18, 2012, consulted February 4,
2013: <http://www.razon.com.mx/spip.php?article80753>.

33 Jameson points to machines as icons, "they are still visible emblems,
sculptured nodes of energy which give tangibility and figuration to the
motive energies of that earlier moment of modernisation", Fredric
Jameson, "Postmodernism, or The Cultural Logic of Late Capitalism",
The New Left Review, 1/46, July-August 1984, 78; Deena Weinstein, *Heavy
Metal: The Music and its Culture* (New York: Da Capo Press, 2000).

Anabel Hernández: In the Dungeons of the Mexican Government

1 See Anabel Hernández, "The Hours of Extermination", *Sorrows of Mexico,*
167–91. Students of the Raúl Isidro Burgos Rural Teachers College in the
municipality of Ayotzinapa are known as *normalistas.*

Lydia Cacho: Fragments from a Reporter's Journal

1 Jacinto, Rodríguez Munguía. *La otra guerra secreta: Los archivos prohibidos
de la prensa y el poder* (The Other Secret War: The forbidden archives of
the press and power) (Mexico City: Debate, 2007).

2 Mexico: Random House Mondadori, 2005.

3 L.C. is here referring *Los Demonios de Edén: el poder detrás de la
pornografía infantil* (The Demons of Eden: The power behind child
pornography) and other books she has written.

Sergio González Rodríguez: Mexico – Return to the Abyss

1 Sergio González Rodríguez, *Huesos en el desierto* (Barcelona: Editorial
Anagrama, 2005), 334; Sergio González Rodríguez, *The Femicide Machine*
(Cambridge, MA: Semiotext(e)/ MIT Press, 2012), 136.

2 <http://www.corteidh.or.cr/docs/casos/articulos/seriec_205_esp.pdf>.

3 Julia E. Monárrez Fragoso y Luis E. Cervera Gómez, *Special Rapporteur
on extrajudicial, summary or arbitrary executions United Nations Human
Rights Office of the High Commissioner for Human Rights, Ciudad Juárez*
(2013), 23.

4 <https://es.wikipedia.org/wiki/Ecatepec_de_Morelos>.

5 Jana Vasil'eva, et al., *Violencia de género y feminicidio en el Estado de
México: La percepción y las acciones de las organizaciones de la sociedad
civil* (México: CIDE, 2016), digital edition, without page numbers.

6 <http://archivo.eluniversal.com.mx/nacion-mexico/2014/

ecatepec-34foco-rojo-34-por-ninias-desaparecidas-1024477.html>.

7   <http://www.proceso.com.mx/332860/edomex-la-calle-de-la-pesadilla>
    <http://alsanguines.blogspot.mx/2011/06/problemas-ambientales-en-el-
    municipio.html>.

8   <http://www.sinembargo.mx/07-11-2015/1541883>.

9   <http://joveneshaciendohistoria.wikispaces.com/
    HISTORIA+DE+ECATEPEC>.

10 <http://www.dineroenimagen.com/2014-12-03/47312>.

11 <http://www.elmanana.com/estalla_pipa_de_gas_en_ecatepec-2068195.
    html>.

12 <http://www.udlap.mx/igimex/> <http://www.vanguardia.com.mx/articulo/
    en-cada-dia-del-2015-asesinaron-51-personas-en-mexico> <http://www.oem.
    com.mx/elsoldetijuana/notas/n3429535.htm>; Homero Campa, "En este
    sexenio, 13 desaparecidos al día", *Proceso*, February 8, 2015, 8–19.
    También: Federico Mastrogiovanni, *Ni vivos ni muertos* (México: Editorial
    Grijalbo, 2014), 232.

13 Christy Thorton and Adam Goodman, "How the Mexican Drug Trade
    Thrives on Free Trade", *The Nation*, cf <http://www.thenation.com/
    article/180587/how-mexican-drug-trade-thrives-free-trade#>.

14 <http://www.informador.com.mx/mexico/2016/641159/6/es-mexico-el-
    mas-corrupto-entre-los-paises-de-la-ocde.htm> <http://www.informador.com.
    mx/mexico/2016/641159/6/es-mexico-el-mas-corrupto-entre-los-paises-de-
    la-ocde.htm>.

15 Daniel Sada, *Porque parece mentira la verdad nunca se sabe* (México:
    Editorial Tusquets, 1999).

16 <http://www.elfinanciero.com.mx/sociedad/miles-protestan-en-ecatepec-
    contra-la-inseguridad.html> <http://archivo.eluniversal.com.mx/
    notas/642273.html>.

17 *Observatorio Ciudadano Nacional del Feminicidio, Estudio de la
    implementación del tipo penal de feminicidio en México: causas y
    consecuencias*, 2012 and 2013, 112 ff.

18 Ibid., 115.

19 <http://www.elfinanciero.com.mx/sociedad/21-cuerpos-son-hallados-
    durante-el-drenado-del-gran-canal-en-edomex.html>

20 <http://www.sinembargo.mx/13-10-2014/1141967>.

21 <http://www.theguardian.com/world/2015/apr/15/mexico-missing-
    girls-canal>.

22 Ibid.

23 <http://eleconomista.com.mx/sociedad/2015/07/28/decretan-alerta-
    genero-feminicidios-edomex>.

24 <https://www.imta.gob.mx/gaceta/anteriores/g04-08-2007/sistema-drenaje-mexico.html>.

25 Armando Ramírez, *Violación en Polanco* (México: Editorial Grijalbo, 1980), 151.

26 Humberto Padgett y Eduardo Loza, *Las muertas del Estado* (México: Editorial Grijalbo, 2014), 416.

27 <http://www.contralinea.com.mx/archivo-revista/index.php/2015/02/10/impune-feminicidio-en-mexico/> <http://www.animalpolitico.com/2014/03/6-mujeres-son-asesinadas-al-dia-en-mexico-la-mitad-es-feminicidio/>.

28 <http://www.elfinanciero.com.mx/archivo/casi-70-de-los-mexicanos-se-siente-inseguro-y-desconfia-de-sus-autoridades-inegi.html>.

29 Sergio González Rodríguez, *Campo de guerra* (Barcelona: Editorial Anagrama, 2014), 168; Sergio González Rodríguez, *El robo del siglo* (México: Editorial Grijalbo, 2015), 150; Sergio González Rodríguez, *Los 43 de Iguala. México: verdad y reto de los estudiantes desaparecidos* (Barcelona: Anagrama, 2015), 157.

30 Sergio González Rodríguez, *Extreme Violence as Spectacle: I Within* (Los Angeles: Semiotext(e), 2014), 18.

31 The circumstances of this episode can be found in: González Rodríguez, *Huesos en el desierto*, 274 ff.

32 <http:Con//www.jornada.unam.mx/ultimas/2015/02/24/en-15-anos-103-periodistas-asesinados-y-otros-25-desaparecidos-informe-9674.html>.

33 <http://www.proceso.com.mx/417092/caso-narvarte-sin-movil-y-con-indicios-torales-extemporaneos-articulo-19>.

34 Instagram: @espinosafoto.

35 <http://www.elfinanciero.com.mx/nacional/cidh-visita-veracruz-ante-altos-indices-de-violencia.html>.

36 Email from Koral Carballo to S.G.R., January 26, 2016.

37 VV. AA., *Detonar y develar. Fotografía en México circa 2016* (México: CONACULTA/ Centro de la Imagen, 2015).

Juan Villoro: Street Children

1 <https://stats.oecd.org/Index.aspx?DataSetCode=ANHRS> (published in 2014 and consulted May 20, 2016).

NOTES ON THE AUTHORS

Lydia Cacho Ribeiro is a Mexican journalist, feminist and human rights activist, whose reporting focuses on violence against and sexual abuse of women and children. Despite being incarcerated, brutally tortured and threatened by corrupt officials for her work, she has become a leader of the freedom of expression and human rights movement in Mexico. She is also the author of a number of books of which *Los demonios del Edén* / Monsters in Eden (Grijalbo, 2005) and *Memorias de una Infamia* / Memoirs of an Outrage (Debate, 2008) caused a national furore, while *Slavery Inc.: The Untold Story of International Sex Trafficking* (Portobello, 2013) has appeared in many languages throughout the world. She has received numerous international awards for her journalism, including the Civil Courage Prize, the Wallenberg Medal, the Olof Palme Prize, the Amnesty International Ginetta Sagan Award for Women and Children's Rights and the Hrant Dink Award. In 2010, she was named U.N.A.N.I.M.A. World Press International Hero 2010 (for the International Press Institute in Vienna) and in March 2016 was awarded the A.L.B.A./Puffin Award for Human Rights Activism. Her most recent book, *En busca de Kayla* / In Search of Kayla (Sexto Piso, 2013), is an illustrated short story to teach children about the power they have over their own safety on the internet and how to tackle human trafficking.

Sergio González Rodríguez studied Modern Literature at the Autonomous National University of Mexico (U.N.A.M., 1978–82), and has a degree from the Carlos Septién García School of Journalism (2010), and a master's in criminal justice from the University of Almería in Spain (2011). He also has a master's in criminal justice and public security from Mexico's University of the Humanities, and is completing a Ph.D. on the History of Thought in the School of Philosophy at the Panamerican University (Mexico). His non-fiction books include *Huesos en el desierto / Bones in the Desert* (Anagrama, 2005), *El hombre sin cabeza / The Man without a Head* (Anagrama, 2009) and *The Femicide Machine* (Semiotexte/ MIT Press, 2012). In 2013 he won the Iberoamerican Prize for Freedom of Expression, awarded by the Casa Amèrica de Catalunya, and in 2014, he received the Anagrama essay prize in Barcelona for his book *Campo de guerra / Battlefield* (Anagrama, 2014). In 2015 he published *Los 43 de Iguala: México: verdad y reto de los estudiantes desaparecidos / The Iguala 43. Mexico: the truth and the challenge of the disappeared students* (Anagrama, 2015). Most recently he was awarded the Fernando Benítez National Tribute to Cultural Journalism, which was awarded at the Guadalajara Book Fair in 2015. He is a member of the National System of Creators of Art of Mexico.

Anabel Hernández is a Mexican journalist known for her investigative journalism in newspapers, magazines and books, including works on slave labour, sexual exploitation, political corruption and abuse of power and the drug cartels. She started her career as a reporter at *Reforma*, later reporting for the national newspapers *Milenio*, *Reforma*, *El Universal* and its supplement, *La Revista*. Today she is a contributing journalist for the online publication *Reporte Indigo* and *Proceso* magazine. Her editorial on the importance of a Free Press in Mexico, called "The Perverse Power of Silence", in which she wrote, "If we remain silent we kill freedom, justice and the possibility that a society armed with information may have the power to change the situation that has brought us to this point" won her the World Association of Newspapers and News Publishers' Golden Pen of Freedom in 2012. Her books include *Narcoland: The Mexican Drug Lords and their Godfathers* (Verso, 2013).

Diego Enrique Osorno is a Mexican reporter and writer, who has witnessed some of the principal twenty-first-century conflicts in Mexico and other countries of Latin America. He has received many awards for his work, including Italy's *Stampa Romana* "A mano disarmata" prize, the Latin American prize for journalism about drugs, *Proceso*'s International Journalism prize and Mexico's 2013 National Journalism prize. His books include *El Cártel de Sinaloa* / The Sinaloa Cartel (Grijalbo, 2009), *La guerra de los Zetas* / The War against the Zetas (Grijalbo, 2012) and *Contra Estados Unidos* / Against the United States (Almadía, 2014). He has also made films like "El alcalde" (with Emiliano Altuna and Carlos Rossini), as well as leading social regeneration initiatives based in local journalism like ElBarrioAntiguo.com. He currently teaches at the University of Monterrey, and was appointed a Truth Commissioner for Oaxaca to investigate and remand public officials involved in extrajudicial killings, acts of torture and other serious human rights violations. His most recent book is *Slim. Biografía política del mexicano más rico del mundo* / Slim: A Political Biography of the Richest Mexican in the World (Debate, 2015).

Elena Poniatowska is Mexico's greatest living writer. She was born in Paris in 1932, began writing for newspapers at eighteen and was the first woman to receive Mexico's National Journalism Prize. Her many books include *La noche de Tlatelolco* / Massacre in Mexico (1971), about the army's massacre of students in Tlatelolco Square in 1968. It was immediately recognised as a classic and awarded the Xavier Villaurrutia Prize, but she rejected the award in an open letter to the president, asking who would give a prize to the murdered students. She is also the author of novels, story collections, testimonies and biographies, including *La flor de lis* / Fleur de Lys, *Hasta no verte Jesús mío* / Here's to You Jesusa!, *Querido Diego* / Dear Diego, a life of Diego Rivera, *Tinísima* / Tinisima, a life of Tina Modotti, *La piel del cielo* / The Skin of the Sky (Alfaguara Fiction Prize, 2001) and *El tren pasa primero* / *The Train Passes First* (Rómulo Gallegos International Novel Prize, 2007) about the life of the Mexican railroad workers, and *Leonora* / *Leonora*, a novel about the life of Leonora Carrington (Premio Biblioteca Breve Seix Barral, 2011). She has received honorary degrees from the Autonomous National University of Mexico (U.N.A.M.) and The Autonomous Metropolitan University (U.A.M.) in Mexico, and numerous others including from the New School of Social Research in New York, the Sorbonne in Paris and, most recently, the Complutense University of Madrid. She has been decorated with the French Legion of Honour, Chile's "Gabriela Mistral" award and the "Courage Award" of the International Women's Media Foundation. On November 19, 2013, she received Spain's highest literary award, the Cervantes Prize.

Felipe Restrepo Pombo is a Colombian journalist, editor and author. He studied Literature and started his career as a journalist at the news magazine *Cambio*, under the direction of Gabriel García Márquez. He is the author of the novel *Formas de evasión* (Seix Barral, 2016) and two collections of journalistic profiles: *16 retratos excéntricos* / *16 Eccentric Portraits* (Planeta, 2014) and *Nunca es fácil ser una celebridad* / *It's Never Easy Being a Celebrity* (Planeta 2013). He is also the author of a biography of Francis Bacon (*Francis Bacon: Retrato de una pesadilla* / Francis Bacon: Portrait of a Nightmare (Panamericana, 2008). He is the editor behind the books: *Crónica en latinoamérica* / Narrative Journalism in Latin America (U.N.A.M., 2016), *15 años de Gatopardo: historias y personajes* / *15 Years of Gatopardo* and *Mundo Maya* / Mayan World (Editorial Mapas, 2011). He has been Latin American editor of *Esquire*, cultural editor at *Semana*, director of *Arcadia*, a columnist at *El Espectador* and *Gente* magazine, and has contributed to numerous Latin American publications, including *GQ*, *Travesías*, *El Universal*, *SoHo*, *Qué Pasa*, *La Nación* and *La Tercera*. He teaches narrative journalism at several universities throughout the continent and is currently the editor-in-chief of the acclaimed *Gatopardo* magazine in Mexico City.

Emiliano Ruiz Parra studied Hispanic Literature at the National Autonomous University of Mexico (U.N.A.M.) and took a master's in Political and Legal Theory at University College London. He is the author of *Ovejas negras, rebeldes de la iglesia mexicana del siglo XXI* / Black Sheep: Rebels of the Mexican Church in the Twenty-First Century (Océano, 2012) and of *Los hijos de la ira, las víctimas de la alternancia mexicana* / Children of Anger: Victims of the New Mexican Politics (Océano, 2015). Both books tells stories of social resistance against the political violence which started in Mexico in recent years, and which picked up momentum with the declaration of the so-called war on drugs by ex-president Felipe Calderón in 2006. He was a reporter on the daily news paper *Reforma* (2004–08), is on the staff of *Gatopardo* and his journalism has appeared in various anthologies on migration, the disappearances of the forty-three Ayotzinapa students and on narco-politics. In 2010 he was shortlisted for the Gabriel García Márquez Foundation's New Latin American Journalism Prize. Currently he is working on a film about a Mexican slum called Golondrinas on the outskirts of Mexico City, and since 2015 he has taught a course in medieval Spanish literature at U.N.A.M.

Marcela Turati is a freelance journalist dedicated to covering human rights, and since 2008, the so-called "war on drugs", especially disappearances and massacres of migrants. She writes mainly for *Proceso*, a national magazine focusing on political and drug trafficking issues. She is the author of *Fuego cruzado: las víctimas atrapadas en la guerra del narco* / Crossfire: The Victims of the War on Drugs (2010) and co-editor with Daniela Rea of *Entre las cenizas: Historias de vida en tiempos de muerte* / Written in Bones: Stories of Life in Times of Death (2012) and *Periodistas con Ayotzinapa* /

Journalists for Ayotzinapa – so-called because the forty-three students who disappeared at Ayotzinapa have come to stand for all such disappearances. She is the co-founder of the Periodistas de a Pie network, created by women journalists in 2006 and committed to the training and support of reporters, the defence of freedom of expression, human rights and journalism. She has been awarded a number of international prizes, including F.N.P.I. a la Excelencia, the Louis M. Lyon prize for conscience and integrity in journalism, a L.A.S.A. Media Award and a W.O.L.A (Washington Office on Latin America) Human Rights Award.

Juan Villoro is the author of several novels, short story and essay collections, plays, chronicles and children's books. He is also a weekly columnist for the Mexican newspaper *Reforma* and is called upon frequently to contribute to *El País* and *El Periódico de Catalunya* as well as other national and international print media. A graduate in Sociology from the Metropolitan University Iztapalapa, he has been Professor of Literature at Mexico's National University, and a Visiting Professor at Yale, Princeton, and the Pompeu Fabra University in Barcelona. His books have won him many awards, including the Herralde Prize in Spain for his novel *El testigo* (*The Witness*, Anagarama, 2005), the King of Spain Prize for Journalism and the Antonin Artaud Prize for his collection of short stories, *Los culpables* (Alamadía, 2007) (*The Guilty*, George Braziller, 2015) and *God Is Round* (Restless Books, 2016), among others. His novel for young adult readers, *El libro salvaje* (Fondo de Cultura Económica, 2008) (*The Savage Book*), which has sold more than one million copies in Spanish, has been translated to French, Italian, German and Portuguese. Today, Juan Villoro is increasingly recognised as one of the leading writers of contemporary Latin America.

NOTES ON THE TRANSLATORS

Jennifer Adcock is a poet and translator working in English and Spanish. Her translations of Juan Rulfo, Elena Poniatowska and David Huerta have appeared in Princeton University's *Inventory* journal, *Words Without Borders* and *Asymptote*. Under the pen name Juana Adcock, her work has appeared in publications such as *Magma Poetry*, *Shearsman*, *New Writing Scotland* and *Words Without Borders*, among others. Her first book, *Manca*, explores the anatomy of violence in Mexico and was named by *Reforma*'s distinguished critic Sergio González Rodríguez as one of the best poetry books published in 2014. In 2016 she was selected as one of the Ten New Voices from Europe by Literature Across Frontiers. She lives in Glasgow.

Thomas Bunstead's translations have appeared in *Granta*, *Music & Literature*, *Paris Review Daily* and *Vice*, and include work by Agustín Fernández Mallo, Yuri Herrera and Enrique Vila-Matas. His translation of Juan Villoro's collected football writing has been published by Restless Books under the title *God Is Round*. In 2015, he guest edited a Mexico feature for *Words Without Borders* with Sophie Hughes, and was nominated for an Arts Foundation Fellowship. He is currently an editor at the biannual translation journal *In Other Words*, and writes for *The Times Literary Supplement*, the *Independent* and literary websites, including ready-steadybook.com and Bammagazine.com. He lives in East Sussex.

Peter Bush has translated many Catalan, Spanish and Latin American writers including Carmen Boullosa, Chico Buarque, Juan Carlos Onetti, Najat El Hachmi, Leonardo Padura Ramón del Valle-Inclán, Teresa Solana, Joan Sales and Mercè Rodoreda. He received the Valle-Inclán Prize (for *The Marx Family Saga* and *Exiled from Almost Everywhere* by Juan Goytisolo), the Calouste Gulbenkian Prize (for *Equator* by Miguel Sousa Tavares) and the Ramon Llull Prize (for *The Gray Notebook* by Josep Pla). The Spanish government awarded him the Cross of the Order of Civil Merit in 2012 and the Generalitat, the St George's Cross in 2015, for his translation and promotion of Spanish and Catalan literature respectively. He lives in Oxford.

Nick Caistor is a British translator of many books from Latin America, Spain and France. He has won the Valle-Inclán translation prize for Spanish three times (for *The Sleeping Voice* by Dulce Chacón, 2006, *The Past* by Alan Pauls, 2008, and *An Englishman in Madrid* by Eduardo Mendoza, 2014). He is the author of *Mexico City: A Cultural History* (Signal Books) and the forthcoming *Guide to Mexico City* (Reaktion Books), as well as of biographies of Octavio Paz, Fidel Castro and Ernesto "Che" Guevara. He lives in Norwich and London.

David Frye has published more than twenty books in translation, ranging from *A Planet for Rent* (2014) and *Super Extra Grande* (2016) by the Cuban science-fiction novelist and heavy metal rocker Yoss to the classic *First New Chronicle and Good Government*, written in 1615 by the Andean native chronicler Guaman Poma de Ayala, and the early picaresque novel *El Lazarillo de Tormes* from 1552. His translations of two short novels by the Spanish writer Elia Barceló, *The Goldsmith's Secret* and *Heart of Tango*, appeared from MacLehose Press in 2011. When he is not translating, David Frye teaches Latin American culture and society at the University of Michigan.

Lucy Greaves translates from Spanish, Portuguese and French. She won the 2013 Harvill-Secker Young Translators' Prize and during

2014 was Translator in Residence at the Free Word Centre in London. Her work has appeared in *Granta* and *The White Review*, among other publications, and her translation of María Angélica Bosco's *Death Going Down* is forthcoming from Pushkin Press in late 2016. She lives in Bristol.

Ángel Gurría-Quintana is a historian, journalist and literary translator from Spanish and Portuguese. He is a regular contributor to the books pages of the *Financial Times* and has written for the *Observer*, the *Guardian*, *Prospect*, the *Economist* and *Paris Review*. He edited and translated *Other Carnivals: New Stories from Brazil* (Full Circle Editions, 2013), which included works by Beatriz Bracher, João Anzanello Carrascoza, Bernardo Carvalho, Andrea del Fuego, Ferréz, Marcelino Freire, Milton Hatoum, Tatiana Salem Levy, Adriana Lisboa, Reinaldo Moraes, André Sant'Anna and Cristovão Tezza. His translation of Dulce Maria Cardoso's novel, *The Return* (Maclehose, 2016), was awarded a PEN Translates grant. He is co-curator of FlipSide Literary Festival, in Suffolk. He lives in Cambridge.

Daniel Hahn is a writer, editor and translator, with more than forty books to his name. His translations include fiction from Europe, Africa and the Americas, and non-fiction by writers ranging from the Portuguese Nobel laureate José Saramago to Brazilian footballer Pelé. His work has won the Independent Foreign Fiction Prize (for *The Book of Chameleons by* José Eduardo Agualusa, 2007) and the Blue Peter Book 'Best Book about Facts' Award (for *The Ultimate Book Guide*, 2004) among others, and has been shortlisted for the Man Booker International Prize (for *A General Theory of Oblivion* by José Eduardo Agualusa, 2016). He is a former chair of the Translators Association and the Society of Authors, and a board member of a number of organisations that work with literature, human rights and free speech. Recent publications include the new *Oxford Companion to Children's Literature* (2015). He lives in Brighton.

Rosalind Harvey's translation of Juan Pablo Villalobos' novel *Down the Rabbit Hole* was shortlisted for the 2011 Guardian First Book Award and the Oxford-Weidenfeld Prize. Her co-translation with Anne McLean of *Dublinesque* by Enrique Vila-Matas was shortlisted for the 2013 Independent Foreign Fiction Prize, and longlisted for the 2014 IMPAC Dublin Literary Award. In 2016 she was shortlisted for the Arts Foundation Award. She is founding member and chair of the Emerging Translators Network, associate translation teacher at the University of Bristol, and is currently working on *After the Winter*, a novel by the Mexican author Guadalupe Nettel, to be published by MacLehose Press in 2017. She lives in London.

Amanda Hopkinson has translated some thirty works from Spanish, Portuguese and French, the majority from Latin America. She has translated across genres, ranging from testimonies in the 1980s, to a series including poetry and novellas, and anthologies of stories, emerging from the Latin American women's movement. She has also translated catalogues for art and photography exhibitions, and monographs on Martín Chambi, Manuel Álvarez Bravo and Graciela Iturbide. Most recently, she translated the fictionalised biography of British Surrealist Leonora Carrington, by Elena Poniatowska; and novels by Sergio Bizzio, Ricardo Piglia, Isabel Allende (with Nick Caistor), Claribel Alegría, Dominique Manotti and Paulo Coelho. She is Professor of Literary Translation at City University. She lives in London and Norwich.

Sophie Hughes' translations and reviews have appeared in various publications, including the *Guardian*, the *White Review*, *The Times Literary Supplement*, *Music & Literature* and *Literary Hub*. She has worked as an editor-at-large for *Asymptote Journal* and translation correspondent for *Dazed & Confused*, and in 2015 she guest edited a *Words Without Borders* feature on contemporary Mexican literature with Thomas Bunstead. In 2015 she was awarded a British Centre for Literary Translation Mentorship and in 2016 she received an Arts Foundation Fellowship shortlist grant for Literary Translation. She has translated novels by several Spanish and Latin American authors, including Iván Repila's *The Boy Who Stole Attila's Horse* (Pushkin Press), Jon Bilbao's *Still the Same Man* (Hispabooks), one of Hay Festival's "México 20" most outstanding young Mexican writers Laia Jufresa's *Umami* (Oneworld) and one of Granta's Best Young Spanish-Language Novelists Rodrigo Hasbún's *Affections* (Pushkin Press).

Catherine Mansfield is a translator, copy editor and communications professional. Her translations include *China's Silent Army* by Juan Pablo Cardenal and Heriberto Araujo (Penguin Press, 2013) and *A History of the World for Rebels and Somnambulists* by Jesús del Campo (Telegram, 2008). She has also translated short works of fiction and non-fiction by authors including Brenda Lozano, Rafael Pérez Gay and Juan Pablo Anaya for *Words Without Borders* and *México20* (Pushkin 2015). She is co-founder of a creative translation agency called ZigZag Translations, which she set up while living in Bogotá, Colombia, and now lives in London.

Megan McDowell has translated many works by Latin American and Spanish writers, with a particular focus on Chilean and Argentine literature. Her published and forthcoming translations include books by Alejandro Zambra, Samanta Schweblin, Lina Meruane, Mariana Enriquez, Alejandro Jodorowsky, Carlos Busqued, Arturo Fontaine, Juan Emar, Diego Zúñiga, Carlos Fonseca and Álvaro Bisama. Her translations of Zambra have been featured in *The New Yorker*, *The Paris Review*, *Harper's*, *Tin House*, *McSweeney's* and *Vice*, among others, and her translation of Zambra's novel *Ways of Going Home* won a 2013 PEN Award for writing in translation. She is from Kentucky and lives in Santiago, Chile.

Anne McLean has translated works by many Spanish and Latin American authors including Héctor Abad, Julio Cortázar, Carmen Martín Gaite, Ignacio Martínez de Pisón, Enrique Vila-Matas and Tomás Eloy Martínez. She has been awarded the Independent Foreign Fiction Prize (for *Soldiers of Salamis* by Javier Cercas, 2004, and *The Armies* by Evelio Rosero, 2009), the Premio Valle-Inclán (for *Soldiers of Salamis*, 2004, and *Outlaws*, 2016, both by Javier Cercas) and the IMPAC Dublin Literary Award (for *The Sound of Things Falling* by Juan Gabriel Vásquez, 2014). In 2012 she was awarded the Spanish Cross of the Order of Civil Merit in recognition of her contribution to making Spanish literature known to a wider public. She lives in Toronto.

Samantha Schnee's translation of Mexican author Carmen Boullosa's *Texas: The Great Theft* (Deep Vellum, 2014) was long-listed for the International Dublin Literary Award, short-listed for the PEN America Translation Prize, and won the Typographical Era Translation Award. She won the 2015 Gulf Coast Prize in Translation for an excerpt from Boullosa's *The Conspiracy of the Romantics* (forthcoming Deep Vellum, 2017). Her translation of Spanish author Laia Fàbregas's *Landing* is due from HispaBooks. She is the founding editor of *Words Without Borders* and currently edits the biannual translation journal *In Other Words*. She is also a trustee of English PEN, where she chairs the Writers in Translation committee. Born in Scotland and raised in Texas, she lives in London.